CW01066964

The Sociology of Higher Education

The Sociology of Higher Education: Reproduction, Transformation and Change in a Global Era provides an exciting and conceptually rich approach to the sociology of higher education. It offers innovative perspectives on the future of universities within the new and emerging research sub-field of the sociology of global higher education. The twenty-first century has witnessed wide-ranging structural and ideological transformations in higher education which have created both a sense of opportunity, as well as crisis and loss in the urgent debates around the legitimate roles of the university. The chapters represent a diverse and vibrant field, illustrating a sociological imagination and a dynamic engagement with the key challenges facing higher education, and confirming continuing inequalities through internationalisation.

This book is a compilation of articles originally published in the *British Journal of Sociology of Education*.

Miriam David is Professor Emerita of Education at the Institute of Education, University of London, UK.

Rajani Naidoo is Senior Lecturer at the University of Bath School of Management, UK.

British Journal of Sociology of Education
Chair of the Executive Editorial Board: **Madeleine Arnot**, University of Cambridge, UK

The *British Journal of Sociology of Education,* which was founded in 1980 by Len Barton, is one of the most renowned international scholarly journals in the field. It has created and serves an established well-informed international audience, publishing original, theoretically informed analyses of the relationship between education and society.

The journal has an outstanding record of addressing major global debates about the social significance and impact of educational policy, provision, processes and practice. Its vitality is sustained by its ambition to offer independent evaluations of the ways in which education interfaces with local, national, regional and global developments, contexts and agendas. With a strong commitment to the promotion of social justice and economic development, the journal provides an important internationally recognised space for this critical perspective.

The *BJSE* is published six times a year. Its editorial board comprises the leaders of sociological studies in education who are solely responsible for reviewing all submissions and ensuring the quality of sociological writing. The journal's book reviews, and symposia which focus on significant publications in the field offer opportunities to reflect on the latest publications, whilst special issues turn the spotlight on particularly important contemporary debates.

This series of book titles represent a careful selection of influential, theoretically rigorous and methodological innovative articles which were published in the *BJSE* mostly within the last five years. The editors hope that such collections will encourage educationalists and professionals to discover the richness in quality, the continuity and the important shifts in thinking in the international tradition of sociological research in education.

Book titles from the British Journal of Sociology of Education

The Sociology of Disability and Inclusive Education
Edited by Madeleine Arnot

The Sociology of Higher Education
Edited by Miriam David and Rajani Naidoo

The Sociology of Higher Education

Reproduction, Transformation and Change in a Global Era

Edited by
Miriam David and Rajani Naidoo

Routledge
Taylor & Francis Group

LONDON AND NEW YORK

First published 2013
by Routledge
2 Park Square, Milton Park, Abingdon, Oxon, OX14 4RN

Simultaneously published in the USA and Canada
by Routledge
711 Third Avenue, New York, NY 10017

Routledge is an imprint of the Taylor & Francis Group, an informa business

© 2013 Taylor & Francis

This book is a compilation of articles originally published in the *British Journal of Sociology of Education*. The Publisher requests to those authors who may be citing this book to state, also, the bibliographical details of the issue on which each chapter was based.

Trademark notice: Product or corporate names may be trademarks or registered trademarks, and are used only for identification and explanation without intent to infringe.

British Library Cataloguing in Publication Data
A catalogue record for this book is available from the British Library

ISBN13: 978-0-415-65966-6

Typeset in Times New Roman
by Taylor & Francis Books

Publisher's Note
The publisher would like to make readers aware that the chapters in this book may be referred to as articles as they are identical to the articles published in the journal. The publisher accepts responsibility for any inconsistencies that may have arisen in the course of preparing this volume for print.

Contents

Citation Information

The chapters in this book were originally published in the *British Journal of Sociology of Education*. When citing this material, please use the original issue information and page numbering for each article, as follows:

Chapter 1

Global field and global imagining: Bourdieu and worldwide higher education
Simon Marginson
British Journal of Sociology of Education, volume 29, issue 3 (May 2008) pp. 303-315

Chapter 2

Equity and diversity: towards a sociology of higher education for the twenty first century?
Miriam David
British Journal of Sociology of Education, volume 28, issue 5 (September 2007) pp. 675-690

Chapter 3

Elite destinations: pathways to attending an Ivy League University
Ann L. Mullen
British Journal of Sociology of Education, volume 30, issue 1 (January 2009) pp. 15-27

Chapter 4

Disability studies, disabled people and the struggle for inclusion
Mike Oliver and Colin Barnes
British Journal of Sociology of Education, volume 31, issue 5 (September 2010) pp. 547-560

Chapter 5

Accidental achievers? International higher education, class reproduction and privilege in the experiences of UK students overseas
Johanna Waters and Rachel Brooks
British Journal of Sociology of Education, volume 31, issue 2 (March 2010) pp. 217-228

Chapter 6

Aspiration for global cultural capital in the stratified realm of global higher education: why do Korean students go to US graduate schools?
Jongyoung Kim
British Journal of Sociology of Education, volume 32, issue 1 (January 2011) pp. 109-126

Chapter 7

Higher education and linguistic dualism in the Arab Gulf
Sally Findlow
British Journal of Sociology of Education, volume 27, issue 1 (February 2006) pp. 19-36

Chapter 8

Qualitative research as a method for making just comparisons of pedagogic quality in higher education: A pilot study
Andrea Abbas and Monica McLean
British Journal of Sociology of Education, volume 28, issue 6 (November 2007) pp. 723-737

Chapter 9

Research assessment as a pedagogical device: Bernstein, professional identity and education in New Zealand
Sue Middleton
British Journal of Sociology of Education, volume 29, issue 2 (March 2008) pp. 125-136

Chapter 10

Kindness in pedagogical practice and academic life
Sue Clegg and Stephen Rowland
British Journal of Sociology of Education, volume 31, issue 6 (November 2010) pp. 719-735

Notes on Contributors

Andrea Abbas, University of Teesside, UK

Colin Barnes, Centre for Disability Studies, School of Sociology and Social Policy, University of Leeds, Leeds, UK and Department of Health and Social Sciences, University of Halmstad, Sweden

Rachel Brooks, Department of Political, International and Policy Studies, University of Surrey, Guildford, UK

Sue Clegg, Centre for Research into Higher Education, Carnegie Research Institute, Leeds Metropolitan University, Cavendish Hall, Leeds, UK

Miriam David, Institute of Education, University of London, UK

Sally Findlow, Keele University, UK

Jongyoung Kim Department of Sociology, Kyung Hee University, South Korea

Simon Marginson, Centre for the Study of Higher Education, University of Melbourne, Victoria, Australia

Monica McLean, University of Nottingham, UK

Sue Middleton, Department of Policy, Culture and Social Studies in Education, School of Education, University of Waikato, New Zealand

Ann L. Mullen, Department of Sociology, University of Toronto, Ontario, Canada

Rajani Naidoo, School of Management, University of Bath, UK

Mike Oliver, University of Greenwich, London, UK

Stephen Rowland, Higher Education, University College London and Institute of Education, London University, London, UK

Johanna Waters, Department of Geography, University of Liverpool, Liverpool, UK

Introduction

Miriam David and Rajani Naidoo

The twenty-first century has witnessed wide-ranging transformations in Higher Education (HE) with structural, cultural and ideological changes encapsulated by the terms 'globalisation' and the 'knowledge economy'. In a context where the nation state's competitive edge in the global economy has been linked to knowledge innovation, HE's role as an engine for economic development has jostled for dominance with other nationally circumscribed social and cultural roles (Brennan *et al,* 2008). HE has also been deployed to exert political and cultural influence in the global context in a multipolar world characterised by the rise of Asian countries, China especially, which has the capacity to challenge existing global power relations (Naidoo, 2011).

Research on the transformation of HE reveals that, in many countries, there is a trend away from forms of funding and regulation based on the 'social compact' that had evolved between HE, the state and society in the 20th century. The belief that universities require a relative independence from political and corporate influence to function optimally, that was, in turn, linked to guaranteed state funding and autonomy for the academic profession, has been eroded. These developments, together with retractions in public policy away from Keynesian welfare state settlements, have resulted in the implementation of new funding and regulatory frameworks that revolve around neo-liberal market and new public management mechanisms (Deem, 2001; Slaughter and Rhoades, 2004). With exceptions such as the rising powers of China and India, there has been a world-wide decline in state funding for research and teaching. We have also witnessed the tightening of state control over core aspects of academic life through external regulatory bodies and the extension of competition and quasi-market mechanisms. Global competition has been reinforced through global rankings while international organisations such as the World Bank have been active in global governance (Shahjehan, 2012).

These developments have contributed to rapid expansion and diversification in all arenas of HE: student numbers have grown exponentially. Developed economies like the US, Canada and Japan which achieved participation rates of the relevant age cohorts of 18-24 year olds of 50 per cent and over have been caught up or indeed overtaken by countries like South Korea. The most ambitious plans to expand HE have come from India and China (Brown, Lauder and Ashton, 2011). The growth of private and for-profit HE has contributed to this expansion and differentiation. In addition, cross-border HE including collaborative partnerships for competitive advantage between high and rising income countries have been accelerated by technological advances and pressing needs for revenue generation. Research is both expanding and diversifying and we are witnessing the creation of new disciplinary forms and new forms of student engagement and pedagogy.

These transformations have created a sense of opportunity tinged with crisis and loss in the urgent debates around the legitimate roles of HE in the 21st century (Barnett, 2011; David *et al*, 2011). They have attracted the attention of sociologists situated in different institutional locations, and critical lenses have focused on the inter-relationship between global and national socio-political and economic developments occurring in diverse academic settings. Other interests have also emerged including questioning HE's role in national skills strategies, educational inequality, pedagogy, curriculum and student engagement, the academic profession and governance. In the BJSE, these topics have been elaborated to advance theory and empirical research in the field. Several lines of specialisation including the internal structuring of knowledge and its role in the reproduction of inequality (Maton, 2000; Moore and Muller, 2002) have been addressed. The journal has drawn on several intellectual and methodological legacies while retaining a focus on the relationship between macro socio-political and economic forces, power relations within the academy and social consequences. Dominant ideologies and managerial trends in HE have also been rigorously challenged.

The articles on HE published, therefore, represent a diverse and vibrant field and this special issue does not provide a comprehensive overview. We do not engage in an artificially constructed competition for the best articles published but rather we have selected papers to illustrate theoretical developments, geographic and topic diversity, a sociological imagination and a dynamic engagement with the key challenges facing HE.

We begin with Simon Marginson's '*Global field and global imagining: Bourdieu and worldwide higher education*' which builds on previous BJSE studies (Tomusk, 2000; Naidoo, 2004; Reay, 2004). Marginson extends Bourdieu's theory to encompass the global and its relationship with differentiated national domains and he also draws on Gramsci's notion of hegemony to analyse the dominance of US universities. Noting Bourdieu's tendency of leaning towards the structural and deterministic, both Sen and Appadurai's work on self-determining identity and global imagining, flows and 'scapes' are incorporated. Marginson concludes that the dynamics of Bourdieu's competitive field of HE continue to play out globally, but are located within a larger and more disjunctive relational setting with more dynamic possibilities than suggested.

Miriam David in '*Equity and diversity: towards a sociology of higher education for the twenty first century?*' presents a wide-ranging analysis of the transformations in global HE and research. She shows how economic changes have influenced the growth of HE leading to contestation in what counts as HE and the practices and divisions between teaching and research. She illustrates the expansion of sociology to include a diverse range of themes and suggests that while globalisation has malign effects, new forms of 'academic capitalism' (Slaughter and Rhodes, 2004) also allow for potentially inclusive forms of HE. She concludes that while ethnicity and gender are still on the agenda through critical and feminist research and pedagogies (Arnot, 2002; David, 2005; Morley, 2011) these diverse forms of HE nevertheless lead to inequities in the distribution of possibilities and privileges which are reproduced within and between local and global contexts.

To what extent, then, have transformations of elite HE in fact challenged social inequality? Social research reveals that while absolute chances of entry for disadvantaged students have increased, government policy, the socialisation of students and institutional arrangements have combined to maintain relative inequalities between classes and ethnic groups. Anne Mullen in *'Elite destinations: pathways to attending an Ivy League University'* contributes to work on class-based differences in student choice (Ball *et al,* 2002) showing the effects of social class, schools and peers on student pathways to Yale University. She demonstrates how choosing an Ivy League college becomes normalised in wealthy and highly educated families while socially disadvantaged students place these types of college outside the realm of the possible. Less privileged students with exceptional academic credentials must, therefore, overcome substantial hurdles to arrive at such a college.

A dominant strand of sociological studies are about theories of stratification, neo-Marxist and feminist work, incorporating ways of understanding diversities such as ethnicity (Shiner and Modood, 2002) migrant status, gender and/or masculinity (Skelton, 2005; Burke, 2007) and disability. Mike Oliver and Colin Barnes in *'Disability studies, disabled people and the struggle for inclusion'* replace medical approaches to disability with a social model, locating the cause of disadvantage in how society restricts the opportunities of disabled people to participate in mainstream economic and social activities. Drawing on Len Barton's work, it is argued that the links between disability activism and the academy had an important influence on mainstream sociology and policy. They conclude, however, that greater impact needs to be achieved and that the need for meaningful inclusion is urgent.

National studies have also been widened to focus on how international education programmes reproduce and transform national and global hierarchies. Johanna Waters and Rachel Brooks in *'Accidental achievers? International higher education, class reproduction and privilege in the experiences of UK students overseas'* find that UK students undertaking a degree abroad are not motivated by 'strategic' concerns but are seeking goals such as 'adventure'. The spatially uneven and socially exclusive nature of international HE is illustrated by showing how even with such ostensibly 'disinterested' objectives, UK students studying abroad remain a highly privileged group and their experiences serve only to facilitate the reproduction of their privilege.

Jongyoung Kim's *'Aspiration for global cultural capital in the stratified realm of global higher education: why do Korean students go to US graduate schools?* combines the concept of global positional competition with Bourdieu's theory of cultural capital. She shows how Korean students pursue degrees in the US to succeed in the global positional competition within Korea and in the global labour market. Korean students internalize US hegemony as it reproduces the global hierarchy of HE, but, at the same time, see US HE as a means of liberation that resolves some of the inner contradictions of Korean HE, including gender discrimination and an authoritarian learning culture. Korean students' aspirations for global cultural capital are, therefore, linked to complex and irregular structures and relations of class, gender, nationality and HE that extend across national, international and global dimensions.

'Higher education and linguistic dualism in the Arab Gulf' by Sally Findlow also links to these wider sociological themes of globalisation and neo-imperialism. She examines the spread of English as a medium of HE in the Arab world. Drawing on ethnographic research, she documents how Arabic and English have been implicated in the re-configuring of collective identities against a context of rapid modernisation and a regional undercurrent of pan-Arab and Islamist-tinged nationalism. She examines how far the resulting dualism amounts to a loss of linguistic-cultural diversity, and how far there is a linguistically-framed discourse of resistance. Her conclusion is that such linguistic

dualism, which enables two identities to be claimed at once, offers insights into the potential for both language and HE to act as tools for cultural transformation and for resistance.

The interaction of political dynamics and policies with institutional frameworks and academic responses is our next theme. The academic profession which has traditionally been governed by a distinctive mix of professional self-regulation and limited forms of bureaucracy is faced by new forms of accountability and market mechanisms which rely on competition, performance measurement, audit systems and hierarchical management (Gleeson and James, 2007; Ball, 2008; Enders and de Weert, 2009). Abbas and Mclean in *'Qualitative Research as a Method for Making Just Comparisons of Pedagogic Quality in Higher Education: A Pilot Study'* draw on their sociological analysis of two contrasting English universities to illustrate how quality assurance systems, ostensibly concerned with quality and global equality, contribute to reproducing inequality. They argue that future European and global hierarchies are complex and biases are likely to be more difficult to uncover. They conclude by suggesting that an examination of pedagogic quality drawing on Bernstein's framework could play a role in promoting social justice.

Sue Middleton in *'Research assessment as a pedagogical device: Bernstein, professional identity and education in New Zealand'* also draws on Bernstein and Beck and Young (2005) to explore how the official assessment of research in New Zealand affects academic professional identities in a university Department of Education. She historicises education's changing official identities to illustrate how academic identities are both enabled and constrained in the quality evaluation process. Academics who had published in high status journals experienced the assessment as affirming existing internal identities while those with records of advancing knowledge through 'service roles' were undermined. She concludes that the requirement for all degree teaching staff to be researchers could undermine Education's other mandates reproducing binaries in theory and practice.

Sue Clegg and Stephen Rowland in *'Kindness in pedagogical practice and academic life'* exemplify how research published in BJSE attempts to counter the dominant instrumental versions of HE to reveal alternative values and to create space for a continuing ethical commitment. The authors focus on the concept of kindness as an expressive component that is silenced in accounts of teaching excellence but that can be subversive of neo-liberal assumptions that place value on utility and cost. Their theorisation of kindness as encompassing cognitive as well as affective dimensions resists the dualisms which see cognitive capacity in opposition to the embodied and experiential. They conclude by suggesting that what is subversive in thinking about HE practice through the lens of kindness is that it cannot be regulated or prescribed through performance measures, regulation or surveillance.

These 10 articles illustrate the rich theoretical and methodological diversity of sociological studies of HE and bear witness to the unintended consequences of transformations in global HE and the prospects for creative responses to such seismic changes.

References

Arnot, M. (2002) *Reproducing gender? Essays on educational theory and feminist politics* (London, Routledge).

Ball, S., Davies, J., David, M., and Reay, D. (2002) Classification and judgement: the cognitive structures of choice in higher education, *British Journal of Sociology of Education*, 23(1), 51-72.

Ball, S. (2008) Performativity, Privatisation, Professionals and the State. In Cunningham B. (ed.) *Exploring Professionalism*. (London, Institute of Education, University of London).

Barnett, R. (2011) *Being a University* (London, Routledge)

Beck, J. and Young, M. (2005) The assault on the professions and the restructuring of academic and professional identities: a Bernsteinian analysis *British Journal of Sociology of Education* 26 (2),183-197.

Brennan, J., Enders, J., Mousselin, C., Teichler, U. and Valimaa, J. (2008) Higher education looking forward: An agenda for future research (Strasbourg, France, European Science Foundation).

Brown, P., Lauder, H. and Ashton, D. (2011) *The global auction: the broken promise of education, jobs, and incomes* (Oxford, Oxford University Press).

Burke, P. and Jackson, S. (2007) *Reconceptualising Lifelong Learning: Feminist Interventions* (London, Routledge).

David, M. (2005) Feminist values and feminist sociology as contributions to higher education pedagogies and practices, in: S. Robinson and C. Katulushi (eds.,) *Values in higher education* (Glamorgan, Aureus Publishing Limited for the University of Leeds).

David, M., Hey, V. and Morley, L. (2011) (eds.,) Challenge, Change or Crisis in Global Higher Education, special issue *Contemporary Social Science: Journal of the Academy of Social Sciences* 6 (2).

Deem, R. (2001) Globalisation, new managerialism, academic capitalism and entrepreneurialism in universities: is the local dimension still important? *Comparative Education*, 37(1), 7-20.

Enders, J. and de Weert, E. (eds.) (2009) *The Changing Face of Academic Life. Analytical and Comparative Perspectives* (Houndsmill, Basingstoke: Palgrave).

Gleeson, D. and James, D. (2007) The paradox of professionalism in English Further Education: A TLC Project Perspective, *Educational Review*, 59(4), 451-467.

Maton, K. (2000) Languages of Legitimation: the structuring significance for intellectual fields of strategic knowledge claims, *British Journal of Sociology of Education*, 21(2), 147-167.

Morley, L. (2011) Misogyny Posing as Measurement: disrupting the feminisation crisis discourse, *Contemporary Social Science* 6(2), 1–17.

Moore, R. and Muller, J. (2002) The growth of knowledge and the discursive gap, *British Journal of Sociology of Education* 23(4), 627-639.

Naidoo, R. (2004) 'Fields and institutional strategy: Bourdieu on the relationship between higher education, inequality and society', *British Journal of Sociology of Education*, 25(4), 446-472.

Naidoo, R. (2011) Higher education and the new imperialism: Implications for development in Marginson, S. King, R. and Naidoo, R. (eds.,) *Higher Education and Globalisation Reader* (London, Edward Elgar).

Reay, D. (2004) 'It's all becoming a habitus': Beyond the habitual use of Pierre Bourdieu's concept of habitus in educational research, *British Journal of Sociology of Education* 25(4), 431-444.

Shahjahan, R.A. (2012) The roles of international organizations (IOs) in globalizing higher education policy in J. Smart and Paulsen, M. (eds.) *Higher Education: Handbook of Theory and Research* (Vol. 27) pp. 369-407 (Dordrecht: Springer).

Shiner, M. and Modood, T. (2002) Help or hindrance? Higher education and the route to ethnic equality, *British Journal of Sociology of Education*, 23(2), 209–232.

Skelton, C. (2005) The self-interested woman academic: A consideration of Beck's model of the individualised individual, *British Journal of Sociology of Education*, 26(1), 5-16.

Slaughter, S. and Rhoades, G. (2004) *Academic capitalism and the new economy: markets, state and higher education* (Baltimore, MD, John Hopkins University Press).

Tomusk, V. (2000) Reproduction of the State Nobility in Eastern Europe: Past patterns and New Practices, *British Journal of Sociology of Education* 21(2), 269-283.

Global field and global imagining: Bourdieu and worldwide higher education

Simon Marginson

Centre for the Study of Higher Education, University of Melbourne, Victoria, Australia

This paper maps the global dimension of higher education and associated research, including the differentiation of national systems and institutions, while reflecting critically on theoretical tools for working this terrain. Arguably the most sustained theorisation of higher education is by Bourdieu: the paper explores the relevance and limits of Bourdieu's notions of field of power, agency, positioned and position-taking; drawing on Gramsci's notion of hegemony in explaining the dominant role played by universities from the United States. Noting there is greater ontological openness in global than national educational settings, and that Bourdieu's reading of structure/agency becomes trapped on the structure side, the paper discusses Sen on self-determining identity and Appadurai on global imagining, flows and 'scapes'. The dynamics of Bourdieu's competitive field of higher education continue to play out globally, but located within a larger and more disjunctive relational setting, and a setting that is less closed, than he suggests.

Introduction

Worldwide higher education is a relational environment that is simultaneously global, national and local (Marginson and Rhoades 2002; Valimaa 2004). It includes international agencies, governments and national systems, institutions, disciplines, professions, e-learning companies and others. Although most activity in higher education is nation-bound, a distinctive global dimension is growing in importance, connecting with each national system of higher education while also being external to them all.

Although the global dimension has many roots, it above all derives from the worldwide roll-out of instantaneous messaging, complex data transfer and cheapening air travel. The cross-border dealings of research-intensive universities and the relations between governments on higher education are something more than a mass of bilateral connections. There are networked global systems with commonalities, points of concentration (nodes), rhythms, speeds and modes of movement. In research there is a single mainstream system of English-language publication of research knowledge, which tends to marginalise other work rather than absorb it. There are converging approaches to recognition and quality assurance, such as the Washington Accords in Engineering. The Bologna agreement facilitates partial integration and convergence in degree structures and the diploma supplement in Europe.

The practices that distinguish higher education from other social formations are the credentialing of knowledge-intensive labour, and basic research. We can understand the global dimension of higher education as a bounded domain that includes institutions with cross-border activities in these areas. Although this domain is frayed at the edges by diploma mills, corporate 'universities' and cross-border e-learning – and despite its connections with other social formations – its boundedness and disinctiveness are irreducible. A dual of inclusion/exclusion shapes the outer and inner relationships of the domain. This suggests Pierre Bourdieu, who terms such domains as 'fields of power'. Such as field is 'a space, that is, an ensemble of positions in a relationship of mutual exclusion' (Bourdieu 1996, 232).

Any theorisation of this global higher education domain must account for two elements. One is cross-border *flows*: flows of people (students, administrators, academic faculty); flows of media and messages, information and knowledge; flows of norms, ideas and policies; flows of technologies, finance capital and economic resources. Global flows in higher education are exceptionally dynamic and uneven. In the decade from 1995 to 2004 the number of students enrolled outside their country of citizenship rose from 1.3 million to 2.7 million (Organization for Economic Cooperation and Development 2006, 287). Cross-border research collaborations and institutional partnerships are expanding rapidly (for example, Vincent-Lancrin 2006); when networks grow, the cost rises in linear fashion but the benefits rise exponentially via the increasing number of connections, while 'the penalty for being outside the network increases' (Castells 2000, 71). Global flows constitute relatively visible lines of effect. The other less explicit element is the worldwide patterns of *differences* that channel and limit global flows: lateral diversity in languages, pedagogies and scholarship, and in organisational systems and cultures; vertical diversity including competitive differentiation, hierarchy, inclusion, exclusion and unequal capacity. Global higher education is not a level playing field.

This paper is concerned with a synthetic mapping of the global dimension of higher education and research in terms of relations of power, including self-determining human agency, in order to contribute to understandings of global transformations (Held et al. 1999) in and through higher education. The paper draws on theorisations by Bourdieu and Antonio Gramsci and on discussions of global ontology and agency by Arjun Appadurai and Amartya Sen. Although this is not an empirically-driven study, data from OECD (2006), World Bank (2007) and other sources are used.[1] The paper considers higher education without interrogating its relations with other fields of power in the economy, military, government, polity, communications and elsewhere. Those are matters for further synthesis.

Bourdieu and the global field of higher education

Arguably Bourdieu's work on higher education (including Bourdieu 1984, 1988, 1993, 1996) is the most sustained of any major social theorist. Rajani Naidoo (2004) uses Bourdieu to analyse the differentiation of higher education institutions in South Africa. She notes, however, that Bourdieu's argument developed in the context of a relatively stable compact between higher education, society and nation-state (Naidoo 2004, 468–469); and he has little to say about the structuring and content of knowledge. Further, much of his empirical research was in the 1960s prior to contemporary globalisation. Can Bourdieu assist our imaginings of global higher education given he is nation-bound and knowledge formation is both primary to universities and quintessentially global? Yes, with some qualifications. The qualifications will be discussed below but Bourdieu's notion of field of power, with agents 'positioned' and 'position-taking' within the field, continue to be a useful starting point.

Polar structure of the global field

For Bourdieu a field of power is a social universe with its own laws of functioning. It enjoys a variable degree of autonomy, defined by its ability to reject external determinants and obey only its own specific logic. In *The Field of Cultural Production* (Bourdieu 1993, 38–39) he finds that the field is structured by an opposition between the elite subfield of restricted production, and the subfield of large-scale mass production tending towards commercial production. Each subfield has its distinctive principle of hierarchisation. In the elite subfield, where outputs are scarce, the principle of hierarchisation is cultural status, autonomous and specific to the field. In mass or 'popular' institutions the principle of hierarchisation involves economic capital and market demand and is heteronymous, although mass institutions renew themselves from time to time by adapting ideas from the elite sector. Between the subfields are found a range of intermediate institutions that combine the opposing principles of legitimacy in varying degrees and states of ambiguity.

Bourdieu's polarity helps to explain relations of power within national systems, where heteronomy is shaped by governments, market forces and both together. The contrast in South Africa between the more autonomous white English-language universities focused on products for the intellectual field and more heteronomous black universities and white Afrikaans-medium universities (Naidoo 2004, 461) is replicated in the differentiation of the Australian system with its polarity between more autonomous and selective 'sandstone' universities that see themselves as global research players, and more heteronomous vocational and regional institutions (Marginson and Considine 2000, 175–232). Other examples can be cited. Far from making a universal journey from elite to mass higher education (Trow 1974), national systems contain both kinds of institution simultaneously and/or sustain the Bourdieuian polarity inside single institutions. However, the point here is that this Bourdieuian polarity is apparent also in the global field.

In the global subfield of restricted production are the American doctoral universities led by Harvard, Stanford, MIT, Yale, Princeton, Berkeley and others, plus Cambridge, Oxford and a handful of the Russell group. Ultimately they derive global predominance from their position within their own national/imperial systems. *The Economist* (2005) christened them the 'Global Super-league'. These institutions constitute advanced careers almost anywhere in the world. Places are prized by both students and academic faculty. Selectivity is enhanced by modest student intakes, and they concentrate knowledge power to themselves by housing most leading researchers. They head the world in research outputs as measured by the Shanghai Jiao Tong University (SJTU) (SJTU Institute of Higher Education 2007).[2] The top 20 SJTU universities are 17 from the USA, and Cambridge, Oxford and Tokyo. Largely autonomous, their agency freedom is enhanced by the globalisation of knowledge and their pre-eminence displayed in the web, global university rankings and popular culture. The global power of these institutions rests on the subordination of other institutions and nations.

In the opposite subfield are institutions solely focused on revenues and market share. This includes not only for-profit vocational universities such as the University of Phoenix, now active in a dozen countries, but in their global teaching function non-profit universities in the United Kingdom and Australia that provide international education on a commercial basis.

There is a range of institutions in intermediate positions (Figure 1). Some universities have elite roles in their national field and compete in the global research stakes while building high volumes of full fee-paying international students (category 2b); some other national leaders lack a strong global presence (category 4a). Beneath both groups are ostensibly teaching-research universities for whom the research mission is subordinated to cross-border revenues (category 4b). For-profit institutions vary in the extent to which they sustain a global role (categories 3, 6, and 8). Other institutions are solely nation-bound but nevertheless affected by the global field, for they are subordinated by it (categories 7 and 9).

Bourdieu's notion of a differentiating field of power that includes/excludes is closer to the dynamics of higher education than is the neo-liberal imaginary of a universal market. However, in some respects the polarity differs from Bourdieu's description. Anglo-American universities have not adopted the French division between high intellectual schools and those preparing the

AUTONOMOUS SUB-FIELD* of elite research universities, prestige- not profit-driven Notes 1. autonomy relative to global field 2. elite teaching-only liberal arts colleges feed into category 1					HETERONOMOUS SUB-FIELD of institutions providing commercial vocational cross-border education (includes for-profits & revenue-driven units of non-profits)
	1 The 'Global Super-league': Much of American doctoral sector and a few high prestige universities in UK. Prestige derived from stellar research reputation and global power of degrees [Harvard U, Cambridge etc.]	**2b Elite non U.S. national research universities with strong cross-border roles:** Prestige-driven non profit research universities at national level. Global presence in research; cross-border students some on for-profit basis [U Sydney, U of Warwick]	**4b Teaching-focused export universities:** Lesser status non-profit universities, commercial players in global market: lower cost/quality foreign education at scale. May have minor research role [Oxford Brookes, U Central Queensland]	**3 Elite and globally focused for-profits:** Prestigious fully for-profit institutions operating globally, largely teaching focused with some research. National exclusivity and global power creates autonomy vis a vis 6. Very small group. [Indian IITs, IMs]	**6 Lesser prestige teaching only global for-profits:** Fully commercial operators actively building export markets, low cost mass production, no research [U Phoenix, DeVry, various global e-Us]
	2a Less globally engaged American doctoral universities Global prestige and some research, marginal foreign engagement and cross-border students [some U.S. state universities]	**4a Nationally-bound elite research universities:** Prestige providers in one nation. Research intensive, varying global research roles. Inward looking. Nationally competitive with segment 2b, not 1. [U Buenos Aires, many in Europe and Japan]	**5 Teaching-focused national universities** Largely teaching focused institutions, marginally global in research and/or cross-border teaching [most Malaysian public universities, some Canadian community colleges, etc.]		**8 For-profits with minor global functions:** Commercial operators focused on local market with some cross-border students. [some private industry training in Australia]
			7 Non-profits without global agendas: teaching-focused, local demand orientation. No cross-border role. [largest group, especially in importing nations]		**9 For-profits without global agendas:** local degree mills, no cross-border students. Large category in some nations [Brazil, Philippines]

Figure 1.   Polar field of global higher education, after Bourdieu.
Note: Horizontal axis maps autonomy/heteronomy. Vertical axis maps degree of global engagement. Numbers signify order of status in the global field.

business elite. The Super-league universities combine the two functions, increasing their weight and integrating them closely at the centre of economic and political power. Further, elite universities, particularly the US Ivy League, are not just status dominant but *economically* dominant *vis-à-vis* mass producers. The Super-league command extraordinary resources: for example, the Harvard endowment, the commercial presence of American research universities in bio-science. Nevertheless Bourdieu is right to state that more autonomous universities are less commercial in temper. Super-league universities do not expand willy-nilly to maximise market share like a capitalist business. Their authority derives not from their equity price but from their selectivity and knowledge. They maximise not sales but research impact. Their lodestone is not revenues but social power. Where they run commercial suboperations, the resulting tensions are absorbed within the institution, playing out inside research programmes that are alternately fundamental and commercial (the two are mixed together almost irretrievably in bioscience) and in the cultural differences between arts/disciplinary science and business studies.

Position and position-taking

Within a field of power, agents compete for resources, status or other objects of interest. Bourdieu describes an inter-dependency between the prior positions of agents and the position-taking strategies they select.

> Every position-taking is defined in relation to the *space of possibles* which is objectively realized as a *problematic* in the form of the actual or potential position-takings corresponding to the different positions; and it receives its distinctive *value* from its negative relationship with the coexistent position-takings to which it is objectively related. (Bourdieu 1993, 30; emphasis in original)

Position-taking is the 'space of creative works' (p. 39). This is not an open-ended free-wheeling creativity. Only some position-takings are possible, identified by agents as they respond to changes in the settings and the moves of others in the competition game. Agents have a number of possible 'trajectories', the succession of positions occupied by the same agent over time, and employ semi-instinctual 'strategies' to achieve them. Agents respond in terms of their 'habitus', their acquired mix of beliefs and capabilities, and in particular their 'disposition' that mediates the relationship between position and position-takings (Bourdieu 1993, 61–73).

This schema is consistent with much of the evidence on the decisions of university executives as they strive for relative advantage (for example, Marginson and Considine 2000, 68–95). Bourdieu's concepts of positioned/position taking can be applied in situated case studies (Deem 2001) of the strategies of universities each with its distinctive habitus. Specific national trajectories can be identified in, say, China, Singapore and Australia (Marginson 2007). Nevertheless, there are questions about how much room is left for self-determining agency. Bourdieu claims a reciprocity between structure and agency. 'Although position helps to shape dispositions, the latter, in so far as they are the product of independent conditions, have an existence and an efficacy of their own and can help shape positions' (Bourdieu 1993, 61). 'The scope allowed for dispositions' is variable, being shaped by the autonomy of the field in relation to other fields, by the position of the agent in the field, and by the extent to which the position is a novel and emerging one, or path-dependency has been established (1993, 72). But the 'in so far as' creates ambiguity. Bourdieu also fails to distinguish hierarchy from overwhelming power within a field such as higher education. This problem will considered first, before returning to agency.

Gramsci and global university hegemony

Here Bourdieu is usefully supplemented by Antonio Gramsci with his notion of *egemonia* (hegemony). Gramsci couples and contrasts two regimes of power. The first is domination or coercion by the open state machine, the 'State-as-force' (Gramsci 1971, 56). The second is hegemony, 'the "spontaneous" consent given by the great masses of the population to the general direction imposed on social life by the dominant fundamental group' (1971, 12). Hegemony is secured primarily in civil society, including education (Gramsci 1971, 12). It is a social construction in the realms of intellectual reason, institutions and popular culture in which a certain way of life and thought is diffused. There are parallels with Foucault's (1991) distinction between political sovereignty and government as the conduct of conduct permeating all aspects of life. Like Foucault, Gramsci emphasises that the two regimes constitute mutually dependent strategies. Rule by consent is ultimately underpinned by rule by force (Gramsci 1971, 10).

Civil institutions like universities are analytically distinct from the state (political society) but intertwined with it. Tradition is an active, shaping force in making hegemony. Certain meanings and practices are selected into the common tradition. Elite universities secure their role as manufacturers of tradition, distinct from other universities, with symbols of venerability such as roman numerals and baroque stone. Does Gramsci see hegemony with its grounding in city states and nations as potentially global? Yes.

> Every relationship of 'hegemony' is necessarily an educational relationship and occurs not only within a nation, between the various forces of which a nation is composed, but in the international and worldwide field, between the complexes of national and continental civilizations. (Gramsci 1971, 350)

In one respect, however, Gramsci's theorisation has dated. He saw the USA as lagging behind because it 'has not yet created a conception of the world or a group of great intellectuals to lead the people within the ambit of civil society' (1971, 272). This is no longer the case. American not European universities lead global civil society, installing a conception of the world consistent with American economic, political and military power. More to the point, Gramsci remarks that hegemony can vary in the degree of integration it facilitates. Although hegemony mostly presupposes that account is taken of the interests and tendencies of the groups over which it is exercised, there is the hegemony of the Italian *Risorgimento*, which does not feel the need to secure concordance between its interests and those of the dominated groups or engage with their specificities such as languages and ways of life 'They wished to "dominate" and not to "lead"' (Gramsci 1971, 104–105). This argument is more contemporary, more indicative of the forms of American hegemony.

Manifestations of American hegemony

The instrumental strength of the United States in higher education is massive compared with all other nations. It has the third largest population, the largest Gross Domestic Product (GDP) and a GDP per head of almost US$42,000, and spends the highest proportion of GDP on tertiary education – 2.9%, about $360 billion, in 2003. The next largest spender is Japan at $51 billion. The United States invests seven times as much on tertiary education as the next nation (Table 1).

This overwhelming concentration of resources explains little in itself but is a condition for many things. How is US hegemony in higher education manifest? Hegemony is not top-down in the manner of a military command. It is accumulated in worldwide networks dominated by American institutions that define not just scholarly and managerial agendas but the idea of a university in this era. Hegemony is enabled by and expressed in American global geo-strategic mobility; that freedom to go anywhere and intervene in other national sites while maintaining territorial control of the homeland. This paper notes four aspects of US hegemony: research concentration and knowledge flows, the global role of English, and American universities as people attractors and as exemplars of ideal practice.

Table 1. US GDP, GDP per head, spending on tertiary education, leading researchers and research universities, compared with the next 10 OECD nations on spending and the five largest nations.

	Population, 2005 (millions)	GDP in PPP terms, 2005 (US$ billion)	GDP per capita PPP, 2005 (US$)	Proportion of GDP on tertiary education, 2003 (%)	Spending on tertiary education PPP (estimated), 2003/2005 (US$ billion)	Thomson-ISI 'HiCi' researcher, 2007	Research universities in SJTU ranking, 2006		
							Top 50	Top 200	Top 500
USA	296.5	12,409.5	41,854	2.9	360	3837	37	84	167
Japan	128.0	3943.8	30,811	1.3	51	246	2	9	32
Korea	48.3	1056.1	21,868	2.6	27	3	0	1	9
Germany	82.5	2417.5	29,309	1.1	27	243	0	15	40
France	60.7	1829.6	30,120	1.4	26	157	1	6	21
Canada	32.3	1061.2	32,885	2.4	25	175	2	8	22
United Kingdom	60.2	1926.8	32,007	1.1	21	444	5	23	43
Italy	57.5	1667.8	29,019	0.9	15	75	0	6	23
Mexico	103.1	1052.4	10,209	1.3	14	14	0	1	1
Spain	43.4	1133.5	26,125	1.2	14	18	0	1	9
Australia	20.3	643.0	31,642	1.5	10	105	0	6	16
China[a]	1311.4	8787.2	6701	n.a.	n.a.	18	0	2	14
India[b]	1095.6	3815.6	3483	0.7	27	11	0	0	2
Brazil	186.4	1627.3	8730	0.8	13	4	0	1	2
Russia	143.2	1559.9	10,897	0.7	11	5	0	1	2
Indonesia[b]	221.6	847.4	3842	0.3	3	0	0	0	0

Note: PPP, purchasing power parity; n.a., data not available. [a]Includes Hong Kong, excludes five universities from Taiwan. [b]Proportion of GDP spent on tertiary education in 2004 for India and Indonesia. Spending on tertiary education estimated using 2005 GDP data and the 2003 proportion of GDP allocated to tertiary education.
Sources: World Bank (2007), OECD (2006), Thomson-ISI (2007), and SJTU Institute of Higher Education (2007).

First the flows, concentrations and asymmetries in research knowledge. In 2001 US scientists and social scientists published 200,870 journal papers, Japan 57,420, the United Kingdom 47,660, Germany 43,623, China 20,978 and India 11,076. In Indonesia, the world's fourth most populous nation, there were 207 papers. Not much knowledge flows from Indonesia to the USA (National Science Board 2006). Further, whereas in 2001 the USA produced less than one-third of articles it accounted for 44% of citations in the scientific literature (Vincent-Lancrin 2006, 16). US institutions employ 3930 of the Thomson Publishing/Institute for Scientific Information (Thomson-ISI) 'HiCi' researchers that shape the SJTU rankings, compared with 456 in the United Kingdom, 256 in Germany, 253 in Japan, 18 in China, 11 in India and zero in Indonesia. Harvard has 183 HiCi researchers, more than France; Stanford has 134 and UC Berkeley has 85. There are 45 such researchers at Cambridge, and 29 at Oxford (Thomson-ISI 2007).

Second, American universities are the global hub of the communicative environment and are supreme in and through academic language. Institutions in all world regions have partial linkages with other regions but routinely link to US universities (Castells 2001). In hegemony 'great importance is assumed by the general question of language, that is, that is, the question of collectively attaining a single cultural "climate"' (Gramsci 1971, 349). Bourdieu puts it more sharply (1993, 20): establishing a canon is an act of 'symbolic violence' that occludes the norms it displaces and the underlying power relations sustaining it. Certain practices are legitimated as naturally superior and made especially superior to those who do not participate (Bourdieu 1993, 24). English is the first language of one-sixth of the world but the sole global language of research, marginalising Latin, German, French and Russian. It is often used in Masters programmes in non-English-speaking Europe and Asia. It dominates the managerial literature and the Internet.

Third, US universities are extraordinary global attractors of talent. American institutions are open and flexible. They provide superior scholarships and salaries. Foreign doctoral assistants have become essential to American research; the United States is the main site for postdoctoral places and short-term academic visits, and also draws later career migration. Universities in the American doctoral sector focus less on generating revenues from foreign students than on attracting the best people. Whereas 13.4% of all students enrolled in UK tertiary education in 2004 were foreigners, in the USA the proportion was 3.4% (OECD 2006, 303). But almost one-third of the foreign students entering American doctoral universities were doctoral students. In 2004/05 the American doctoral sector enrolled 102,084 foreign doctoral students. Almost two-thirds received financial assistance from their US university (Institute for International Education 2006). Having positioned itself as the world graduate school the USA then keeps one-half of its foreign doctoral graduates, including more than one-half of those from the UK. From 1987 to 2001 the stay rate for foreign doctoral graduates in science and engineering rose from 49% to 71%, reaching 96% for China (OECD 2004, 159). In 2003 three-quarters of European Union citizens who obtained a US doctorate said they had no plans to return to Europe (Tremblay 2005, 208). Net brain-drain in higher education is a problem for all nations except the USA. In using global people flows in higher education to boost knowledge power rather than accumulate capital, American universities decisively positions themselves in Bourdieu's subfield of restricted production as against mass or commercial production, distinguishing themselves from other English-speaking countries.

Fourth, there is the primarily American content of the norms of university and system organisation. The policy imagination everywhere is infused with two idealised institutional models that embody Bourdieu's opposing subfields and are based on a selective reading of US practices. One is the high-status not-for-profit private research-intensive university; selective, a magnet for donors and focused on research and graduate education (the Ivy League). The other is the for-profit vocational institution with broad-based training in business studies and perhaps technologies, health and education; expansionary, spare and efficient, 'customer-focused' without academic frills like research (the University of Phoenix). In policy circles these two ideal types have each been earmarked for organisation as a particular global market. Global hegemony extends not just to normalisation of a single model but to the continuing reconstitution of the global field as a whole.

Yet these ideal types confront very diverse national systems and institutions, such as: the participatory universities of Latin American that take in a large slice of national economic, social, political and cultural life (e.g. the University of Buenos Aires and UNAM in Mexico); the German *Fachhochschulen* and high-quality vocational sectors in Finland and Switzerland; and research institutes in France and Germany. These other types and systems are marginalised by world university league tables, which codify the supremacy of the leading Anglo-American institutions, normalise selective science-intensive universities, and favour English language nations because English is the global research language. Like research publication, global rankings are a technology for securing hegemony (Marginson 2007).

Open and bounded

American research-intensive universities are not organised as a national system and are unusually open to foreign personnel, but American exceptionalism and the periodic American isolationism sustain a firm boundary with the rest of the higher education world and American institutions exhibit a remarkable cultural coherence in their dealings with it. Open and bounded. Openness is expressed in the free mobility of talent into the USA and the outward flows of American knowledge, a gift that no one can refuse. Boundedness is sustained by the American-dominated system of research and publishing in English and the abiding sense of national superiority. This is the *Risorgimento*. Rather than engaging closely with non-American institutions to learn the languages of use and build capability, US universities mostly ignore them, leaving them to evolve towards US templates according to their capacity and 'merit'. Scholars outside the USA are under-cited. The worldwide Carnegie survey of the academic profession found that while over 90% of scholars from other nations believed it necessary to read foreign books and journals, only 62% of Americans agreed, much the smallest level among developed nations (Altbach 2005, 148–149). The non-American world is on the periphery of American vision. But, for the rest of higher education, the great American universities loom large in the landscape.

American hegemony in higher education and university research rests above all on knowledge concentrations and flows. (Bourdieu's neglect of knowledge formation helps to explain his neglect of hegemony.) US university hegemony is akin to US domination of communications and the contents of film, television and hand-held media; and to American financial and technological might. It is almost akin to the US global domination of military capacity. Perhaps a case can be made for Anglo-American hegemony in higher education given the role of English, UK research strength and the worldwide authority of Cambridge and Oxford (although middling UK universities have less global clout than their American counterparts). But if there is an Anglo-American hegemony, the United Kingdom is a very junior partner.

Is there a way out? How solidly fixed are worldwide power relations in higher education? This goes to questions of global agency and ontology.

Agency in the global field

From time to time, university and research leaders engage in off-the-wall innovations not fully explained by prior positions and conditions, especially in the global field: for example, the first branch campuses in importing nations, the global schoolhouse strategy in Singapore, the MIT open courseware initiative. Here limits of Bourdieu's theorisation of agency are apparent, with implications also for his theorisation of the field of power. The problem is not just that the changes in the global setting, the emergence of a worldwide communicative system and a single system of published research have transformed the map of positions and the position-taking options. Bourdieu himself would make that point. Rather, the problem is that he sees agency freedom, self-determining identity, as bound *a priori* by the stratification of class power lodged in the unconscious.

In *Distinction* Bourdieu talks about an opposition between 'the tastes of luxury (or freedom) and the tastes of necessity' (1984, 177). The potential for self-determination is confined to freedom from material necessity.[3] However, while self-determination *is* conditioned by resources and historical relations of power and it is essential to understand these conditions, they do not close the list of possibilities. Self-determining freedom is conditioned also by agency itself, by the imagination and the capacity of agents to work on their own limits. Gramsci knew this, with his emphasis on the will and individual initiative. Likewise Amartya Sen (1985, 1992) distinguishes self-determining agency freedom from resources, freedom from constraint and its other conditions. When these conditions are held constant, the range of choices may still be expanded; in the first instance by thought. To the long list of elements that differentiate self-determination in higher education and condition the map of power, including national GDP and investment, research capacity, language, the volume and intensity of cross-border engagements, and so on, we can add the *creative imagination* of governments, universities, disciplines, groups and individuals. In contrast, for Bourdieu 'strategy' is not based on conscious imagining and deciding so much as on learned dispositions, the habitus. The range and limits of possible position-taking strategies, appropriate to the position of each agent, is burned into the mind and conditions every action. Agents move instinctively in response to changing possibilities. 'Because position-takings arise quasi-mechanically – that is, almost independently of the agents' consciousnesses and wills – from the relationship between positions, they take relatively invariant forms' (Bourdieu 1993, 59). Conscious 'lucidity is always partial and is, once again, a matter of position and trajectory within the field' (1993, 72). This reifies not just human reflexivity but the reciprocity between structure and agency on which Bourdieu's system turns. He becomes trapped on the structure side of a dual he has created, before the dual can be re-reconciled. If the scope for action is decisively confined by limitations to our inner mental horizons installed by a prior materiality, self-determination has been locked.

A further difficulty is that Bourdieu universalises competition. There is no respite from the relentless war of all against all that continually eats into our conditions of possibility. Yet intersubjective relations in global higher education are often cooperative. Bourdieu's pre-structuring of agency and conscious imagining also leaves insufficient scope for the multiple investments in both fields and identity characteristic of the open global setting (Sen 1999), in which positionality is continually made and remade by strategic action.

Global ontology

Arjun Appadurai (1996) discusses this broader range of possibilities, envisioning the global as a zone of new imaginings and the construction and self-construction of identity. Emphasising mobility, plurality 'and in general, agency', he describes 'a new global cultural economy ... a complex, overlapping, disjunctive order' (1996, 32) with 'interactions of a new order and intensity' (Appadurai 1996, 27) in which human agents generate global cultural flows, and flows generate and transform agents. Diasporic populations use media, communications and return travel to create hybrid identities within more malleable configurations of locality, breaking the monopoly of nation-states over modernisation (Appadurai 1996, 10). Appadurai famously specifies 'five dimensions of global cultural flows': ethnoscapes, mediascapes, technoscapes, financescapes and ideoscapes (1996, 33ff.) that are 'building blocks' of these 'imagined worlds'. Each scape has its own logic, and intersects with and conditions the other scapes in unpredictable ways. 'The suffix -scape allows us to point to the fluid, irregular shapes of these landscapes' (Appadurai 1996, 33). Global flows are structured but their structures are uneven, overlapping, disjunctive, asynchronous, temporary and contingent. This contrasts with not only Bourdieu's attenuated notion of agency but also his more robust notion of fields, which requires bounded-ness, predictability and a certain insularity.

The global dimension of higher education is in continuous formation, the map of positions is continually being reworked and novel positions are emerging. Why this greater ontological openness in the global setting? One factor is the growth, extension, reciprocity, dynamism, insta-bility and contingency of cross-border flows. As the fluid ever-moving metaphor of 'flows' suggests, flows generate change on a continuous basis even as they themselves are changing. These effects are conditioned by permeable national borders, the transience of global networks and the flaky borders of the global field; and lacunae in the governmental regulation of cross-border relations and room for spontaneous association this creates. Above all there are the expanded potentials for agency freedom created by the global transformations in space and time: more multiple locations; faster passage between them; instantaneous, expanded, intensified and multi-associating communications; multiple and variously articulated spheres of action. All of this loosens relations of power.

Yet Appadurai's suggestive reading of flows, scapes and disjuncture also has limits for understanding global higher education (Marginson and Sawir 2005). He argues 'the nation-state ... is on its last legs', and that 'globalisation does not necessarily or even frequently imply homogenisation or Americanisation' (Appadurai 1996, 17). Claims that the nation-state is vanishing and hegemony is a paper tiger are less convincing since the assertion of American military-security globalisation after 9/11; and implausible in the higher education sector where capacity is shaped by patterns of national investment. The larger point is that it is unhelpful to consider the global as a single space, open and volatile, which contains the whole of human action. It is one identifiable space where human action is played out, suffused with unpredict-ability in the manner of Appadurai's scapes. It sits alongside the national and local spaces and connects with them at many points. Working across all three of these relatively open spaces we find more bounded and predictable (although no longer closed) domains such as law, govern-mental regulation and finance. These domains of practice have their own global aspect or dimen-sion, and they intersect with Appadurai's global scapes, but they are not reducible to the global (still less the national) 'as a whole'. Grounded in traditions and institutions, domains such as law and government tend to be more regular and stable and tightly bordered than scapes. Neverthe-less in a more global era they are bigger and less stable than they once were, and infused with greater dynamism and unpredictability by the scapes. One such domain of practice is higher education and the associated research. Within such domains, Bourdieu's notions of field of power and position-taking retain the larger part of their potency.

Even so, if the global space is immersed in the multiple and unpredictable with ever-growing scope for imagining, this places a question mark alongside American hegemony. Hegemony is a bold effort to impose form on flux, to stop time and centre control in particular sites. How could any such project ever be anything but provisional? How could it not fail 'in the long run'? That does not mean that US university hegemomy is ephemeral or incapable of present domina-tion, only that the project must be continually made and remade as Gramsci saw until its capacity for renewal is finally undermined, fragmented or exhausted. Appadurai (1996) implies that hegemony can be subverted from below, in hybrid academic forms created in the gaps left by American exceptionalism and isolationism. There is more potential for hybridity in some practices than others. People movement, where the US fosters openness, readily generates complex identities. Organisational models are nested in historical conditions and open to local self-determination and variation. In teaching there is plurality of languages of use, including the heterogeneous 'Englishes', hybrid responses to tenacious cultural traditions. However, and despite the fluidity of intellectual discourse, there is less scope for hybridity in research and knowledge. As noted, it is here, above all, that elite status and global power in higher education are secured. A tight binary logic of inclusion/exclusion assigns worldwide academic labour to one of two categories: part of the global research circuit that uses the dominant language and publishes in the recognised outlets; or 'not global', outside the hegemonic circuit, the bearer of knowledge obsolete or meaningless and doomed to be invisible. Will this hold? Appadurai's argument nests the closure of research within the larger openness of mobility and scapes. The global research system is layered over the top of a vast potential for imaginings. More concretely, there is pluralisation in the rise of China and other Asian science powers (China doubled investment in R&D as a share of GDP during 1995–2005) and the potential of Spanish and Arabic as global languages.

The expanded and more open global ontology is experienced differentially. Some have more freedoms of action than others. Bourdieu's point is that autonomy, capacity and scope for strategy are concentrated in the high academic subfield. Here an individual institutional break with hegemony is telling, but few will risk losing their place in the sun. The point about concentration is right but not the end of the story. All structures are open to change including hegemonic structures. Especially in the global field, any structural dynamic must be considered partial, relativised by the other parts of the field, provisional and in continuous transformation. There is no closure. One element always at play in the field and a primary source of this ontological openness is the imagination and will of agents.

Acknowledgements

This is a revised version of a paper delivered in the ESRC-funded seminars 'Geographies of Knowledge/ Geometries of Power: Global Higher Education in the 21st Century', 5–7 February 2007, Gregynog, Wales. Grateful thanks to Debbie Epstein, Rebecca Boden, Rajani Naidoo and others present, and the two referees.

Notes

1. The work is also informed by 12 case studies of the cross-border practices of research-intensive national universities in the Asia-Pacific, the Americas and Western Europe (for example, Marginson and Sawir 2005).
2. The SJTU Institute of Higher Education (2007) measures include publication and citation in leading journals, and the location of highly cited researchers, and of winners of Nobel Prizes and field medals in mathematics.
3. In *On Freedom* Zyggy Bauman (1988) makes a similar argument.

References

Altbach, P. 2005. Academic challenges: the American professoriate in comparative perspective. In *The professoriate: Portrait of a profession,* ed. A. Welch. Dordrecht: Springer.
Appadurai, A. 1996. *Modernity at large: Cultural dimensions of globalisation.* Minneapolis: University of Minnesota Press.
Bauman, Z. 1988. *Freedom.* Milton Keynes: Open University Press.
Bourdieu P. 1984. *Distinction: A social critique of the judgment of taste.* London: Routledge & Kegan Paul.
———. 1988. *Homo academicus.* Cambridge: Polity.
———. 1993. *The field of cultural production.* New York: Columbia University Press.

————. 1996. *The State Nobility.* Cambridge: Polity.

Castells, M. 2000. *The rise of the network society.* 2nd ed. Oxford: Blackwell.

————. 2001. *The Internet galaxy.* Oxford: Oxford University Press.

Deem, R. 2001. Globalisation, new managerialism, academic capitalism and entrepreneurialism in universities: Is the local dimension still important? *Comparative Education* 37, no. 1: 7–20.

The Economist. 2005. The brains business, September 8.

Foucault, M. 1991. Governmentality. In *The Foucault effect: Studies in governmentality,* ed. G. Burchell, C. Gordon and P. Miller. London: Harvester Wheatsheaf.

Gramsci, A. 1971. *Selections from the prison notebooks.* New York: International Publishers.

Held, D., A. McGlew, D. Goldblatt, and J. Perraton. 1999. *Global transformations.* Stanford, CA: Stanford University Press.

Institute for International Education. 2006. Data on US international education. http://opendoors.iienetwork.org/?p=69736 (accessed August 17, 2006).

Marginson, S. 2007. Global university rankings. In *Prospects of higher education: Globalisation, market competition, public goods and the future of the university,* ed. S. Marginson. Rotterdam: Sense Publishers.

Marginson, S., and M. Considine. 2000. *The enterprise university: Power, governance and reinvention in Australia.* Cambridge: Cambridge University Press.

Marginson, S., and G. Rhoades. 2002. Beyond national states, markets, and systems of higher education: A glonacal agency heuristic. *Higher Education* 43: 281–309.

Marginson, S., and E. Sawir. 2005. Interrogating global flows in higher education. *Globalization, Societies and Education* 3, no. 3: 281–310.

Naidoo, R. 2004. Fields and institutional strategy: Bourdieu on the relationship between higher education, inequality and society. *British Journal of Sociology of Education* 25, no. 4: 446–72.

National Science Board. 2006. Science and engineering indicators 2004. http://www.nsf.gov/statistics/seind04/ (accessed September 30, 2006).

Organization for Economic Cooperation and Development. 2004. *OECD science, technology and industry outlook.* Paris: OECD.

————. 2006. *Education at a glance 2006.* Paris: OECD.

Sen, A. 1985. Well-being, agency and freedom: The Dewey lectures 1984. *The Journal of Philosophy* 82, no. 4: 169–221.

————. 1992. *Inequality reexamined.* Cambridge, MA: Harvard University Press.

————. 1999. Global justice: Beyond international equity. In *Global public goods: International cooperation in the 21st century,* ed. I. Kaul, I. Grunberg, and M. Stern. New York: Oxford University Press.

Shanghai Jiao Tong University Institute of Higher Education. 2007. Academic ranking of world universities. http://ed.sjtu.edu.cn/ranking.htm (accessed February 19, 2007).

Thomson Publishing/Institute for Scientific Information. 2007. Data on highly cited researchers. ISIHighly Cited.com. http://hcr3.isiknowledge.com/home.cgi (accessed August 9, 2007).

Tremblay, K. 2005. Academic mobility and immigration. *Journal of Studies in International Education* 9, no. 3: 196–228.

Trow, M. 1974. Problems in the transition from elite to mass higher education. *Policies for higher education.* From the General Report on the Conference on Future Structures of Post-Secondary Education. Paris: OECD.

Valimaa, J. 2004. Nationalisation, localisation and globalisation in Finnish higher education. *Higher Education* 48: 27–54.

Vincent-Lancrin, S. 2006. What is changing in academic research? Trends and futures scenarios. Draft paper. Paris: OECD-CERI.

World Bank. 2007. World Bank data and statistics. http://www.worldbank.org/data (accessed February 28, 2007).

Equity and diversity: towards a sociology of higher education for the twenty-first century?

Miriam David[a]

Institute of Education, University of London, UK

Introduction

When I agreed to write a review essay on social change and higher education, I did not fully appreciate quite what a complex and diverse field of studies I would have to consider, and this essay thus represents a very brief commentary on a huge field. I felt I had an overview of the research in higher education (David, 2003) both as a sociologist of education and as a critical educational researcher reflecting upon pedagogies and practices of teaching both undergraduate and postgraduate students of education and social science, and through doctoral education and research training. My involvement in developing new fields of study such as women's studies and feminist sociology and reflecting upon how to transform the academy to engage new kinds of students, and academics, women especially, through feminist pedagogies and practices also contributed (David, 2005). Finally, my brief as associate director for higher education within the Economic and Social Research Council's Teaching and Learning Research Programme provided me with an overview of new research on widening participation in higher education in the United Kingdom, the links with forms of post-compulsory schooling (and especially the transforming field of further education and education for 14–19 year olds) and sociological research within higher education and lifelong learning. Perhaps as one totally immersed in academia and educational research, I had not quite appreciated the far-reaching but often unintended consequences of globalization for higher education itself and how these social and political global transformations seem to be creating constant change, both conceptually and organizationally. However, I was aware of how contested some critical and feminist perspectives on higher educational changes, especially in policy arenas, were (Watson, 2007).

As Deem (2004) cogently argued at an international conference on sociology of education, there is nevertheless still no field that can really be called the sociology of higher education, despite the increasing engagement by social scientists in issues of research, policy and practice in higher education. However, a brief review of *British Journal of Sociology of Education* provides a clear indication of the diversity of emerging studies on higher education merely within sociology of education. At the time of writing, in the three issues for volume 28 in 2007 about one-half of the articles are about the topic or subject of higher education, with international pieces ranging from studies on access to, choices or preparation for participation in forms of higher education, student retention, doctoral studies and issues about academic staff and promotion as well as innovative social theory about the information revolution and reviews of changing practices in higher education. By contrast, in the recently published volume (Barton, 2007) to celebrate 25 years of the journal (1979–2004) only two articles out of 16 chosen to illustrate the themes across the field over this period are on questions of higher education, both relatively recently published and about inequalities and ethnic or class 'barriers' to higher education (Lynch & O'Riordan, 1998; Shiner & Modood, 2002, in Barton, 2007).

Transformations in global higher education and research in the twenty-first century

In the twenty-first century alone, we have witnessed massive global social and economic change that has influenced all of our conceptualizations and understandings of higher education in relation to the economy, society, states, work or labour, markets and knowledge (Slaughter & Leslie, 1997; Barnett, 2000, 2003; Delanty, 2001; Slaughter & Rhoades, 2004; Burgan, 2006; Frank & Gabler, 2006; Lauder *et al.*, 2006; Rhoads & Torres, 2006; Raffe & Spours, 2007; Sagaria, 2007; Shavit *et al.*, 2007). Moreover, as economic changes have influenced the growth and spread of forms of post-compulsory schooling, what counts as higher and/or university education is increasingly contested and the practices and divisions between teaching and research in higher education challenging and challenged (Bok, 2003, 2005; Brew, 2001, 2006; Ramsden, 1998; Rowland, 2006; Jenkins *et al.*, 2007). As higher education has expanded and become more diversified, so too have the social sciences and sociology within social sciences (Becher & Trowler, 2002; Barnett & Coate, 2005; Lauder *et al.*, 2006; Shavit *et al.*, 2007). How we conceptualize and understand these transformations, and research studies within sociology around equality, equity and diversity, take on new meanings and perspectives, as do studies within sociology of education (Morley, 2003; Arnot, 2002; Hey, 2004; Sagaria, 2007). Knowledge and methodological approaches to notions of research for and on/in higher education have also increasingly become contested (Barnett, 2003; Barnett & Coate, 2005; Clegg & David, 2006; Rhode, 2006). Not only have the discourse of higher education and policies and practices within higher education been transformed towards notions of pedagogies and teaching and learning (Walker, 2006; McLean, 2006), but there is also a question of the role of the disciplines within and across the social sciences, as well as for the arts and natural sciences and applied or vocational subjects (Becher & Trowler, 2002). In other words, the landscape of higher education has been completely transformed for what counts as students or learners, teachers or academics and researchers or research (Morley, 2003; David, 2005; Rowland, 2006; Walker, 2006; McLean, 2006).

On the other hand, there have also been moves to professionalize higher education and the practices of teachers within and across higher education, drawing on either explicitly or implicitly the social sciences, developing new forms of teaching and learning or academic practices and development (for example, Fry *et al.*, 2003). Whilst much of this draws on the sociology of education, there remains a challenging debate about the contributions of the disciplines of the social sciences and sociology of education; in particular, to the practices of academic development. Perhaps this new debate mirrors the debates in the 1980s about the contributions of the sociology of education to teacher education for schoolteachers (Acker, 1997; Dillabough & Acker, 2002). However, now, the debate about discipline or subject teaching in higher education draws on rival approaches to the history and practices of traditional universities and notions of academic enquiry (Slaughter & Rhoades, 2004; Rowland, 2006; Maher & Treteault, 2007). Indeed, the massive expansion of postgraduate work and research training produces a profound contradiction around methods and methodologies of research across the disciplines and the emerging inter-disciplinarity within and across universities and the broader field of higher education nationally and internationally (Delamont *et al.*, 1998, 2000; Leonard, 2001; McWilliam *et al.*, 2002; Morley, 2003; Tinkler & Jackson, 2004; Maher & Treteault, 2007).

Some of the most interesting yet challenging international studies in the twenty-first century have used sociological theories and methodologies, making the field of higher education intellectually creative and innovative, despite the more forbidding and negative socio-political context of globalization and neo-liberalism (Evans, 2004/05; Slaughter & Rhoades, 2004; Maher & Treteault, 2007). These educational and social research studies on higher education can be organized around four themes, namely: (i) equity, social stratification and social mobility; (ii) diversity as a changing concept in relation to ethnicity/race, social class and gender for individuals and institutions; (iii) globalization and higher education nationally or internationally; and (iv) discourses around teaching and learning, pedagogies and academic practices. These illustrate the rich diversity of social theories and methodologies of higher education, and I explore these briefly below.

Equity, social stratification and mobility: the role of higher education

Historically, within sociology there has been a major concern with how education, and higher education in particular, contributes to social mobility and equal opportunities, mainly with respect to the students involved. Indeed many of the now classic studies are of this kind of approach (Halsey *et al.*, 1956, 1980; Halsey & Trow, 1971; Trow, 2005), whether through sociological analyses or policy concerns. Olive Banks (1955), a pioneering British sociologist of education (and a founder member of this

journal), innovatively addressed the question of how an education system that stratified schools in relation to a stratified labour market in the early post-war period could
provide 'parity of prestige', to use term she coined over 50 years ago in respect of
secondary rather than higher education.

There remains a vitally important question about whether Banks' view of the
relationships of secondary schools to the labour market in the early 1950s holds true
for evidence about universities today. She argued precisely that:

> The nation's *secondary* education had to be understood through its relationship with the
> labour market which rewarded educational skills and qualifications according to a social
> hierarchy. The two or three different types of education could not possibly result in each
> school enjoying 'parity of prestige'. *'If ... the prestige a school derives from the social and
> economic status of the occupations for which it prepares, then equality of prestige is clearly
> impossible.*(Banks, 1955, p. 30, emphasis added)

There is clearly sociological evidence, within a revised theoretical and methodological
framework, which demonstrates how social mobility and stratification are strongly
related to educational processes and systems. For example, a major new edited collection, drawing on this as a traditional approach while also providing a revised conceptual framework (Lauder *et al.*, 2006), continues to argue the importance of education
for social mobility. Similarly Fiona Devine's (2004) comparative sociological study of
various middle-class families in Boston and Manchester presents an analysis within
this tradition, showing that parents, whether professional doctors or teachers, strive
to get 'good jobs' for their children. Drawing on work with Savage (Savage *et al.*,
2005) and his emerging methodological framework (Savage, 2003), her approach
remains a dominant concern within particular approaches to the field of social
mobility.

More importantly from the point of view of traditional sociological studies within
a quantitative research paradigm, and in relation to higher education, there is a major
new comparative text using international empirical evidence from higher education
systems in 15 different countries. This edited collection both reviews the field and
provides individual country analyses contained within highly focused essays. The
editors (Shavit *et al.*, 2007) argue that:

> research on social stratification, particularly on the relation between education and strati-
> fication, has for decades recognized the importance of cross-national comparisons ...
> Much of this past work was carried out by members of the Research Committee on social
> stratification (RC28) of the International Sociological Association, an important intellec-
> tual forum for the exposition and discussion of ideas and findings contained in this schol-
> arship ... the distinctive focus of this book is on higher education ... [and] changes in
> stratification and higher education through the 1990s ... in light of conceptual develop-
> ments in the last decade. (p. xi)

The editors present a theoretical overview of the field in their substantive and
substantial introduction, entitled 'More Inclusion Than Diversion: Expansion,
Differentiation, and Market Structure in Higher Education' (Arum *et al.*, in Shavit
et al., 2007, pp. 1–35), following which there are chapters grouped together through
an analytical lens addressed in the introduction, namely: *diversified* systems of Israel,

Japan, Korea, Sweden, Taiwan and the United States; *binary* systems of Great Britain (*sic*), France, Germany, The Netherlands, Russia and Switzerland; and, finally, *unitary* and other systems of Australia, The Czech Republic and Italy. The argument around 'the key question about educational expansion is whether it reduces inequality by providing more opportunities for persons from disadvantaged strata, or magnifies inequality by expanding opportunities disproportionately for those who are already privileged' (Shavit *et al.*, 2007, p. 1). In other words, the editors address a question similar to that posed by Banks about secondary education and whether or not different education systems produce a highly stratified labour force in relation to their different educations. Indeed, in reviewing the literature and social and economic arguments, they present a range of different hypotheses about the relationships between '… expansion and differentiation' and whether 'higher education expansion is primarily a process of *diversion* [*sic*], channeling members of the working class to lower-status postsecondary opportunities in order to reserve higher-status opportunities for the elite (Brint and Karabel 1989) or a … process of *inclusion*' (Shavit *et al.*, pp. 5–6). They therefore develop the argument by reference to three different types of higher education system; namely that different social and political processes have produced different new systems of higher education, ranging from what they call 'diversified systems' to 'binary' to 'unitary and other systems'. More importantly, the researchers in all the countries used similar data-sets based upon educational expansion and change in the 1990s, and they reach rather complex findings about the three-fold relationship between expansion, differentiation and diversification. Their over-arching conclusions are complex too, but they argue that 'findings from this project provide evidence of the relations among institutional expansion, differentiation and privatization, and stratification of individual educational opportunity' (Shavit *et al.*, 2007, p. 27). They find overall *persistent inequality* (*sic*) (Shavit *et al.*, p.29) but that it may have policy implications about how to transform class inequalities in an expanding situation where they 'reach a more optimistic conclusion' (p. 29).

This very worthy and interesting comparative research study, however, is based upon a methodological approach to data collection through statistical case studies and, with the benefit of hindsight, out-dated data on the 1990s, given the constantly changing higher education systems. Nevertheless, their conclusions are in line with previous studies of comparative educational systems that show educational expansion does not necessarily lead to more equality or even inclusion, but rather to greater diversification or diversion (to coin their terms). In other words, expanding education and opportunities may, and indeed does, in this study lead to maintaining broad social inequalities, despite the changing economic and social structures and systems.

The authors, however, also notice a major flaw in their approach and insert 'a note on gender inequality' within their introduction (Shavit *et al.*, 2007, pp. 25–26). They say:

> although it was not the main focus of our inquiry, *we would be remiss if we did not mention the findings related to variation in gender inequality* … consistent with other researchers … our findings indicate that men's advantages in educational attainment declined

dramatically during the second half of the twentieth century. The erosion of male advantage is especially pronounced for participation in postsecondary education. In all countries for which data are available, and in both the conditional and unconditional models, men's relative advantage declined ... In sum, our data show an average widening of the gender gap in higher education favoring women, and indicate that the gap expanded fastest in systems where attendance rates expanded most. While there are differences across systems in the rate of change, overall there is a fairly uniform pattern of women's increasing participation in higher education, closing the gap, and then often coming to outperform men in higher education enrollment. (Shavit *et al.*, 2007, pp. 25–27; emphasis added)

This then seems to be a very serious flaw in their approach, since not only is there a massive array of sociological and policy evidence internationally of women outperforming men in enrolments but also achievements at first-degree level (Lauder *et al.*, 2006), although these may not translate into gender equity in labour force participation. Indeed, in commenting upon the case study on the United Kingdom (Cheung & Egerton, 2007), as an example of a binary system, the editors make the comment that 'perhaps the most dramatic change between these two cohorts was the complete disappearance of the male advantage in eligibility for upper tertiary education and in postsecondary attainment conditional on eligibility' (Arum *et al.*, 2007, p. 32). This kind of finding is now dominating current UK policies on post-compulsory education, especially in recent debates about policies such as widening access or participation and *AimHigher*. For example, a report for the Higher Education Funding Council for England on the subject of 'Young participation in higher education' in January 2005 found that:

> Inequality of the sexes in young participation has risen steadily: by the end of the period studied, young women in England are 18 per cent more likely to enter higher education than young men. This inequality is more marked for young men living in the most disadvantaged areas, and is further compounded by the fact that young men are less likely than young women to successfully complete their higher education courses and gain a qualification ... (Higher Education Funding Council for England, 2005, p. 13)

The report also found that the participation rate in higher education (whether universities or higher education colleges) of young people (aged 18 or 19) in England was around 30% at the end of the period studied (2003/04) while 53.7% of first-year undergraduates were aged 21 or over, or one can argue that the majority of students enrolled on first degrees were in their twenties and (technically at least) mature students.

Whilst the findings on gender equality may come as a surprise to Shavit *et al.* (2007), they are certainly no surprise in the British educational policy arena where social commentators have seen these concerns as the 'poor boys' debate' (Alldred & David, 2007). Women have outnumbered men since 1996/97, and in 2006/07 women were 60% of the full-time student population in British universities (although there are differences across the regions of the United Kingdom; namely English, Irish, Scottish and Welsh differences) (Office of National Statistics, www.ons.org.uk, accessed March 2007). However, men remain the majority in overseas undergraduate and postgraduate enrolments in 2006/07. Moreover, in 2005/06 women were 61.4% of part-time students and 64.2% of mature students (over 21 years old). Even more importantly, women with qualifications to enter higher education (two or more GCE A-levels) more than doubled their proportions from 20% in 1992/93 to 43% in 2005/06, whereas the proportionate increase for men in 2005/06 to a little over one-third (34%) was from a lower base of 18% in 1992/93. Thus the gender performance gap in entry qualifications in 2005/06 was nine per cent compared with just less than two per cent in 1992/93.

These British statistics of gender changes in access to higher education over the past 15 years confirm the note on gender inequality (Shavit *et al.*, 2007), and make it more important as a conceptual and analytical issue than merely an addendum. While these figures and trends are drawn from British policy documents, they clearly illustrate a strong trend in changing features of social class analysis, although not necessarily within a social scientific paradigm (Gorard *et al.*, 2006). However, despite the considerable work by feminists and other gender and critical analysts over the past 20 or 30 years (for example, Arnot *et al.*, 1999; Arnot, 2002; Reay *et al.*, 2005; Savage *et al.*, 2005) the more sophisticated sociological approaches have not been taken up within the policy arena. Critical and/or feminist work has led to an array of sociological studies about students' access and choice of higher education (for example, Bowl, 2003; Reay *et al.*, 2005; Langa Rosado & David, 2006) that deal not only with questions of social class but in relation to gender, ethnicity or race and, separately, by religion or faith (for example, Arthur, 2006).

Diversity as a changing concept in relation to ethnicity/race, social class and gender for individuals and institutions

One of the key features of the emerging literature on higher education is the conceptualization of diversity, and its varied meanings in relation to these studies. Shavit *et al.* (2007) used the concept in relation to systems and institutions but others use it in relation to individuals and their various social characteristics. Whilst until the twenty-first century diversity was usually taken to mean issues in relation to race and ethnicity within educational research and policy studies (see, for example, the seminal study by Ladson-Billings [2001]), this is no longer simply the approach. Studies on diversity in the USA range from work on systems to individuals around their ethnicity (Parker, 2007). For example, Sylvia Hurtado (2007), in her Presidential address to Association for the Study of Higher Education, developed an argument about how to link notions of diversity with the broader educational and civic missions of higher education, conceptualizing diversity as about ethnicity and race. Similarly, Rhoads and Torres' (2006) edited text also contained a range of studies about ethnic diversity in not only the USA but other countries of the Americas—in particular, using the notion in relation to Latin America. Yet other studies within and across different types and levels of post-compulsory or tertiary education have focused upon conceptions of equity in relation to ethnicity rather than class or gender (for example, Bailey & Morest, 2006).

Shavit *et al.* (2007) struggled with their conceptualizations of social class, gender and stratification, through a conception of diversion and/or inclusion, whilst there are far more sophisticated sociological approaches in the emerging literature. A particularly intriguing and interesting study is that entitled *Privilege and Diversity in the Academy* by American feminist sociologists Frances Maher and Mary Treteault (2007). Using a sociological framework of analysis, and drawing on Dorothy E. Smith's (1999) institutional ethnography, they argue that:

> we have chosen the terms *privilege* and *diversity* as a framework for our work. For much of the past 30 years, discussions of these issues have taken the form of a rhetorical opposition between the supposed two poles of diversity and *excellence*, where excellence is a code word for commonly agreed-on high standards of academic performance—in other words, rigorous scholarship with universal applicability—and a deservedly high stature for those who meet these standards. Diversity has then meant a spreading out of, a dilution of, and a threat to those standards. However, to us the use of the term excellence is employed not so much as a mark of quality as a mark of privilege—that is, the power of elites to control the norms of the scholarly enterprise in such a way as to keep new people, new topics, and new methodologies at bay. (Maher & Treteault, 2007, pp. 3–4)

They go on to say how difficult they have found it to write about privilege because they see it as embedded in normal practices, and unspoken or like the 'air we breathe': 'It means rarely having to be conscious of your gender, race, class or sexuality. A pervading emphasis on individual experience and achievement ...' (Maher & Treteault, 2007, p. 4). Nevertheless, they provide a careful and intricate analysis of three very different and distinctive American universities—an elite private university (Stanford, CA), a research-intensive public university (Michigan) and a comprehensive and diverse public university (Rutgers)—and their individual and institutional struggles around diversity and excellence/privilege. They also explore then new discourses and meanings of diversity within each university, and draw conclusions around how these lead to different engagements with new research and educational agendas for the twenty-first century. They also draw on the innovative new approaches of other scholars such as Slaughter and Rhoades (2004) on the concept of 'academic capitalism'. The authors conclude that:

> looking at the dynamics of privilege and diversity with this national lens ... we are both puzzled and energized. We are puzzled about how to explain the wide discrepancies between the warnings sounded by national publications about the 'kept university' or 'academic capitalism' versus the sense of autonomy and scholarly integrity ... as for progress of diversity initiatives ... another perspective ... show[s] that the 35 years between the sex discrimination suits of the 1970s and today is too short a period of time to overcome long-entrenched sexism and racism of the academy ... It may take the innovators of this generation, ... of faculty and administrators to fully institutionalize diversity. (Maher & Treteault, 2007, pp. 194–195)

While this conclusion is relatively bleak and gives a long timeframe for change, it chimes in with the similar scholarly work of feminist sociologists in the United Kingdom. For example, Louise Morley's (2003) study of changing practices around equality and quality assurance is also rather pessimistic, and Mary Evans' (2004/05) trenchant critique about the processes of change in British higher education provides little by way of hope for a more creative future. While she does not employ the same concepts of privilege and diversity, she nevertheless argues similarly:

The present woes of higher education can be listed as fourfold: the brutalization of the culture of the academy through assessment and appraisal exercises, the creation of further harsh hierarchy and division between universities where none needs exist, the intensification of social difference through the 'culture wars' and finally the overall diminution of the essential function of the universities which is to educate not train ... (Evans, 2004/05, p. 151)

Globalization and policy changes for higher education nationally or internationally

In this respect, there have been a diverse range of studies of the influences and effects of globalization and neo-liberalism on the transforming academy, perhaps best exemplified by the important work by Slaughter and Rhoades (2004) on 'academic capitalism'. Again, drawing on social theorists such as Castells and Foucault (Slaughter & Rhodes, 2004, p. 14), they argue that:

At the turn of the 21st century the rise of the 'new' global knowledge or information society calls for a fresh account of the relations between higher education institutions and society. Our analysis of these relations has led us to develop a theory of academic capitalism which explains the process of college and university integration into the new economy. The theory does not see the process as inexorable; it could be resisted ... nor ... 'corporatized' ... sees actors ... as using a variety of state resources to create new circuits of knowledge that link higher educational institutions to the new economy ... it moves beyond thinking of the student as consumer to considering the institution as marketer. (Slaughter & Rhodes, 2004, p. 1)

They also use new discourses to specify the shifts and changes as: 'colleges and universities shifting from a public good knowledge/learning regime to an academic capitalist knowledge/learning regime' (Slaughter & Rhodes, 2004, p. 7).

Slaughter and Rhoades (2004, pp. 10–11) build on and develop their theory from a previous study (Slaughter & Leslie, 1997), which was about globalization and its global reach in higher education. The aim of their new study is to concentrate on how academic capitalism in the United States is 'blurring the boundaries among markets, states and higher education' (Slaughter & Rhodes, 2004, p. 11). They argue that 'the new economy is central to the rise of academic capitalist knowledge regime it is not causal. Universities find it difficult to separate from the new economy because they richly contribute to its development' (Slaughter & Rhodes, 2004, p. 15). Even more dramatically they argue that:

the growth of the internet and world-wide web which originated in academia has intensi-fied the global dimension of scholarship and ... half of all graduate students in science and engineering are foreign nationals, constituting a global labor force in US universities. (Slaughter & Rhodes, 2004, p. 17)

The notion of a global labour force *within* higher education is innovative and intriguing, all the more so since this remains a goal for UK higher education. More-over, their conclusions chime in with the work of British scholars such as Evans (2004/05) when they argue that 'the academic capitalist knowledge/learning regime in the early 21st century is in the ascendant, displacing but not replacing public good knowledge or liberal learning regime' (Slaughter & Rhodes, 2004, p. 305) and that 'we conceptualize how higher education as an institution embodies the changing social understanding of what is "public"' (p. 305), confirming her argument. They also make the point that diversity is also central to their conception of 'academic capitalism' as with capitalism itself and this leads to many contradictory processes around equity and diversity; namely, examples of 'increased access for underserved populations and expansion of opportunities for women and minorities' (Slaughter & Rhodes, 2004, p. 336). However, their conclusions are less pessimistic than those of Evans, since they argue that there are 'possibilities of networks for socially productive purposes' (Slaughter & Rhodes, 2004, p. 338)

Perhaps Evans' pessimistic conclusions derive from a different policy and practice arena of the United Kingdom. Certainly, other social scientists have found similar pessimism with the public policy changes recently (Acker & Armenti, 2004). For example, Jennifer Bone and Ian McNay (2006) conducted a survey of academics in higher education in the United Kingdom for a celebration of the work of the sociologist, Roy Niblett. They found first that there had been a shift in values of academics in concert with those of policy-makers that had occurred from the 1980s, and second they argued that there is:

> a weariness with trying to deliver bricks without straw for harsh taskmasters. It may also result from trying to reconcile two sets of values—a major cause of stress … such a defence, based upon efficiency and productivity, does risk drifting to acceptance of an industrialised, commercial view of Higher Education, emphasising economic and instrumental outputs and values. (Bone & McNay, 2006, pp. 33–34)

Yet other writers have also been concerned about the work of academics, such as Burgan's study of changing faculty (Burgan, 2007) and a major quantitative and descriptive survey of all the changes in the so-called 'American Faculty' (Schuster & Finkelstein, 2006). However, some of the recent feminist and gender studies have painted a much more optimistic picture of the future for women as academics and researchers in higher education both globally and locally. For example, Sagaria (2007) has edited a collection of essays reviewing women's contributions to scholarly work and managerial changes in higher education in Europe and the USA. Many of the contributors to the study are sociologists (e.g. Teresa Rees, Louise Morley and myself) using these frameworks for analysis. As the numbers of women as social scientists and feminists has grown both within the academy as a whole (Glazer-Raymo, 2003) and especially in managerial or senior administrative positions (for example, Nidiffer, 2000), these frameworks are beginning to influence both frameworks for analysis (Quinn, 2003; Hey, 2004; Jackson, 2004; Britzman, 2006; Leathwood & Francis, 2006; Mirza, 2006). However, the arguments about the possibilities and limitations are complex. For example, Magda Lewis (2005), reviewing the changes in feminist action and theories over a 30-year period, argued that:

> the world wide antifeminist backlash aimed at clawing back the gains towards equity and social participation that women had made over the thirty years since the second wave of the feminist movement … some salient critiques … even those advanced by well informed

and socially conscious critics, the feminist framework falls out of the discussion. (Lewis, 2005, p. 7)

On the other hand, Hey (2004) argued more realistically that: 'The conditions of the contemporary academy put the ethical practice of feminism in extreme contradiction with the contrasting ethical practice and moral regulation of audit and accountability. Feminist academics live between these spaces … (p. 37).

Perhaps even more interestingly, women and feminist social scientists are populating diverse positions within the academy, including in the upper reaches of administration, with feminist scholars reaching senior positions as presidents, including of Ivy League universities in the USA. Examples include both Amy Gutman, a political scientist, President of the University of Pennsylvania since 2001, and Drew Gilpin Faust, a social historian and women's studies scholar appointed as the next President of Harvard University in February 2007. Diversification of higher education has clearly begun to include gender and feminist scholarship at some levels and institutions, including in the new practices and pedagogies of higher education.

Teaching and learning as new discourses for higher education pedagogies and academic practices

A key feature of new forms of higher education is the move to professionalize teaching especially for undergraduate students, and at the same time to consider research and graduate training as part of capacity-building within higher education. Here again, sociological theories and methodologies have been used as the frameworks for these new endeavours. As Evans (2004/05) and Morley (2003) among others have pointed out, these moves and measures are part of discursive shifts within higher education, such that the concept of teaching and learning has replaced the notion of education as the processes within higher education, as much as within schools (for example, Epstein *et al.*, 2003).

A recent example of this move is that Harvard University (2007) set up a task force or working party to develop its approach to improve teaching and learning within its arts and sciences faculty for undergraduates. The working party was, intriguingly, chaired by a world-class scholar and sociologist, Theda Skocpol. Its report suggested strategies to enable graduate students especially to learn to teach undergraduates, to train graduate students and for all faculty to continue to work with the Bok centre on teaching and learning while still retaining the traditional American notion of 'instruction'. The task force report argued that:

2006–7 is a good year for the Faculty of Arts and Sciences to re-think institutional practices surrounding teaching and pedagogical improvement … At the University's helm this year as Interim President is Derek Bok, a revered leader of Harvard and well-known advocate for the improvement of teaching and learning in universities and colleges … A national commission sponsored by the U.S. Secretary of Education Margaret Spellings issued a report in July 2006, calling upon colleges and universities to do a much more thorough job of measuring what students actually learn. Although experts do not find it easy to pinpoint changes in student skills and knowledge, there are growing bodies of research and practice that can help faculty members actively engage students in ways that promote understanding and mastery (sic), rather than passive (in)attention. Harvard has the expertise and resources to provide leadership in this area. (Harvard University, 2007, pp. 10–11)

A key concept that has been developed to some extent from sociological theorizing is that of pedagogy or pedagogical improvement, and yet the notion remains highly contested. Using Habermas' social theories as a way to expound her thesis, Monica McLean (2006) has developed an excellent argument about how this concept might be used to further social justice moves within the university in her *Pedagogy and the University*. She asks how university teachers can practise pedagogy that is attentive to how their students as citizens might influence politics, culture and society in the direction of justice and reason; defining critical pedagogy as changes in society in the direction of social justice (McLean, 2006, p. 1). Indeed, she also challenges contemporary constructions of good teaching and learning as a technical–rational pursuit for economic purposes, such as the measures being taken by Harvard University, seeing an alternative as intellectually challenging and emancipatory (McLean, 2006, p. 3).

McLean goes through the development of critical theory to demonstrate precisely how it can be used by teachers and others in higher education to create social just approaches to studies within the academy. She argues that:

> although it could be argued that to incorporate critical pedagogic principles in mainstream education poses quite a different challenge, I have wanted to show that good university teaching (of which there are many renditions all over the world) is not far away from critical pedagogy. What, though, can be done to make the odds shorter of forging university education for communicative reason? I think a judicious mix of dissent or defensiveness at national levels and determined creation at the level of institutions would, at least, improve matters in the direction of developing communicative reason. In broad terms, a starting point is Habermas's dictate that universities should 'embody an exemplary form of life, in which its members share intersubjectively' (1989, p.101). The exemplary form of life he refers to is the core work of producing and reproducing human culture, society and identity (the human lifeworld) through research, teaching, professional preparation and public enlightenment. (2006, p. 164)

Yet another complementary approach to university education can be found in a recent publication by Stephen Rowland (2006) in his reflective and thoughtful study of *The Enquiring University*. Rowland, like McLean and Walker, comes from an academic development background and so develops an argument about how to transform university pedagogies and practices to sustain and maintain links between teaching and research, seeing this as the essence of *university*. He too argues from social theories and inter-disciplinary perspectives to think about the balances between what he calls compliance and contestation. He concludes that:

> higher education needs to write itself a new story based more closely upon intellectual and moral values connecting participants with the wider society… In my attempts to contribute to such a new story I have developed the concept of the university's role as one of critical service, recognizing that at present the emphasis appears to be on service, or rather servility, with little critique. Hope is nevertheless possible. Despite the increasing dominance of bureaucracy and managerialism, participants of the academic community

are still motivated by educational values, albeit ones that go largely unrecognized in the accounts that higher education is required to give of itself. Fundamental to these is a conception of academic enquiry based upon the intellectual love that motivates learners, teachers and researchers. (Rowland, 2006, pp. 117–118).

Conclusions about equity and diversity in the field of higher education

In the early twenty-first century, there are clearly rich and diverse studies about and on higher education within a sociological methodological framework. While many of the studies point to the malign effects of globalization and neo-liberalism on the processes of managerialism and bureaucracy, masquerading as quality assurance, within higher education they also celebrate the ways in which the new forms of 'academic capitalism' allow for a diverse and potentially inclusive form of higher education. Given all these transformations, it is also clear that there are a diversity of forms of 'knowledge' and knowledge transfer, as well as forms of learning. This also allows spaces for critical and reflective thought, and continuing commitment to intellectual and moral ideas, through diverse forms of enquiry. Intellectual love, as Rowland puts it, or love of one's subject and one's academic work as critical clearly remains possible within the interstices of a fragmented and fragmenting higher education. Nevertheless, these diverse forms lead to inequities and injustices in the distribution of possibilities and privileges, as Maher and Treteault argue so cogently. While gender and ethnicity are clearly on the agendas of higher education for students and academics or researchers, through both diverse and critical or feminist pedagogies and practices, nevertheless the diverse types of higher education maintain inequalities and injustices within and between local and global contexts. It remains an open question about what the future of higher education may hold for subsequent generations into the twenty-first century: equity or diversity or both?

References

Acker, S. (1997) Becoming a teacher educator: voices of women academics in Canadian faculties of education, *Teaching and Teacher Education*, 13(1), 65–74.

Acker, S. & Armenti, C. (2004) Sleepless in academia, *Gender and Education*, 16(1), 3–24.

Alldred, P. & David, M. E. (2007) *Get real about sex: the politics and practice of sex education* (Maidenhead, McGraw Hill), in press.

Arnot, M. (2002) *Reproducing gender? Essays on educational theory and feminist politics* (London, Routledge).

Arnot, M., David, M. E. & Weiner, G. (1999) *Closing the gender gap: post-war education and social change* (Cambridge, Polity Press).

Arthur, J. (2006) *Faith and secularization in religious colleges and universities* (New York & London, Routledge).

Arum, R., Gamoran, A. & Shavit, Y. (2007) Introduction, in: Y. Shavit, R. Arum & A. Gamoran (Eds) *Stratification in higher education: a comparative study* (Stanford, CA, Stanford University Press).

Bailey, T. & Morest, V. S. (Eds) (2006) *Defending the community college equity agenda* (Baltimore, MD, John Hopkins University Press).

Banks, O. (1955) *Parity and prestige in English secondary education* (London, Routledge).

Barnett, R. (2000) *Realizing the university in an age of supercomplexity* (Maidenhead, SRHE/Open University Press).

Barnett, R. (2003) *Beyond all reason: living with ideology in the university* (SRHE/Open University Press).

Barnett, R. & Coate, K. (2005) *Engaging the curriculum in higher education* (McGraw Hill/Open University Press).

Barton, L. (Ed.) (2007) *Education and society. 25 years of the* British Journal of Sociology of Education (Routledge).

Becher, T. & Trowler, P. (2002) *Academic tribes and territories* (SRHE/Open University Press).

Bok, D. (2003) *Universities in the marketplace: the commercialization of higher education* (Princeton, NJ & Oxford, Princeton University Press).

Bok, D. (2005) *Our underachieving colleges* (Cambridge, MA, Harvard University Press).

Bone, J. & McNay, I. (2006) *Higher education and human good.* Report of a consultation held at Sarum College, Salisbury, 3–4 March, inspired by the work of Professor Roy Niblett, and informed by a survey of academic staff in UK higher education (Bristol, Tocklington Press).

Bowl, M. (2003) *Non-traditional entrants to higher education. 'They talk about people like me'* (Trentham Books).

Brew, A. (2001) *The nature of research: inquiry in academic contexts* (London, Routledge Falmer).

Brew, A. (2006) *Research and teaching: beyond the divide* (Palgrave Macmillan).

Britzman, D. P. (2006) *Psychoanalytic studies of learning and not learning* (Peter Lang).

Burgan, M. (2006) *What ever happened to the faculty? Drift and decision in higher education* (Baltimore, MD, John Hopkins University Press).

Cheung, S.Y. & Egerton, M. (2007) Great Britain: Higher education expansion and reform— changing educational inequalities, in: Y. Shavit, R. Arum & A. Gamoran (Eds) *Stratification in higher education: a comparative study* (Stanford, CA, Stanford University Press), 195–220.

Clegg, S. & David, M. (2006) Passion, pedagogies and the project of the personal in higher education, *21st Century Society; Journal of the Academy of Social Sciences*, 1(2), 149–167.

David, M. (2003) *Personal and political. Feminisms, sociology and family life* (Stoke on Trent, Trentham Books).

David, M. (2005) Feminist values and feminist sociology as contributions to higher education pedagogies and practices, in: S. Robinson & C. Katulushi (Eds) *Values in higher education* (Glamorgan, Aureus Publishing Limited for the University of Leeds).

Deem, R. (2004) Sociology and the sociology of higher education: a missed call or disconnection?, *International Studies in Sociology of Education*, 14(1), 21–46.

Delamont, S., Atkinson, P. & Parry, O. (1998) *Supervising the PhD: a guide to success* (SRHE/Open University Press).

Delamont, S., Atkinson, P. & Parry, O. (2000) *The doctoral experience: success and failure in graduate school* (Routledge).

Delanty, G. (2001) *Challenging knowledge: the university in the knowledge society* (Buckingham, Open University Press & SRHE).

Devine, F. (2004) *Class practices: how parents help their children get good jobs* (Cambridge, Cambridge University Press).

Dillabough, J.-A. & Acker, S. (2002) Globalisation women's work and teacher education: a cross-national analysis, *International Studies in Sociology of Education*, 12(3), 227–260.

Epstein, D., O'Flynn, S. & Telford, D. (2003) *Silenced sexualities in schools and universities* (Trentham Books).

Evans, M. (2004/5) *Killing thinking: the death of the universities* (London, Continuum).

Frank, D. J. & Gabler, J. (2006) *Reconstructing the university: worldwide shifts in academia in the 20th century* (Stanford, CA, Stanford University Press).

Fry, H., Ketteridge, S. & Marshall, S. (Eds) (2003) *A handbook for teaching & learning in higher education: enhancing academic practice* (2nd edn) (Routledge/T&F).

Glazer-Raymo, J. (2003) *Shattering the myths: women in academe* (Routledge).

Gorard, S., Smith, E., May, H., Thomas, L., Adnett, N, & Slack, K. (2006) *Review of widening participation research addressing the barriers to participation in higher education.* Report by the University of York, the Higher Education Academy and the Institute for Access Studies. Available online at: www.hefce.ac.uk/rdreports/2006/rd_1306/ (accessed May 2007).

Halsey, A. H. & Trow, M. (1971) *British academics* (Oxford, Oxford University Press).

Halsey, A. H., Floud, J. & Anderson, R. (1956) *Education, economy and society: a reader in the sociology of education* (Oxford, Oxford University Press).

Halsey, A. H., Heath, A. & Ridge, J. M. (1980) *Origins and destinations: family, class and education in modern Britain* (Oxford, Oxford University Press).

Harvard University (2007) *A compact to enhance teaching and learning at Harvard.* Task Force on Teaching and Career Development to the FAS, chaired by Theda Skocpol. President and Fellows of Harvard College, January.

Hey, V. (2004) Perverse pleasures' identity work and the paradoxes of greedy institutions, *Journal of International Women's Studies,* 5(3), 33–43.

Hurtado, S. (2007) Linking diversity with the educational and civic missions of higher education, *The Review of Research in Higher Education., Journal of the Association for the Study of Higher Education,* 30(2), 185–197.

Jackson, S. (2004) *Differently academic? Developing lifelong learning for women in higher education* (Kluwer Academic Publishers).

Jenkins, A., Healey, M. & Zetter, R. (2007) *Linking teaching and research in disciplines and departments* (York, The Higher Education Academy).

Ladson-Billings, G. (2001) *Crossing over to Canaan: the journey of new teachers in diverse classrooms* (San Francisco, Jossey Bass).

Langa Rosado, D. & David, M. E. (2006) 'A massive university or a university for the masses?' Continuity and change in higher education in Spain and England, *Journal of Education Policy,* 21(3), 343–365.

Lauder, H., Brown, P., Dillabough, J.-A. & Halsey, A. H. (Eds) (2006) *Education, globalization and social change* (Oxford, Oxford University Press).

Leathwood, C. & Francis, B. (Eds) (2006) *Gender and lifelong learning: critical feminist engagements* (London, Routledge/Falmer).

Leonard, D. (2001) *A woman's guide to doctoral studies* (Maidenhead, Open University Press).

Lewis, M. (2005) More than meets the eye: the underside of the corporate culture of higher education and possibilities for a new feminist critique, *Journal of Curriculum Theorizing,* 21(1), 7–26.

Lynch, K. & O'Riordan, C. (1998) Inequality in higher education: a study of class barriers, *British Journal of Sociology of Education,* 19(4), 445–478.

Maher, F. A. & Treteault, M. K. T. (2007) *Privilege and diversity in the academy* (New York & London, Routledge/T&F).

McLean, M. (2006) *Pedagogy and the university: critical theory and practice* (London, Continuum).

McWilliam, E., Taylor, P. G., Thomson, P., Green, B., Maxwell, T., Wildy, H. & Simons, D. (2002) *Research training on doctoral programs what can be learned from professional doctorates?* (Australian Commonwealth Department of Education, Science and Training).

Mirza, H. (2006) The in/visible journey: black women and lifelong lessons in higher education, in: C. Leathwood & B. Francis (Eds) *Gender and lifelong learning critical feminist engagements* (London, Routledge/Falmer).

Morley, L. (2003) *Quality and power in higher education* (Buckingham, Open University Press).

Nidiffer, J. (2000) *Pioneering deans of women: more than wise and pious matrons* (Columbia University, NY, Teacher's College Press).

Parker, L. (Ed.) (2007) Difference, diversity, and distinctiveness in education and learning, *Review of Research in Education,* 31(1), xi–xv.

Quinn, J. (2003) *Powerful subjects? Are women really taking over the university?* (Stoke on Trent, Trentham Books).

Raffe, D. & Spours, K. (Eds) (2007) *Policy-making and policy learning in 14–19 education* (Bedford, Way Papers IOE).

Ramsden, P. (1998) *Learning to lead in higher education* (London, Routledge Falmer).

Reay, D., David, M. E. & Ball, S. J. (2005) *Degrees of choice: class, race and gender* (Stoke on Trent, Trentham Books).

Rhoads, R. A. & Torres, C. A. (Eds) (2006) *The university., state., and market The political economy of globalization in the Americas* (Stanford, CA, Stanford University Press).

Rhode, D. L. (2006) *In pursuit of knowledge: scholars., status and academic culture* (Stanford, CA, Stanford University Press).

Rowland, S. (2006) *The enquiring university: compliance and contestation in higher education* (Buckingham, Open University Press).

Sagaria, M. A. D. (2007) *Women, universities and change: gender equality in the European Union and the U.S.* (London, Palgrave Macmillan).

Savage, M. (2003) A new class paradigm?, *British Journal of Sociology of Education,* 24(4), 535–541.

Savage, M., Warde, A. & Devine, F. (2005) Capitals, assets, and resources: some critical issues, *British Journal of Sociology,* 56(1), 31–47.

Schuster, J. H. & Finkelstein, M. J. (2006) *The American faculty: the restructuring of academic work and careers* (Baltimore, MD, John Hopkins University Press).

Shavit, Y., Arum, R. & Gamoran, A. with Menahem, G. (Eds) (2007) *Stratification in higher education: a comparative study* (Stanford, CA, Stanford University Press).

Shiner, M. & Modood, T. (2002) Help or hindrance? Higher education and the route to ethnic equality, *British Journal of Sociology of Education,* 23(2), 209–232.

Slaughter, S. & Leslie, L. (1997) *Academic capitalism: politics., policies and the entrepreneurial university* (Baltimore, MD, John Hopkins University Press).

Slaughter, S. & Rhoades, G. (2004) *Academic capitalism and the new economy markets., state., and higher education* (Baltimore, MD, John Hopkins University Press).

Smith, D. E. (1999) *Writing the social* (Toronto, University of Toronto Press).

Tinkler, P. & Jackson, C. (2004) *The doctoral examination process* (SRHE & Open University Press).

Trow, M. (2005) Reflections on the transition from elite to mass to universal access: forms and phases of higher education in modern societies since WWII, in: P. Altbach (Ed.) *International handbook of higher education* (Kluwer).

Walker, M. (2006) *Higher education pedagogies* (SRHE & Open University Press).

Watson, Sir D. (2007) *Whatever happened to the Dearing Report? UK higher education 1997–2007.* A professorial lecture at the University of London Institute of Education, January.

Elite destinations: pathways to attending an Ivy League university

Ann L. Mullen

Department of Sociology, University of Toronto, Toronto, Ontario, Canada

As higher education expands and becomes more differentiated, patterns of class stratification remain deeply entrenched, in part due to class-based differences in college choice. A qualitative study of 50 Yale students shows the effects of social class, high schools and peers on students' pathways to college. For students from wealthy and highly educated families, the choice of an Ivy League institution becomes normalized through the inculcated expectations of families, the explicit positioning of schools, and the peer culture. Without these advantages, less-privileged students more often place elite institutions outside the realm of the possible – in part because of concerns of elitism. These findings suggest that even low-socioeconomic status students with exceptional academic credentials must overcome substantial hurdles to arrive at an Ivy League university.

Introduction

In spite of a prevailing rhetoric of equality of opportunity, access to higher education in many parts of the world continues to vary by social background, race, ethnicity and gender (Usher and Ceverman 2005). Further, in those countries with highly differentiated systems of higher education (such as those with an elite tier alongside several progressively less-selective tiers), access to the upper tiers is also found to be influenced by social background (Shavit, Arum, and Gamoran 2007). Surprisingly, while students' previous academic achievement explains some of this variation, even when academic ability is held constant, more advantaged youth hold a disproportionate share of places at top-tier institutions (Bowen and Bok 1998). While institutional gate-keeping may explain part of this imbalance (Karabel 2005; Soares 2007), studies also find that low-socioeconomic status (SES) students are considerably less likely to apply to elite institutions compared with their more privileged peers (McPherson and Schapiro 1991; Spies 2001). Thus, patterns of stratification in higher education may be explained in part by qualified students' educational decision-making.

A number of qualitative studies have explored students' choice of higher education institution (McDonough 1997; Reay, David, and Ball 2001, 2005; Power et al. 2003; Brooks 2003). These studies offer compelling views of class and race-based differences and identify several factors that may dissuade low-SES students from applying to elite institutions. The current study adds to this literature by examining the pathways taken by a group of students to Yale University, one of the eight Ivy League institutions in the United States. While nearly all of the literature has focused on the decision-making of high school students, this retrospective study offers several advantages. While previous literature leads us to expect low-SES students to be dissuaded from applying to elite institutions, we know very little about those that actually do apply. This study illuminates the pathways of those traditionally under-represented students. Further, because all of the students in this study met the high admissions standards of Yale, we can assume a similarity in their achievement levels. Thus, the findings cannot be explained by differences in academic ability. Finally, this study casts light on the important case of elite institutions. Because attending an Ivy League university promotes connections to the top reaches of the stratification hierarchy, elite higher education facilitates the reproduction of class privilege and contributes to the dynamic whereby a system charged with ensuring equality of opportunity may in fact promote the reproduction of inequality.

Choice in higher education

Studies on educational decision-making point to three sets of factors that may affect students' choices. The first of these is the family. Parents' educational expectations for their children have been found to influence children's expectations of themselves (Looker and Pineo 1983). In addition, parental cultural capital has been found to be an important predictor of attendance at an elite versus non-elite college, after controlling for academic ability (Kaufman and Gabler 2004). Knowledge of the application process, and in particular of the elite sector of education, is a form of cultural capital more commonly held by privileged families (Lamont and Lareau 1988). McDonough (1997) shows this form of cultural capital at work, with the high-SES families in her study demonstrating more perspicacity concerning the process of admissions and the means to increase their children's likelihood of acceptance, through such tactics as employing private college admissions counselors and SAT tutors. Families with less higher education experience not only lack knowledge of these processes, but may also express ambivalence about their children attending college or leaving home for colleges in other cities (Lubrano 2004). One possible additional influence concerns the effect of legacy status. Some privileged families foster a tradition of sending their children to the same elite institutions they themselves attended. Institutions acknowledge this process through giving 'legacy' students preferences in admissions. Thus, in the case of elite universities, we may find a different kind of family influence at work: that of parents conveying the expectation to their children that they attend their *alma mater* or inculcating this expectation through familiarizing their children with the institution through campus visits for alumni functions.

A second source of influence on students' choices occurs through their high schools. Both McDonough (1997) and Reay, David, and Ball (2001, 2005) document differences in the college application support provided to students by their schools. High schools attended by higher-SES students tend to provide more extensive guidance counseling and support through the college application process. High schools, through school culture or institutional habitus (Power et al. 2003; Reay, David, and Ball 2005), may also convey particular views of higher education opportunities to their students, which include 'tastes' for specific institutions. These influences connect with family-based resources to situate the framework for the college choice process.

Besides these general school effects, there is also a strong link between elite high schools and elite universities, well documented in the United States and Britain. These schools not only provide their students with the rigorous academic training necessary to meet the admissions requirements at elite institutions, they also supply an important form of socialization that helps prepare their students to assume positions of power in society, beginning with their education at a top-tier university (Cookson and Persell 1985). Finally, many private schools have long-standing relationships with elite colleges, which increase their students' chances of admission (Cookson and Persell 1985; Reay, David, and Ball 2001; Power et al. 2003; Karabel 2005).

A final influence on students is friendship (McDonough 1997; Brooks 2003). Friends that come from the same social circle tend to hold similar aspirations and help reinforce each other's goals and plans. Friends can also be an important source of information on potential colleges and processes of application. In cases where students have friends from a higher-SES group, these friends may provide a pivotal source of support and information often missing from these students' families (McDonough 1997).

Bourdieu's concept of habitus helps explain how these different sets of influences come together to make certain choices unthinkable, possible, or probable (Bourdieu 1984). Habitus expresses itself in 'a practical anticipation of objective limits acquired by experience of objective limits, a "sense of one's place" which leads one to exclude oneself from the goods, persons, places and so forth from which one is excluded' (Bourdieu 1984, 471). In this exploration of the pathways students take to Yale University, I begin by looking at how students describe their choice to apply and comparing the accounts of students from different social backgrounds to identify whether and how pathways differ by social background. I then explore the influence of families, schools, and peers. Finally, I discuss students' anticipation of their 'fit' at an elite institution.

The current study: pathways to the Ivy League

The data for this paper come from in-depth interviews conducted with a random sample of 50 Yale junior and senior students. In the first section of the findings, I characterize students' descriptions of their choice of Yale and relate them to social background differences. In the second part, I explore the factors that influenced these choices.

When asked why they had chosen Yale, students' responses fell into five categories. Eleven students (22% of the sample) explained that they had only considered a small number of Ivy League (or similar) universities. To put this in context, the likelihood of attending an Ivy League is remote (less than 1% of four-year university students attend an Ivy League university). However, these students described their choice of Yale in the context of a range of options limited not just to the Ivy League, but to the most prestigious institutions within the League. For example:

> For me, the only schools that I would have considered would have included probably Yale, Brown and Harvard.

> I've often explained it as if you thought you were gonna go to one of the Ivy League schools unless you did something wrong, and it was a question of which one.

These comments convey an extraordinarily high level of expectations and confidence. It is not simply that they aspired to attend the most elite institutions; rather, they planned on it. As one student in this group explained:

I applied to six schools total, but I really didn't know what I was gonna do if I didn't get in here. I didn't know where else I would have gone.

A second set of students described choosing Yale because it was the 'best' institution to which they had been admitted. Seven students (14%) fall into this category. These students typically applied to a range of institutions, including the Ivies, liberal arts colleges, and selective state universities. Students ranked institutions on the basis of quality or prestige and after learning where they had been accepted, simply enrolled in the best one. This approach is exemplified by the following quote:

When it came down to it, I had a college advisor and I applied to a bunch of different schools, some of the caliber of Yale, some not quite up to that caliber. But my college advisor advised me on what he thought would be good choices and what wouldn't be … and then as it turns out [Yale] was really the best option I had once all the acceptance letters and rejection letters came so I ended up here.

The students in this group employ a certain logic in their decision-making, with the objective of attending the most prestigious institution possible. These students apply to a wider range of colleges, following the technique of including a few 'reaches,' and a few 'safeties,' reasoning that if they are not admitted to their top choices, they have a fall back option.

A third group of students selected Yale on the basis of 'fit.' This is the largest group, with 14 students (28% of the sample). In some cases, these students were seeking a university that offered a particular field of study. For other students, aspects of the campus environment or student body were important to them.

I'm a science major and I always knew I was interested in science but I liked having a liberal arts, good liberal arts education. I liked the mixture of how at Yale, there were so many other courses I could take besides science … There was a lot of different choices, as opposed to like MIT where everybody's a science major.

I chose Yale because it had an archeology major … And I was looking at schools that were sort of small to medium sized on the East Coast (I'm from the West Coast), and so Yale like fit those criteria and has an archeology major and there are very few schools that have archeology majors that aren't combined with anthro[pology].

These students had not always taken for granted that they would attend an Ivy League college and are more practical in their decision. They begin their college search with certain key characteristics in mind, such as size, location and particular program strengths, in part reflecting the practicalities of career planning. There is probably some overlap with the previous category, in that these students may also be limiting their search to the 'best' or most prestigious institutions that meet their criteria. They differ from the previous group, however, in that they offer a specific reason for selecting Yale over other institutions, rather than selecting Yale simply because it is the 'best.'

Seven students (14%) came to Yale because they had been recruited through athletics:

Yale was the only Ivy League school I applied to. I didn't really want to go to Ivy League. I didn't even know what it was basically. I mean, I knew there were good schools up North, but, I knew the baseball coach, before he got a job at Yale, I knew him from … I'd met him earlier in my life. And so, I knew him and then baseball helped me get in to Yale, so that's how I, it kind of crawled in my lap, sort of.

Well, it was basically through football. The team contacted me. They got my name from some list, somewhere and they asked me to send in a tape of my football highlights. And I did that and they got back to me and I, they flew me out here and I had a recruiting trip and liked it, and got in, and I couldn't turn it down. I wouldn't have applied here otherwise. I applied to like Michigan [University of Michigan], Michigan State [University].

Finally, for a fifth group of students, applying to Yale was due to the intervention of a parent, teacher, or guidance counselor or following a whim at the last minute. Choosing Yale was neither an easy assumption nor part of a careful process of choice, but rather one of chance.

Actually, at first, Yale wasn't like my first priority or my first choice. I almost didn't apply to Yale and I applied on like one of the last days, and just randomly like typed an essay or whatever, because at first I thought everyone here was gonna be very snobby and not realistic and not down to earth.

I actually never really thought of Yale seriously. I didn't like Ivy League colleges because they were so prestigious and felt they were all that, and I actually just applied. By the time I started applying, I had changed my mind and just applied to a whole bunch of different colleges, and I actually applied to Yale on a whim, just to see if I could get in.

For these students, even the consideration of Ivy League universities came late in their high school years (a few students explained that they had not known until then what the Ivy League was). For example, one student had moved with her family from Europe when she was a teenager. When asked why she had chosen Yale, she explained:

I never really thought about really applying to Ivy League Schools. I've only been in the country for like about six years now and when I got here I wasn't really aware of Ivy League schools or anything. I didn't really know what that was all about. But, um, you know, I did well in school and when I got to my junior year and started talking about going to college and looking at schools that I wanted to apply, and my guidance counselor actually was the one who pushed me to apply to Ivy League schools. And it was then that I kind of got familiarized with the whole idea of Ivy League and I actually didn't want to apply to Yale, because I thought that I just wouldn't fit in here, but I ended up applying anyways.

Another student, whose parents were not supportive of her decision to attend college, cites the important role played by a teacher:

Well, I had, honestly, a teacher in 6th, 7th, and 8th grades who has been, I guess, the most influential person in my life. And she just constantly drilled into me that I need to go to college and that I would have a choice of the best to go to, so I should take advantage of it. So, I just followed her advice and used her encouragement.

To understand if and how social background may be linked to these different patterns of choice, Table 1 shows how characteristics of students' family background relate to their choice of Yale. The first part of the table considers college choice by the highest level of education obtained by either parent (based on students' survey responses), and the second part considers annual family income.[1]

Several patterns emerge from these data. First, a strong majority of those students who assumed they would attend an Ivy League-type institution come from the most privileged families. Ten of these students come from families where at least one parent has a graduate or advanced degree; seven come from families with incomes in excess

Table 1.   College choice by student's family background.

	Elite only	Best	Best fit	Athletic recruit	Whim or intervention
Total (*n* = 50)	11	7	14	7	11
Highest level of parental education (*n* = 50, three missing cases)					
Less than college degree	1	1	0	2	6
College degree	0	1	1	1	2
Graduate degree	10	4	12	3	3
Annual family income[a] (*n* = 50, 10 missing cases)					
<$40,000	1	0	0	1	4
$40,000–99,999	2	3	3	3	2
$100,000 or above	7	2	7	3	2

Note: [a]The US Census reports that, in 1999, 39% of families had household incomes under $40,000, 46% had incomes between $40,000 and $99,999, and 15% had incomes of $99,999 and above.
Source: http://factfinder.census.gov/servlet/DTTable?_bm=y&-geo_id=01000US&-reg=DEC_2000_SF4
_U_PCT112:001&-ds_name=DEC_2000_SF4_U&-_lang=en&-redoLog=true&-format=&-
mt_name=DEC_2000_SF4_U_PCT112&-CONTEXT=dt

of $100,000. Students choosing Yale because of the fit appear to be similarly well advantaged. Only one student comes from a family with less than a graduate degree and none of the students come from families in the lowest income group. In contrast, it is clear that those students choosing Yale on a whim or after outside intervention come from less-privileged families. Six of the 11 come from families where neither parent has a college degree; four come from families with annual incomes of less than $40,000. Students who were recruited as athletes are a more mixed group. While some come from highly educated and wealthy families, others are first-generation students from low-income families. Finally, those students choosing Yale because it was the 'best,' tend to come from mid-range families. Three of them have annual family incomes of $40,000–99,000 and four of them have at least one parent with a graduate degree.[2]

Table 2 shows the relationship between high school type and students' choices. Almost all of the students who only consider Ivy League type institutions attended private high schools (10 out of 11). This is a high proportion, considering that only 23 out of the sample of 50 attended a private school. Those choosing through whim or intervention were much more likely to graduate from a public or Catholic high school (eight and two out of 11, respectively), while only one attended a private high school. Students choosing for the best fit are equally divided between private and public

Table 2.   College choice by high school type.

High school type	Elite only	Best	Best fit	Athletic recruit	Whim or intervention	Total
Private	10	4	7	1	1	23
Public	1	2	7	3	8	21
Catholic	0	1	0	2	2	5

Note: *n* = 50, one missing case.

schools, while a majority of those selecting for the best institution attended a private school. Three of the athletic recruits attended public school while only one attended a private school.

The first part of these findings shows that students' routes to Yale varied, from those who had assumed Yale (or another Ivy League type institution) without ever making a decision to those who came to Yale through chance, after their own impulsive application or the intervention of someone else. Further, this variation relates to social background. To better understand the circumstances and influences that contributed to these differences in decision-making, the second part of the analysis turns to an exploration of these students' families, schools and peers.

Three of the 11 students who assumed they would attend an Ivy League institution recount instances in their childhoods where their families familiarized them with Yale. For some of these students, their father or brothers had attended Yale, leaving a legacy that helped make Yale a natural choice.

> My dad was Yale class of '68, my brother was Yale class of '93. Not even just Yale, but it was never, it was always just the next step … Just because I'd grown up with 'For God, for country and for Yale.'

> My father went to Yale and it was just kind of like, if that's another question about why I chose Yale, it was that I'd been exposed to it since I was eight years old.

These quotes reveal how the family's experience with Yale contributes directly to the formation of the student's own expectation of Yale as an appropriate destination. Even students who identify as 'middle class' still benefit from the powerful advantage of having a family member graduate from Yale.

> My father went here. I came from a middle class family … In high school, at first … I always talked about going to either Princeton, Yale or Harvard, and I used to say I wanted to go to Harvard, like against my father and then I decided I wanted to go to Yale, like my father. As I became 16, 17, I applied early and I got in and I didn't have any real desire to apply anywhere else. I didn't know that much about Yale, really, but I knew that it was, you know, famous.

The powerful influence of his father's history comes across in the way this student, even without knowing much about Yale, decides to either be 'like' or 'against' his father. In either case, his choice was limited to Harvard, Yale or Princeton. Even when family members have not themselves attended Yale, some families explicitly convey the possibility of Yale to their children through their own knowledge of the university and its importance.

> Yale was a choice, actually, way back in about third grade … we passed by the school and my father said, 'If you can go here, you have done well,' and so I kind of made that my own little challenge.

Whether or not they had family members that attended Yale, what is consistent across these students' accounts is that their families successfully inculcated an aspiration, or 'taste,' for the Ivy League. None of these students report that their family overtly encouraged or pressured them in this direction. As one student explained, 'He [her father] hadn't actively but passively put the idea in my head so it just seemed like something I wanted to do.' It is also not the case that all of the children of legacy families assumed they would go to Yale. Four students whose fathers had graduated from Yale chose Yale for practical reasons or because it was the best institution to which they were admitted.

Family influences can also be found among the less-advantaged Yale students. Here, however, families sometimes impede students' desires. In some cases, family members are not familiar with Yale and do not understand its benefits. One student explained how she had to overcome her mother's reluctance for her to attend Yale because of its distance and expense, compared with the local colleges.

> My mother is very supportive in anything I do. However, she's just, she didn't know what Yale was when I got in. At first she was like, 'Hmm, why can't you just go to the local college, because then I won't have to pay anything, and then you can just go for free.' And I was just like, 'Well, no, no, no, no.'

Other families not only disapproved of their child leaving home to attend college but also questioned the decision to go to college altogether.

> I'm the first person in my family to go to college, so I've had to do a lot of fighting, I guess, to make my parents understand why it's important … I think they would have preferred had I just stayed in my home town … After they accepted the fact that I wanted to go to school, they didn't like that I chose Yale. They wanted me to go to a school in Ohio which is closer. So … this next year, I'm taking off for a year to work, because my parents won't co-sign a loan for me, to pay my tuition. That's how much they don't want me here.

These examples highlight the obstacles faced by some low-SES students. In contrast to the close correspondence of values and expectations experienced by more privileged students and their families, these students contend with sharp differences and even disapproval from their parents. Rather than benefiting from family support, these students face the burden of convincing their parents to accept their choices.

The cross-tabulation presented above demonstrates a relationship between attending a private high school and the kind of decision-making that led to the students' arrival at Yale. Twenty-three out of 50 students in the sample (46%) attended a private, non-parochial high school, compared with only 1.7% of students nationwide (US Department of Education 2002; Broughman and Pugh 2004). Because privileged families are more likely to send their children to private high schools, the influences of high school are also those of family background. The privileged families that invested in their children's education long before beginning to pay Yale's tuition contributed an additional advantage to their children. In this section, I examine the ways that high school environments and peer groups may shape students' aspirations for particular types of colleges as well as the ways some high schools facilitate the application process.

Many private college-preparatory high schools now market themselves to parents on the basis of their track records in matriculation rates of their graduates at top colleges and universities. Perhaps for this reason many students were knowledgeable about the current rates at their own high schools, recounting the exact number of their class attending Yale and the Ivies. The emphasis of these high schools in placing graduates at Ivy League or other prestigious colleges and universities creates an atmosphere among the students that promotes this expectation.

> I went to a top private school where everyone goes to college and where most people go to top colleges. So, I mean, from that sense it's something everyone does.

> There was sort of this Harvard, Princeton, Yale thing at my school, where you would sort of specify which one you really liked and then they would sort of pull for you, and everyone else was like Harvard, Princeton, so I was like, 'Okay, there's no one in the Yale category.'

As the quote above shows, some students choose *which* Ivy League to push for on the basis of their peers. In one case, a student chose Yale, after originally aiming for Princeton, because of his high school friends that also planned to attend Yale. Part of choosing Yale became choosing with which friends he wanted to spend four more years.

> Like freshman year, we, for an English class, we had to write letters to ourselves our freshman year that the teacher then gave back to us senior year. Freshman year, I was like, 'I know I'm going to Princeton, blah, blah, blah,' because that's where everybody who I kind of looked up to, my captains, and everything, a lot of them were going to Princeton, or different places like that. [Later], just the kids that I saw from Deerfield who came [to Yale], it wasn't necessarily my best friends, but it was the people that I wanted to spend four years of my life with ... And I just decided, 'No, I wanted to spend four years of my life with those people.'

These accounts show how choosing an Ivy League college becomes a normalized part of these students' high school experiences. By explicitly working towards preparing and sending their graduates to top colleges, these schools help instill a set of high expectations in their students. These expectations then carry over to the peer culture, and decisions about which Ivy League institution to aim for often become a decision made among friends.

In addition to these advantages, students attending private high schools are more likely to benefit from guidance counselors charged with orchestrating each step of the college application process for every student. As one private high school student related:

> My college counselor was insistent on a rigorous routine which was, you have to have two to three 'reaches,' you have to have two to three 'mids,' and you have to have two to three 'safeties.' ... The policy of the school was that you're only allowed to apply to two Ivy League or Ivy League type schools. We finally settled on MIT, Harvard and Yale.

In his fuller description, he explained that his college counselor coordinated the entire process of college applications, from helping in making the final selection of institutions, to requesting letters of recommendation from his teachers, editing the essay portions of the application, checking all the required forms, and ensuring everything was mailed before the deadlines. This kind of in-depth assistance was absent from students attending most public and parochial schools. The students with parents wealthy and savvy enough to select private high schools for their children reaped a number of benefits, including having the educational aspirations fostered in the family reinforced and refined and receiving intensive, individualized assistance with the college application process.

In contrast to the experiences of students attending private schools, many public school students came from peer groups where college was not the taken-for-granted next step, even less an elite college. A student whose mother 'forced' her to apply to Yale attended a public high school where only one-half of the students went on to college. Another student who credits an influential teacher with her decision to apply to Yale describes her high school peers as follows:

> A lot of students in my school do not go on to college. They get the forty hour a week job, five days a week, get married. So many of my classmates are married already, have kids.

Without the high expectations instilled by the school and reinforced by peers, it becomes clear why intercessions played a critical role in these students' decisions to apply to Yale. Without them, it seems likely they never would have applied.

Taken together, the findings related so far demonstrate some of the ways that families, schools and peer groups contribute towards naturalizing or inhibiting the choice of an Ivy League institution. In the final section, I consider students' subjective evaluations of their likely fit at Yale. Students who came from more privileged families and had attended private college-preparatory high schools were much more likely to feel a sense of belonging in regards to Yale.

> I interviewed at 15, 20 schools and came down here for my interview and stepped on the campus and loved it. And it was just a feeling inside of me that I knew that it was right for me and that I belonged here.

> I feel very much at home … I really feel like this is where I belong.

On the other hand, students from less-advantaged circumstances did not expect to feel comfortable at Yale. A number of them mentioned having concerns of not fitting in or worries of snobbery ('I actually didn't want to apply to Yale, because I thought that I just wouldn't fit in here.') One student-athlete who was recruited mentioned how he had originally discarded the idea of Yale because of these concerns:

> I guess my sophomore or junior year somebody mentioned maybe you might want to think about going to Yale, and I was just like, 'Everybody that goes there is snobs [sic], and they're too smart, and brainy and I'm just not like that,' and so I never thought about it.

This disinclination appears even for students from middle-class families. The following student, whose father is a veterinarian and whose mother has a college degree, describes her initial reluctance:

> And Yale wasn't really one that I was considering, at least junior year, and then my grandmother lives [nearby], and I think I was visiting her, and I thought, 'Oh, well, while I'm here, maybe I'll just go check it out and see what it looks like.' And I really didn't think it was going to be anything that I liked, just because it's, you know, your stereotypic image of Yale as being like real snobby and very elite and not what I would want.[3]

These subjective assessments probably stem from the multiple influences of families, schools and peers. While these data do not allow for the untangling of these various factors on students' predictions of whether they would feel comfortable at a place like Yale, they do show a consistent variation by social background, with low-SES and middle-SES students much more likely to express initial reservations about fitting in at Yale. These concerns, and the feelings of belonging expressed by more privileged students, provide the most direct reflection of students' habitus – a disposition towards a certain choice influenced in part by the likelihood of fitting in. For many, these concerns were enough to eliminate Yale as a possible option until outside forces intervened, in the form of a campus visit or the efforts of athletic recruiters.

Discussion and conclusion

The present research demonstrates marked differences in the pathways students take to Yale and the relationship to social background. Students for whom going to college is synonymous with attending an Ivy League institution come predominantly from wealthy and highly educated families. Students who had not initially considered Yale but applied unexpectedly tend to come from families with much less higher education experience and with fewer economic resources. Families in this study transmit educational advantages to their children in three important ways. First, families with knowledge of Ivy League institutions communicate the importance of attending these institutions to their children, often at an early age. Rather than actively pressuring, these parents successfully inculcate expectations in their children such that children perceive them as their own. Second, through their knowledge and sometimes personal experience with elite education, these families help convey to their children that Ivy League institutions are appropriate destinations. Students then expect to 'feel at home' rather than harboring concerns about feeling out of place. Third, these results underscore the role of private college preparatory high schools. By selecting these high schools, these families ensure that their children spend four years in an environment that helps inculcate prestigious colleges as the norm and provides concrete resources to facilitate their eventual successful application. Taken together, privileged families endow their children with a potent bundling of advantage. The expectations instilled by the family and then reinforced through private schooling collude in developing strong predilections for elite institutions.

In the absence of these resources, it is not surprising that less-privileged students are less likely to develop preferences for elite institutions. What stands out in these students' accounts is how commonly Ivy League institutions were initially not even considered as possible college destinations. These students' descriptions of applying on a whim or just to see if they could get in suggest how students place these institutions outside the realm of the possible. Some less-advantaged students also revealed a striking disinclination to attend elite universities because, instead of imagining feeling at home, they anticipate the discomfort of not fitting in, paralleling recent findings in Britain (Ball et al. 2002; Power et al. 2003).

These findings support Bourdieu's theory of action as mediated through the habitus (Bourdieu 1984, 1990). The students exhibited strong dispositions towards various educational alternatives, and these dispositions – more often than calculated choice – shaped actions. I find evidence for this theory in the non-decisions of the most privileged students, and in the seemingly irrational behavior of the low-SES students in applying on a whim. For the former group, their strong disposition to attend an Ivy League institution rendered a choice unnecessary. For the latter group, their initial disinclination reveals itself in their haphazard application behavior. As Bourdieu predicts, students often excluded the Ivy League from their range of choices because of anticipated social discomfort.

This study raises questions about the place of conscious strategic calculation in habitus. While in most of Bourdieu's writing there appears to be little room for this kind of decision-making, Hatcher (1998) identifies a few occasions where Bourdieu does allow for rational strategic action under certain circumstances. Bourdieu describes momentary disruptions of habitus, claiming that it can be 'superseded ... by other principles, such as rational and conscious computation' (1990, 108). The conscious vying for entrance into the best institution exhibited by some of the respondents in this study may represent the actions produced by a particular type of habitus.

The findings from this study also carry implications for educational policy. The narratives of the low-SES students make clear the capriciousness of their application to Yale. Were it not for a concerned teacher, attentive counselor or determined parent, or for the student's own impulsiveness, most of these students would never have applied. The lack of uniformity in the college counseling received by these high-achieving low-SES students raises the possibility of class-biased sorting processes in their high schools and of subjective evaluations and uneven assistance by school counselors, similar to those found by Cicourel and Kitsuse (1963). Further, the commonality of their fears of 'snobbishness' and social exclusion suggests the possibility that similar students choose not to apply because of these concerns. This indicates that far more could be done in terms of outreach. Ivy League universities could do much more to identify high-achieving, low-SES students, inform them about the possibilities of enrollment and the application process, and work to ease students' concerns by having more campus outreach events.

Acknowledgements

The author wishes to acknowledge the helpful comments of Scott Davies, Paul DiMaggio, Kim Goyette, Eric Grodsky, and Scott Thomas. This research was supported by The National Academy of Education and the National Academy of Education/Spencer Postdoctoral Fellowship Program. The author also thanks Jayne Baker and Rebecca (Sophie) Statzel for assistance with coding the data. An earlier version of this paper was presented at the Annual Meeting of the American Sociological Association, Montreal, Canada, August 2006.

Notes

1. Data for this table are based on interviews with all 50 students. Three students did not provide information on their parents' education and 10 students did not provide family income information.
2. There are also gender differences among the characteristics of choice. Notably, none of the women reported being recruited, in comparison with seven of the men. Women were more likely than men to describe applying because of the fit (10 women versus four men), or on a whim or with an intervention (nine women versus two men). Fewer women than men reported applying only to elite institutions (four women versus seven men) or to the best institutions (two women versus five men).
3. While students expressed these concerns as class-based, racial-minority students also hold reservations about attending a predominantly white institution. The difficulties encountered by minority students, particularly black students, in predominantly white universities have been well documented (Feagin, Vera, and Imani 1996). While none of the respondents in this study articulated these concerns at the application stage, nearly all of the African-American students expressed a range of frustrations when describing their educational experiences at Yale, including dealing with the racism and ignorance of their peers and the tediousness of being continually asked to serve as spokespersons for their race.

References

Ball, S.J., J. Davies, M. David, and D. Reay. 2002. 'Classification' and 'judgement': Social class and the 'cognitive structures' of choice of higher education. *British Journal of Sociology of Education* 23: 51–72.

Bourdieu, P. 1984. *Distinction: A social critique of the judgment of taste.* Cambridge, MA: Harvard University Press.

Bourdieu, P. 1990. *In other words: Essays towards a reflexive sociology.* Stanford, CA: Stanford University Press.

Bowen, W.G., and D. Bok. 1998. *The shape of the river: Long-term consequences of considering race in college and university admissions.* Princeton, NJ: Princeton University Press.

Brooks, R. 2003. Young people's higher education choices: The role of family and friends. *British Journal of Sociology of Education* 24: 283–97.

Broughman, S.P., and K.W. Pugh. 2004. *Characteristics of private schools in the United States: Results from the 2001–2002 Private School Universe Survey.* NCES 2005-305. Washington, DC: National Center for Education Statistics, US Department of Education.

Cicourel, A.V., and J.I. Kitsuse. 1963. *The educational decision-makers.* New York: Bobbs-Merrill.

Cookson, Jr., P.W., and C.H. Persell. 1985. *Preparing for power: America's elite boarding schools.* New York: Basic Books.

Feagin, J.R., H. Vera, and N. Imani. 1996. *The agony of education: Black students at white colleges and universities.* New York: Routledge.

Hatcher, R. 1998. Class differentiation in education: Rational choices? *British Journal of Sociology of Education* 19, no. 1: 5–24.

Karabel, J. 2005. *The chosen: The hidden history of admission and exclusion at Harvard, Yale, and Princeton.* Boston: Houghton Mifflin.

Kaufman, J., and J. Gabler. 2004. Cultural capital and the extracurricular activities of girls and boys in the college attainment process. *Poetics: Journal of Empirical Research on Culture, the Media and the Arts* 32: 145–68.

Lamont, M,. and A. Lareau. 1988. Cultural capital: Allusions, gaps and glissandos in recent theoretical developments. *Sociological Theory* 6, no. 2: 153–68.

Looker, E.D., and P.C. Pineo. 1983. Social psychological variables and their relevance to the status attainment of teenagers. *American Journal of Sociology* 88: 1195–219.

Lubrano, A. 2004. *Limbo: Blue-collar roots, white-collar dreams.* Hoboken, NJ: John Wiley and Sons.

McDonough, P.M. 1997. *Choosing colleges: How social class and schools structure opportunity.* Albany, NY: SUNY.

McPherson, M.S., and M.O. Schapiro. 1991. *Keeping college affordable: Government and educational opportunity.* Washington, DC: Brookings Institution Press.

Power, S., T. Edwards, G. Whitty, and V. Wigfall. 2003. *Education and the middle class.* Philadelphia: Open University Press.

Reay, D., M.E. David, and S. Ball. 2001. 'Making a difference?' Institutional habituses and higher education choices. *Sociological Research Online* 5, no. 4. http://www.socresonline.org.uk/5/4/reay.html (accessed December 1, 2008).

Reay, D., M.E. David, and S. Ball. 2005. *Degrees of choice: Social class, race and gender in higher education.* Sterling, VA: Trentham Books.

Shavit, Y., R. Arum, and A. Gamoran, eds. 2007. *Stratification in higher education: A comparative study.* Palo Alto, CA: Stanford University Press.

Soares, J.A. 2007. *The power of privilege: Yale and America's elite colleges.* Palo Alto, CA: Stanford University Press.

Spies, R.R. 2001. *The effects of rising costs on college choice.* Research Report Series No. 117. Princeton, NJ: Princeton University.

US Department of Education. 2002. *Digest of education statistics 2001.* NCES 2000-130. Washington, DC: National Center for Education Statistics.

Usher, A., and A. Cevernan. 2005. *Global higher education rankings 2005.* Toronto, ON: Educational Policy Institute.

Disability studies, disabled people and the struggle for inclusion

Mike Oliver[a] and Colin Barnes[b]

[a]University of Greenwich, London, UK; [b]Centre for Disability Studies, School of Sociology and Social Policy, University of Leeds, Leeds, UK and Department of Health and Social Sciences, University of Halmstad, Halmstad, Sweden

This paper traces the relationship between the emergence of disability studies and the struggle for meaningful inclusion for disabled people with particular reference to the work of a pivotal figure in these developments: Len Barton. It is argued that the links between disability activism and the academy were responsible for the emergence of disability studies and that this has had an important influence on mainstream sociology and social and educational policy nationally and internationally. It is evident, however, that the impact of these developments has been only marginal and that in light of recent concerns about the global economy, environmental change and unprecedented population growth, the need for meaningful inclusion is more urgent than ever and cannot be dependent on the work of a few key individuals for its success.

Introduction

The development of disability studies as an academic discipline is inextricably linked with the rise of the disabled people's movement that effectively began in the 1970s. In this paper we do not intend to describe this in any detail as it has been discussed elsewhere (Barnes, Oliver, and Barton 2002; Oliver 2009; Barnes and Mercer 2010). Instead we want to discuss the wider implications of this phenomenon for sociology, education and its impact on the lives of disabled people. In so doing we shall use mainly the words of Len Barton, who has played a pivotal role in these developments. Inevitably and unfortunately space will not permit us to discuss the contributions of others who have also been important (see, for example, Albrecht 1976; Finkelstein 1980, 1998: Tomlinson 1982, 1995; Oliver 1981, 1983, 1990; Barnes 1990, 1991, 2003; Davis 1995, 1997, 2006; Shakespeare 1998; Albrecht, Seelman, and Bury 2001). The paper is divided into three parts. We begin with a discussion of the relationship between disability studies, sociology and education policy.

Attention then centres on the links between the academy and activism. The final section examines the impact of these developments with reference to disability policy and practice.

Barton, in a recent interview to discuss the international journal *Disability and Society*, of which he was founding editor, provides a succinct description of the terrain we shall cover herein:

> The journal was created at a period when both nationally and internationally disabled people and their organisations were involved in serious struggles over the establishment of empowering conceptions of disability, rights, citizenship and independent living. Through the development of what is called the social model of disability, which is a creation of disabled people, the question of disability began to be understood as a form of social oppression, and it was connected to issues of equity, social justice and human rights, and as well, at this period, disability studies was beginning to emerge as a distinct study in higher education. (Barton 2009)

Unlike previous traditional individual, medical approaches, the social model breaks the causal link between impairment and disability. The 'reality' of impairment is not denied but is not the cause of disabled people's economic and social disadvantage. Instead, the emphasis shifts to how far, and in what ways, society restricts their opportunities to participate in mainstream economic and social activities rendering them more or less dependent. This approach has been a key influence on social policy in general, and disability policy in particular, although its influence on education policy has been considerably less.

Barton, however, has always attempted to open channels of communication in both academic and policy areas. He was not only founding editor of the journal referred to above but had the same pivotal role in the genesis and development of the *British Journal of the Sociology of Education*. Since the establishment of both journals, Barton has always tried to ensure that there was a dialogue between their respective areas of interest, although to begin with there was little enthusiasm for such a task:

> Mainstream sociology has historically shown little interest in the issue of disability … Sociologists have tended to accept the dominant hegemony with regard to viewing disability in medical and psychological terms. (Barton 1996, 6)

Hence, there was little interest in substantive areas such as education in general and special education in particular. Barton was unapologetic in both drawing attention to this situation as well as spelling out its implications for those who would listen:

> Within Britain, sociological analysis of, for example, special education is a relatively new development. An important basis for such work is that an understanding of the plight of vulnerable people gives some crucial insights into the nature of society. (Barton 1993, 235–236)

He was not solely drawing attention to the nature of society, however; he was also drawing attention to some of the central concerns of the sociological agenda since its foundation in the nineteenth century. Until the 1970s sociologists had been content to leave the personal tragedy halo that surrounded both special education and disability to others, but Barton insisted that sociological concerns about power and politics were essential to their creation and our understanding of them:

> ... there is an orthodoxy abroad which views any reference to the question of politics as being biased, irrelevant and counter-productive. This is particularly applicable to those who would seek to raise the question of politics in relation to special education policy or practice. To do so is to raise doubts about the nature of your commitment and whether you have the proper interests of individuals with learning difficulties in view. (Barton 1988, 5–6)

This orthodoxy was beginning to be challenged outside of the academy, however; some parents' groups were beginning to challenge special education policies and practices that usually segregated their children from the mainstream, often on the basis of irrelevant medical labels. Also disabled people were confronting and questioning professionally-led policies and practices that attempted to provide them with 'care and protection' but very little else. The debates that emerged in academia as a result of this took off in what has come to be called the inclusion/exclusion debate not just in education but in society as well.

The exclusion/inclusion debate

This debate began in education and was initially concerned about the location of children considered to have 'special educational needs' (SEN). Hence it was originally called the integration/segregation debate and focused almost exclusively on where these children should be educated; namely in special or regular mainstream schools. Barton, among others, began to insist however that this was far too narrow and that a broader range of educational, political, social and economic issues needed to be considered. So much so that new terminology was needed in order to move beyond the previous sterile discussions. Consequently the new term 'inclusion' appeared along with Barton's insistence that:

> Inclusive education is about the education of all children which necessitates serious changes, both in terms of society and its economic, social conditions and relations and in the schools of which they are a part. (Barton 1998b, 60)

The disabled people's movement had developed an analytical tool to assist in their political campaigns for a better life. We have already referred to this as the social model of disability, and it was based upon the simple idea that people were not disabled by the functional limitations of their impairments but by the external barriers that prevented their full participation in the societies in which they lived. Without ever calling it that, Barton's writings on education have always insisted that a social model approach should be an essential tool in changing the education system to a more inclusive one:

> Identifying institutional barriers to participation in education – in terms, for example, of the organisation and nature of the system of provision, the curriculum, pedagogy and assessment practice – this is an urgent and crucial task demanding serious and systematic attention. It is an essential part of the process of engagement that the struggle for inclusive policy and practice involves. (Barton 1998b, 61)

Despite these assertions, it is probably true to say that the social model has rarely been *explicitly* used as a tool for producing educational change.

The academy and activism

While the university has usually been a conservative political force at various times, it has on occasion played a key role in producing profound social and political change. Certainly in the latter half of the twentieth century we have seen radical ideas about integration and inclusion being developed both from within and outside academia, but we have also seen reactionary forces seeking to prevent changes from occurring. The rise of social movements promoting inclusion have forced these issues onto academic agendas and forced institutions at least to acknowledge the existence of these external agencies. This has occurred in the areas of race, gender, sexual orientation and disability and has spilled over into debates about education.

Within the academy, theorising and research activity have usually been seen as something for academics to engage in. Tentative attempts to promote alternative approaches based upon people's lived experiences have more often than not been dismissed as lacking objectivity. However, Barton has always insisted that academic debate and research stemming from it must take seriously the views of disabled people themselves:

> It is essential when considering the question of 'voice' in relation to educational research that we are aware of, and seek to learn, from the struggles disabled people have been and still are involved in outside the educational context. (Barton 1998a, 29)

The emergence of disability studies within the academy in recent years began to have an influence on traditional academic agendas:

> The increased interest in disability in the academy should not be surprising, given that there is now growing recognition that it raises a number of important theoretical and empirical questions at both the individual and structural level that are not easily answered with reference to established wisdom. Disability is both a common personal experience and a global phenomenon, with widespread

economic, cultural and political implications for society as a whole. (Barnes, Oliver, and Barton 2002, 2)

Since the 1970s we have seen the creation of more and more undergraduate and postgraduate courses in disability studies as well as the creation of several departments and professorial chairs in the subject. In the United Kingdom, for instance, there are now Chairs in disability-related studies at the Universities of Bristol, Glasgow, Dundee, de Montfort, Lancaster, Northumbria, Leeds, Manchester Metropolitan University and Brunel. Globally the rise in interest in disability studies has been is equally phenomenal. In 2010, for example, there are international disability studies conferences in Philadelphia, USA, in Montreal, Canada, in University of Tokyo, Japan and the UK's Disability Studies Network's fifth bi-annual event will be held 7–9 September at University of Lancaster. This conference is held every other year in conjunction with the Scandinavian Society for Disability Research conference, which is held in alternate years (Disability Studies Network 2010).

Until now, however, despite the influence of disability activism on the subject, one disabled activist has concluded that:

> It would seem that thus far the academic and research agenda and how far it is useful to activists has been to a large degree left to chance and the personal integrity of the individuals concerned. (Germon 1998 quoted in Barnes, Oliver, and Barton 2002, 258)

Yet as the discipline of disability studies becomes institutionalised within the academy, it raises a number of important concerns. Most notably is the issue of colonisation; will academics simply use the subject and the experience of disabled people for their own ends and to build their own careers or will a genuine partnership between the academy and activism emerge?

As mentioned earlier there has been a substantial growth in disability studies programmes across the world and a growing recognition within British sociology that disability is not simply a purely medical problem (Scambler 2004; Giddens 2006: Thomas 2007; Giddens and Sutton 2010). But, with few notable exceptions, the general trend has been toward a more pluralist approach commensurate with orthodox academic concerns rather than the development of a more comprehensive and radical socio/political analysis based around social model insights (Oliver and Barnes 2006; Oliver 2009). This is exemplified by the claim that the social model of disability is an 'outdated ideology' and that Britain's disabled people's movement is no longer representative of the disabled population as a whole (Shakespeare and Watson 2002; Shakespeare 2006).

Policy, practice and disabled people

The social model

Despite such assertions there is no doubt that our understandings of impairment and disability at the policy level have improved considerably as a result of the work described above and the contributions of key individuals like Len Barton for whom the social model has always been central to their work. Key to these understandings is the fact that while impairment may impose personal restrictions, disability is created by hostile cultural, social and environmental barriers. The disabled child in education may well have an impairment but his or her participation in school is restricted by an inaccessible curriculum, negative staff attitudes and physical barriers to getting around. This is clearly evident with reference to the fact that the social model of disability, as it is now called, is now widely recognised at both the national and international levels as the key to understanding and explaining the economic, political and social barriers encountered by disabled people.

Since the launch of the campaign for legislation to outlaw discrimination against disabled people in 1991 by the British Council of Disabled People – the UK's national umbrella for organisations controlled and run by disabled people themselves, and renamed the United Kingdom's Disabled People's Council in 2006 – the language of the social model, independent living and disability rights have become increasingly prominent in the publications produced by national and local government organisations and disability charities both large and small (Oliver and Barnes 2006). For example, the recent Cabinet Office report 'Improving the Life Chances of Disabled People' states clearly that:

'Disability' should be distinguished from 'impairment and ill health'

and defined as:

- disadvantage experienced by an individual …
- … resulting from barriers to independent living or educational, employment or other opportunities …
- … that impact on people with impairments and or ill health. (Prime Minister's Strategy Unit 2005, 8)

The Report also endorsed the importance of the development of policies to enable disabled people achieve independent living so that:

by 2025 disabled people have full opportunities and choices to improve their quality of life and be included and be respected as equal members of society. (Prime Minister's Strategy Unit 2005, 6)

At the European level, a study entitled 'Disability Policies in European Countries' by Vim van Oorschot and Bjorn Hvinden concluded that:

The thinking about disability associated with the Social Model (of disability) appears to have become more widely accepted. (Oorschot and Hvinden 2001, 9)

This is clearly reflected in recent European Union (EU) policy statements on disability, as indicated below:

The EU also sees disability as a social construct. The EU social model of disability stresses the environmental barriers in society which prevent the full participation of people with disabilities in society. These barriers must be removed. (European Commission of the European Communities 2003, 4)

Further afield. Disabled People's International, the international equivalent of the United Kingdom's Disabled People's Council, adopted a similar approach at its inception in 1981 (Driedger 1989). Its influence at the international level, particularly within the United Nations (UN), is indisputable. A social model perspective is implicit if not explicit in various UN documents. The UN 'Standard Rules on the Equalisation of Opportunities for People with Disabilities' (UN Enable 2005) and 'The Convention on the Rights of Persons with Disabilities' (UN 2006) are but two examples (Hurst and Albert 2006). Also, a social model perspective played a key role in the recent 'Rethinking Care from Disabled People's Perspectives' initiative sponsored by the World Health Organisation's Disability and Rehabilitation Team; a two-year project and conference that involved professionals, disabled people, and their families from all over the world (World Health Organisation 2001).

Policy and practice

All of this has led to a number of policy initiatives that at face value appear to address many of the concerns of disabled people and their organisations. In the United Kingdom, for instance, in response to the campaign mentioned above, the Disability Discrimination Act came onto the statute books in 1995 to outlaw discrimination against disabled people. This was followed a year later by the Community Care (Direct Payments) Act to legalise cash payments from local authorities to enable disabled individuals to employ their own personal assistants rather than rely on staff appointed and controlled by professionally led agencies such as local authorities and National Health Service trusts.

Following the election of the New Labour Government in 1997, the Disability Rights Task Force was established in 1999 followed in 2000 by the Disability Rights Commission with the support of the large disability charities and key figures in the disabled people's movement. In 2001 anti-discrimination legislation was extended to include education: The Special Educational Needs and Disability Act (SENDA). The Disability Rights Commission along with the Equal Opportunities Commission and the Commission for Racial Equality was abolished in 2006 and replaced by the Equality and Human Rights Commission with a remit to cover all forms of discrimination including religion and age. Unfortunately, as we indicate below, the Commission has not made a promising start.

After publication of the *Improving Life Chances* report in 2005, the government introduced the 'Disability Equality Duty'. In contrast to previous policies, this was conceived as a proactive measure that requires all public institutions to produce a 'Disability Equality Scheme' outlining plans to make the necessary changes in all policy and practices to facilitate disabled people's inclusion. The intention was that these schemes are reviewed and amended every three years until equality is achieved. The responsibility for ensuring that public organisations and institutions fulfil their obligations under the Disability Equality Duty was the responsibility of the Equality and Human Rights Commission. However, the impact of these initiatives has been only marginal. This is due in large part to the fact that all the legislative measures mentioned above lack teeth and therefore have not been properly enforced. Monitoring and enforcement have been almost none existent.

Research commissioned by the government's Office of Disability Issues on the practices of 35 public authorities across seven policy sectors, including housing, education, health, environment, transport, culture and criminal justice, found that at best the mainstreaming of disability issues had been 'only partly achieved in some organisations, while others have a long way to go' (Ferrie et al. 2008, 14). Similar stories are evident across Europe and the rest of the world (see, for example, Stone 1999; Priestley 2001; Barnes and Mercer 2005; Albert 2006; Katsui 2006; Inclusion Europe 2008; Clements and Read 2008; Yeo and Bolton 2008).

Education

In the United Kingdom, the idea of educating disabled children in mainstream school environments had been around since the Education Act (1944). Nonetheless it created 11 medically based classifications of children and, despite its lukewarm endorsement of integration, facilitated the expanded segregative practices of the past the 'special school' system, which had its roots in the eighteenth century. Hence special schools flourished in the post-1939–1945 war period and continued to expand until the early 1990s despite the publication of the Warnock Report (Warnock 1978) and its implementation through the Education Act (1981).

Following the longstanding critique of segregated educational systems for children and students labelled with 'SEN' (see, for example, Tomlinson 1982, 1995; Barton and Tomlinson 1984; Barton 1988; Rieser and Mason 1990; Oliver 1990, 2000; Barton and Armstrong 2001, 2007), the principle of inclusive education was endorsed in official documents both nationally and internationally (see, for example, UNESCO 1994, 2006, 2007; Department for Education and Employment 1998; UN 2006).

In 1997 the Department for Education and Employment endorsed the UNESCO *Salamanca Statement and Framework for Action on Special Needs*:

> This statement calls on the international community to endorse the approach of inclusive schools by implementing practical and strategic changes. (UNESCO 1994, 1)

This is based on the assertion that

> regular schools with this inclusive orientation are the most effective means of combating discriminatory attitudes, creating welcoming communities, building an inclusive society and achieving education for all. (UNESCO 1994, 1)

Yet despite apparent initial enthusiasm for such an approach by the Labour Government of 1997 and the introduction of SENDA in 2000, progress has been slow. For instance, the proportion of all children attending special schools, that rose to just under 1% at the start of the 1980s, has subsequently declined to only 0.8% (Rustemier and Vaughan 2005; Department for Education and Skills [DfES] 2007). The number of special schools fell from 1830 in 1990/91 to 1391 in 2006/07 (DfES 2007). Moreover, these figures mask considerable variation with segregation increasing slightly in one-third of local education authorities in England (Rustemier and Vaughan 2005).

But mainstream schools are not inclusive, and segregation into special units or classes is not uncommon. With few notable exceptions the dominant discourse emphasises academic success and 'ableist' values (Tomlinson 1995; Benjamin 2003). These are often reinforced by poor environmental access, particularly in secondary schools and colleges (Audit Commission 2002), and restricted opportunities for participation in out-of-school activities (Gray 2002). Major concerns revolve around the continued dominance of standards agendas and examination assessment criteria that prioritise outcomes over process and disregard the appropriateness of an inclusive curriculum (Ofsted 2004; Qualifications and Curriculum Authority 2004).

A longstanding criticism of special educational provision is that it does not provide disabled children with the qualifications and skills for adulthood. Recent research indicates that over 25% of disabled adults have no qualifications or marketable skills whatsoever; more than twice that for non-disabled peers (Office of National Statistics 2005). This gap is particularly evident for those labelled with 'learning difficulties' or 'mental health problems'. While special school results have improved over the past decade, the average examination points score of 50 compares very unfavourably with the 361 average for regular schools (DfES 2007). Children rated as 'SEN' in mainstream schools are more than twice as likely as special school pupils to take GCSE or GNVQ examinations (Audit Commission 2002).

Moreover, despite several international initiatives to ensure that children with accredited impairments are not excluded from mainstream schools following the *Salamanca Statement,* there remains a divergence of views on the meaning of inclusion. Consequently, despite some notable successes (Rieser 2008), many disabled children are educated in segregated school environments (Miles and Singal 2008). Also, there is substantial evidence that disabled children's exclusion from all forms of education is commonplace. Indeed, in some countries disabled girls are denied all of formal schooling. In others, children with 'intellectual disabilities' are considered uneducable

(UNESCO 1995). A recent EFA monitoring report suggests that globally only 10% of disabled children are in school (UNESCO 2007). In the United Kingdom, all disabled children are officially considered educable; consequently there are no known figures for those who may be excluded.

As Barton and others have repeatedly argued, an inclusive education system is a necessary prerequisite for an inclusive society.

Concluding comments

In this paper we have argued that the early development of disability studies was due primarily to the activities of academics such as Len Barton and their links with disability activism and the disabled people's movement – and that these developments have had an important influence on mainstream sociology, social policy and educational policies at both the national and international levels. But whilst the foundations for meaningful change have clearly been made, progress has been limited and the reality of an inclusive society seems as far away as ever. This is especially worrying as both the United Kingdom and the rest of the world face a series of unprecedented challenges that threaten to undermine any hope of future economic, political and social stability and progress toward a truly inclusive global society. Examples include the widening gulf between rich and poor within and across nation-states, overpopulation and environmental degradation (Oliver and Barnes 1998, 2006). If the contributions of committed individuals like Len Barton are not to be wasted, then as we move ever further into the twenty-first century the academy and the disabled people's movement will need to form a much more comprehensive and committed partnership than they have managed so far. This is simply because as Barton pointed out over a decade ago:

> ... there is now an urgency about the need for further attention being given to the development of a political analysis which is inspired by a desire for transformative change and that constitutes hope at the centre of struggles for inclusivity. (Barton 1998b, 53)

Whether the academic community, the disabled people's movement and its allies have the commitment or capacity to rise to this challenge has yet to be seen.

References

Albert, B., ed. 2006. *In or out of the mainstream? Lessons from research on disability and development cooperation.* Leeds: The Disability Press.

Albrecht, G.L. 1976. *The sociology of physical disability and rehabiolitation.* Pittsburgh, PA: The University of Pittsburgh Press.

Albrecht, G.L., K.D. Seelman, and M. Bury, eds. 2001. *Handbook of disability studies.* London: Sage.

Audit Commission. 2002. *Special educational needs – A mainstream issue.* London: Audit Commission.

Barnes, C. 1990. *Cabbage syndrome: The social construction of dependence.* Lewes: Falmer Press. http://www.disability-archive.leeds.ac.uk/.

Barnes, C. 1991. *Disabled people in Britain and discrimination.* London: Hurst and Co. in association with the British Council of Organisations of Disabled People. http://www.disability-archive.leeds.ac.uk/.

Barnes, C. 2003. Disability studies: what's the point? Keynote address presented at the Disability Studies Conference, 3 September, in University of Lancaster, UK. http://www.disability-archive.leeds.ac.uk/.

Barnes, C., and G. Mercer, eds. 2005. *The social model of disability – Europe and the majority world.* Leeds: The Disability Press.

Barnes, C., and G. Mercer. 2010: *Exploring disability: A sociological introduction.* 2nd ed. Cambridge: Polity.

Barnes, C., M. Oliver, and L. Barton, eds. 2002. *Disability studies today.* Cambridge: Polity.

Barton, L., ed. 1988. *The politics of special educational needs.* Lewes: Falmer.

Barton, L. 1993. The struggle for citizenship; The case for disabled people. *Disability and Society* 6, no. 3: 235–48.

Barton, L. 1996. Sociology and disability: Some emerging issues. In *Disability and society: Emerging issues and insights,* ed. L. Barton, 3–17. London: Longman.

Barton, L. 1998a. Developing an emancipatory research agenda: Possibilities and dilemmas. In *Articulating with difficulty: Research voices in inclusive education,* ed. P. Clough and L. Barton, 29–40. London: Paul Chapman Publishing.

Barton, L. 1998b. Sociology, disability studies and education. In *The disability reader: Social science perspectives,* ed. T. Shakespeare, 53–65. London: Cassell.

Barton, L. 2009. Transcript of audio interview with Professor Len Barton. www.informaworld.com/smpp/educationarena_interviewonline_interview5~db= educ.

Barton, L., and F. Armstrong. 2001. Disability, education and inclusion: Cross cultural issues and dilemmas. In *Handbook of disability studies,* ed. G.L. Albrecht et al., 693–710. Thousand Oaks, CA: Sage.

Barton, L., and F. Armstrong, eds. 2007. *Policy experience and change: Cross cultural reflections on inclusive education.* Dordrecht, The Netherlands: Springer.

Barton, L., and S. Tomlinson, eds. 1984. *Special education and political issues.* London: Croom Helm.

Benjamin, S. 2003. What counts as success? Hierarchical discourses in a girls' comprehensive school. *Discourse* 24, no. 1: 105–18.

Clements, L., and J. Read, eds. 2008. *Disabled people and the right to life: The protection and violation of disabled people's most basic human rights.* London: Routledge.

Davis, L.J. 1995. *Enforcing normalcy: Disability, deafness, and the body.* London: Verso.

Davis, L.J., ed. 1997. *The disability studies reader.* London: Routledge.

Davis, L.J., ed. 2006. *The disability studies reader.* 2nd ed. London: Routledge.

Department for Education and Employment. 1998. *Excellence for all children: Meeting special educational needs.* London: DfEE. http://www.dfes.gov.uk/consultations/downloadableDocs/45_1.pdf.

Department for Education and Skills. 2007. *Education and training statistics for the UK, 2007.* London: DfES.

Department of Health. 2009. *Shaping the future of care together.* London: DoH. http://www.dh.gov.uk/en/Consultations/Liveconsultations/DH_102339 accessed 5th January 2010.

Disability Studies Network. 2010. Disability Studies Conference: 5th Biannual Disability Studies Conference, Lancaster University, UK. http://www.disability-studies.net/?content=3 (accessed February 26, 2010).

Driedger, D. 1989. *The last civil rights movement.* London: Hurst and Co.

European Commission of the European Communities. 2003. *Equal opportunities for people with disabilities: A European action plan.* Communication from the Commission to the Council, The European Parliament, The European Economic and Social Committee and the Committee of the Regions, October 30. Brussels: European Commission. http://eur-lex.europa.eu/LexUriServ/LexUriServ.do?uri= COM:2003:0650:FIN:EN:PDF.

Ferrie, J., J. Lerpiniere, K. Paterson, C. Pearson, K. Stalker, and N. Watson. 2008. *An in depth analysis of the implementation of the Disability Equality Duty in England.* London: Office of Disability Issues.

Finkelstein, V. 1980. *Attitudes and disabled people: Issues for discussion.* New York: World Rehabilitation Fund. http://www.disability-archive.leeds.ac.uk/.

Finkelstein, V. 1998: Emancipating disability studies. In *Disability studies: Social science perspectives,* ed. T. Shakespeare, 28–49. London: Cassell. http://www.disability-archive.leeds.ac.uk/.

Germon P. 1998. Activists and academics: Part of the same or a world apart. In *The disability reader: Social science perspectives,* ed. T. Shakespeare, 245–55. London: Cassell.

Giddens, A. 2006. *Sociology.* 6th ed. Cambridge: Polity.

Giddens, A., and P. Sutton, eds. 2010. *Sociology: Introductory readings.* 3rd ed. Cambridge: Polity.

Gray, P. 2002. *Disability discrimination in education: A review of the literature on discrimination across the 0–19 age range.* London: Disability Rights Commission.

Hurst, R., and B. Albert. 2006. The social model of disability: Human rights and development cooperation. In *In or out of the mainstream? Lessons from research on disability and development cooperation,* ed. B. Albert, 24–39. Leeds: The Disability Press.

Inclusion Europe. 2008. *The specific risks of discrimination against persons in situations of major dependence or with complex needs: Report of a European study, Volume 3: Country reports.* Brussels: Inclusion Europe. http://www.inclusion-europe.org/documents/CNS%20Volume%201.pdf.

Katsui, H. 2006. Human rights and disabled people in the South. In *Vammaisten Ihmisoikeuksista Etäiiä,* ed. A. Teittinen, 86–119. Helsinki: Vliopistopaino. http://www.disability-archive.leeds.ac.uk/.

Miles, S., and N. Singal. 2008. The education for all and inclusive education debate. *International Journal of Inclusive Education.* http://www.leeds.ac.uk/disability-studies/archiveuk/miles/IJIE_MilesandSingal_resubmission.pdf.

Office of National Statistics. 2005. *National statistics: Special educational needs in England.* London: ONS. http://dfes.gov.uk/rsgateway/DB/SFR/s000584/SFR24-2005.pdf (accessed November 10, 2006).

Ofsted. 2004. *Special educational needs and disability: Towards inclusive schools.* London: Ofsted.

Oliver, M. 1981. A new model of the social work role in relation to disability. In *The handicapped person: A new perspective for social workers,* ed. J. Campling, 19–32. London: RADAR. http://www.leeds.ac.uk/disability-studies/archiveuk/ index. html.

Oliver, M. 1983. *Social work with disabled people.* Basingstoke: Macmillan.

Oliver, M. 1990. *The politics of disablement.* Tavistock: Macmillan. http://www.disability-archive.leeds.ac.uk/.

Oliver, M. 2000. *Decoupling education from the economy in a capitalist society.* ://www.disability-archive.leeds.ac.uk/.

Oliver, M. 2009. *Understanding disability: From theory to practice.* 2nd ed. Tavistock: Palgrave.

Oliver, M., and C. Barnes. 1998. *Social policy and disabled people: From exclusion to inclusion.* London: Longman.

Oliver, M., and C. Barnes. 2006. Disability politics: Where did it all go wrong. In *Coalition,* 8–13. Manchester: Greater Manchester Coalition of Disabled People.

Oorschot, V., and B. Hvinden. 2001. Introduction: Toward convergence?: Disability policies in Europe. In *Disability policies in European societies,* ed. V. Oorschot and B. Hivnden, 3–12. The Hague: Kluwer Law International.

Peck, S. 2009. Rieser's reservations on ratification. In *Disability now,* 18. April 7. London: Scope.

Priestley, M., ed. 2001: *Disability and the life course: Global perspectives.* Cambridge: Cambridge University Press.

Prime Minister's Strategy Unit. 2005. *Improving the life chances of disabled people: Final report.* London: PMSU, Cabinet Office. http://www.cabinetoffice.gov.uk/strategy/work_areas/disability.aspx.

Qualifications and Curriculum Authority. 2004. *Inclusive learning: 2002/03 annual report on curriculum and assessment.* London: QCA.

Rieser, R. 2008. *Implementing inclusive education: A Commonwealth guide to implementing Article 24 of the UN Convention on the Rights of People with Disabilities.* London: Commonwealth Secretariat.

Rieser, R., and M. Mason. 1990. *Disability equality in the classroom: A human rights issue.* London: Inner London Education Authority.

Rustemier, S., and M. Vaughan. 2005. *Segregation trends – LEAs in England 2002–2004.* Bristol: Centre for Studies on Inclusive Education.

Scambler, G. 2004. Re-framing stigma: Felt and enacted stigma and challenges to the sociology of chronic and disabling conditions. *Social Theory and Health* 2, no. 1: 29–46.

Shakespeare, T., ed. 1998. *Disability studies: Social science perspectives.* London: Cassell.

Shakespeare, T. 2006. *Disability rights and wrongs.* London: Routledge.

Shakespeare, T., and N. Watson. 2002. The social model of disability: an outmoded ideology. *Research in Social Science and Disability* 2: 9–28. http://www.leeds.ac.uk/disability-studies/archiveuk/index.html.

Stone, E., ed. 1999. *Disability and development: Learning from action and research on disability in the majority world.* Leeds: The Disability Press.

Thomas, C. 2007. *Sociologies of disability and illness: Contested ideas in disability studies and medical sociology.* Basingstoke: Palgrave Macmillan.

Tomlinson, S. 1982. *A sociology of special education.* London: Routledge and Kegan Paul.

Tomlinson, S. 1995. *Machine and professional bureaucracies: Barriers to inclusive education.* http://www.disability-archive.leeds.ac.uk/.

UN Enable. 2005. Enable: Standard rules, overview. United Nations. www.un.org/esa/socdev/enable/dissre00.

UNESCO. 1994. *The Salamanca Statement and framework for action on special needs education.* Paris: UNESCO.

UNESCO. 1995. *Overcoming obstacles to the integration of disabled people.* London: Disability Awareness in Action.

UNESCO. 2006. *EFA global monitoring report 2007: Early childhood care and education.* Paris: UNESCO.

UNESCO. 2007. *EFA Global monitoring report 2008: Education for all by 2015. Will we make it?* Paris: UNESCO.

United Nations. 2006. Convention on the rights of persons with disabilities. http://www.un.org/disabilities/convention/conventionfull.shtml.

Warnock, M. 1978. *Report of the Committee of Enquiry into the education of handicapped children and young people.* London: HMSO.

World Health Organisation. 2001. *Rethinking care from disabled people's perspectives.* Geneva: WHO. http://www.disability-archive.leeds.ac.uk/authors_list.asp?AuthorID=188&author_name=World+Health+Organisation+Disability+and+Rehabilitation+Team.

Yeo, R., and A. Bolton. 2008. *'I don't have a problem, the problem is theirs'. The lives and aspirations of Bolivian disabled people in words and pictures.* Leeds: The Disability Press. http://www.disability-archive.leeds.ac.uk/.

Accidental achievers? International higher education, class reproduction and privilege in the experiences of UK students overseas

Johanna Waters[a] and Rachel Brooks[b]

[a]Department of Geography, Roxby Building, University of Liverpool, Liverpool L69 7ZT, UK;
[b]Department of Political, International and Policy Studies, University of Surrey, Guildford GU2 7XH, UK

To date, scholarship on international students has generally focused on flows from non-western economies to the main English-speaking destination countries (such as the United States, the United Kingdom and Australia). In contrast, we draw on a qualitative study of 85 UK students who have either completed or are considering undertaking a degree programme overseas. We found that, in opposition to a common image of 'international students', UK students are not overtly motivated by 'strategic' concerns. Instead, they are seeking 'excitement' and 'adventure' from overseas study and often use the opportunity to delay the onset of a career and prolong a relatively carefree student lifestyle. Despite these ostensibly 'disinterested' objectives, however, UK students remain a highly privileged group and their experiences serve only to facilitate the reproduction of their privilege. The paper calls for a more critical analysis of the spatially uneven and socially exclusive nature of international higher education.

I didn't make any effort, I didn't try, I didn't study, I could not be bothered [...] I grew up in a very spoilt environment, so of course, why did I have to do anything, you know? The world was going to come to me. (Richard, interviewee, completed higher education in Canada)

Introduction

A great deal of work to date on the sociology of education has discussed the concept of 'strategy' in relation to middle-class decision-making around schooling, university and employment (for example, Collins 1979; Bourdieu 1984; Brown 1995; Ball et al. 1995; Brown, Hesketh, and Williams 2003; Ball 2003). The general tenor of many of these arguments is that, with the 'democratisation' of access to formal education, the social advantage of middle-class families has come under threat. They have, consequently, had to find new ways of excluding working-class participants from the most valued and sought-after occupations. Middle-class families can thus be seen, in the words of Brown et al. to employ 'exclusionary tactics [...] at a time of profound personal and social uncertainty' (1997, 14–15), to ensure their social reproduction and to maintain their position in the class structure (Bourdieu 1984). Most frequently, these tactics are portrayed as rational and calculating and undertaken with a fairly clear and explicit understanding of consequences (in terms of the economic and social rewards they will elicit). In national and local educational markets, such strategies might include the use of school league tables, moving house to be within a desired school 'catchment area', paying for a private education, stressing the importance of extra-curricular activities or employing personal tutors to enhance children's achievement. Within higher education, the choice of particular institutions or pursuit of master's-level and doctoral-level qualifications are used to secure one's 'positional advantage' in relation to increasing numbers of others with commensurate undergraduate credentials (Brown and Hesketh 2004).

Such strategies are apparent, although rarely discussed, on an *international* scale (Waters 2006). As the relatively small academic literature on international and immigrant students would suggest, these individuals are equally engaged in the strategic and conscious pursuit of 'advantage' (Li et al. 1996; Ong 1999; Balaz and Williams 2004; Waters 2006; Baas 2006; Collins 2006; Rivza and Teichler 2007). Buoyed by their families, students are deeply concerned with acquiring the 'right' credentials and other embodied traits, which will be ultimately converted into social status and economic capital. Other media and policy accounts point to high levels of strategy amongst international students when it comes to the choice of destination country, institution and subject of study (Shepherd 2008). Subject choices, for example, are usually closely aligned to specific career and 'employability' objectives: Institute of International Education data for the United States show 41% of international students in 2006/07 taking business and management, engineering, or mathematics and computer science (Open Doors 2007). Similarly, British Council data for the United Kingdom claim that 44% of international students are enrolled on business studies, engineering and technology, or physical and mathematical sciences programmes (compared with 9% for social science subjects), whereas in Australia 65% take management/commerce, information technology or engineering (British Council 2004). The demand for business studies is growing fastest and is predicted to increase from 14,000 in 2003 to 74,000 in 2020 (British Council 2004).[1] International students, it would therefore seem, are very aware of the close relationship between credentials and employment outcomes, and the need to secure 'positional advantage' in an increasingly global knowledge-based economy (Brown and Hesketh 2004).

This paper makes an explicit attempt to bring together work in sociology of education around middle-class strategies and an increasingly vibrant research agenda examining the mobilities of international students. Despite this growing agenda, very little is still known about those emanating *from* English-speaking western countries. A small number of academic studies on UK students have examined international movement (for 6–12 months) *within* a UK-based degree (as part of, for example, the Erasmus and Socrates programmes) (King and Ruiz-Gelices 2003; Findlay et al. 2006). However, there remains a significant gap in our knowledge of the motivations and experiences of UK students who choose overseas study for the *whole* of an undergraduate or postgraduate degree. The case of British students is particularly interesting, leaving the United Kingdom – one of the primary student *destination* countries – for study abroad. Based on in-depth interviews, our research has sought to shed light on this hitherto unexplored aspect of international mobility, focusing on UK students seeking overseas education for the whole of an undergraduate or postgraduate degree, in a range of destination countries, as well as their subsequent employment experiences.

Attempts to explain international student migration stress, in different ways, the importance of accumulating 'capital' (Balaz and Williams 2004; Findlay et al. 2006; Waters 2006, 2008). International credentials are the embodiment of both 'human capital' and 'cultural capital', which can subsequently be exchanged for economic capital in the labour market (Bourdieu 1986). One of the most common and widely recognised advantages of an 'overseas' education for many students is the guarantee that it provides of proficiency in a foreign language, notably English (Balaz and Williams 2004; Waters 2006). However, this is unlikely to matter for international students emanating *from* English-speaking countries such as the United Kingdom. Other debates in sociology and education suggest the salience, for UK students and graduates, of issues such as 'employability', credential inflation, overpopulated graduate labour markets, and the consequent need to seek 'positional advantage' (for example, Arthur and Rousseau 1996; Brown and Hesketh 2004; Brown and Lauder 2006; Moreau and Leathwood 2006). None of these discussions, however, engage with debates around *international* education and the possibility that UK students, when faced with the apparent reality of credential inflation, could choose to go overseas for their education. As entry levels to higher education in the United Kingdom reach 40%, an 'international' education, we suggest, may offer British students something scarcer and therefore more valuable than the 'norm' (Bourdieu 1996; Waters 2009) – securing their 'positional advantage' in the competition for graduate jobs.

This paper focuses on the reasons why *UK students* (as opposed to international students more generally) decide to pursue an overseas education, in a climate where 'Education UK' is undoubtedly a desirable and highly sought after global brand (British Council 2004). It begins with a brief look at what we already know about international student mobility. We then introduce the specific case of UK students, suggesting the need to understand their decisions to study overseas in the context of recent debates within British and American sociology around credential inflation, graduate labour markets and employability. The project's methodology is discussed, before providing an in-depth look at the overseas mobility of UK students. We consider the claim that, in the (exceptional?) case of UK students, the 'cultural capital' associated with international education is not sought strategically but is accumulated 'accidentally', or without any conscious attempt to gain an explicit 'advantage' from overseas study. The paper uniquely and productively brings together different literatures and debates emanating from diverse disciplines to examine important emergent geographies of international higher education.

The international mobility of UK students

To date, the internationalisation of education in the United Kingdom has been a rather one-sided process, involving the selling of 'Education UK' to overseas consumers (particularly through the work of the British Council) and the consequent 'importing' of thousands of students. The UK Government's stance on international education was recently formalised through the 'Prime Minister's Initiative on International Education' (PMI) (1999–2004), and the PMI2, which was launched in April 2006. The PMI2 is a five-year strategy (building on the first PMI) with the aim of securing the position of the United Kingdom as a 'leader in international education', with targets that include attracting an additional 70,000 international students to the United Kingdom and significantly growing the number of partnerships between the United Kingdom and other countries, both by 2011. As already noted, along with the United States and Australia, the United Kingdom is the foremost destination country for large numbers of international students, with over 270,000 in UK higher education (British Council 2004). Increasingly, higher education institutions in the United Kingdom are investing heavily in implementing 'internationalisation' strategies – as a number of recent policy reports (Fielden 2007) and dedicated practitioner conferences attest.

Very little attention has been paid, however, in both policy and academic circles, to the implications for the United Kingdom of 'exporting' students, and, aside from piecemeal anecdotal evidence, knowledge of this is scant. The *Times Higher Education* recently included a small feature on UK students overseas, suggesting that 'unprecedented numbers of British teenagers are considering shunning UK universities for US colleges in the hope of a broader, cheaper and more luxurious education' (Shepherd 2008, no pagination). The Fulbright Commission, which funds UK students to study in the United States, reported 700,000 inquiries in 2007, which represents a three-fold increase on the previous year (Shepherd 2008); the latest Institute of International Education (2009) statistics show an increase in the number of UK students in the US. In another media account, concerns over 'cost' and the relatively high tuition fees (particularly at master's and PhD levels) faced by students in the United Kingdom were given as a reason why increasing numbers would seem to be interested in studying abroad. Countries such as Sweden and the Netherlands offer postgraduate tuition in the English language for a fraction of the cost of an equivalent UK-based course (Clark 2006). There is a need, however, for a far more detailed analysis of UK students and their role in global international population flows.

Addressing this gap, the project on which this paper draws included in-depth interviews with 85 UK students and graduates conducted in 2007/08. The sample comprised 40 sixth-formers and undergraduates who were seriously considering study overseas, and 45 graduates who had completed either an undergraduate or postgraduate degree abroad. It was anticipated that choices may be configured differently for individuals studying at undergraduate and postgraduate level, and we therefore included approximately equal numbers of both in the sample. Participants were recruited through diverse channels, including state and private schools in the United Kingdom located in Surrey, Greater Manchester, Merseyside and Cumbria, the Fulbright Commission, the Canadian Rhodes Scholars Foundation, the Commonwealth Scholars Commission, 65 alumni associations, and advertisements placed on university notice pages. The spread of subject areas pursued by students was wide, and included geography, economics, psychology, politics, international relations, literature, Viking studies, zoology, mathematics, nuclear physics, engineering, journalism, shark behaviour and education. However, we recognise that our sampling method may not have captured the total population of UK students overseas, and there is an inevitable bias towards those particular schools and universities that provided us with the most help.

Our data indicate that there was much less geographical diversity in relation to undergraduate study than there was at postgraduate level: high-status universities in the United States (Ivy League) were by far the most common destinations amongst the former group. In contrast, for postgraduate study, many more respondents had considered or were considering institutions outside the United States (although North America as a whole still dominated student choices). Notably, across the sample there were only four respondents who either had studied or were planning to study in a language other than English.

It is also important to note the socio-economic characteristics of our sample. Socio-economic diversity was far more apparent for our 'postgraduates' (i.e. those thinking of studying for, or having completed, a postgraduate degree overseas) than it was at the 'undergraduate' level (i.e. amongst individuals that were thinking of/had completed an undergraduate degree abroad). Nineteen out of 31 of our 'undergraduate' respondents had attended a private school, compared with only 12 out of 54 'postgraduates'. The 'undergraduate' group had all followed a traditional path through school to university, with 'gap years' being the only break in study. In contrast, our 'postgraduate' sample also contained some individuals who had more 'unconventional' educational histories (e.g. mature students). Thus, whilst international education is usually associated with a privileged upbringing (and this aspect is highlighted in this paper), this is not always and necessarily the case. Nevertheless, taken as a whole, the characteristics of the respondents indicate that international students from the United Kingdom do represent a highly privileged group, with access to significant amounts of capital (social, cultural and economic). Interviews demonstrated privilege in a number of different ways, including the degree of parental support and involvement in education, familial expectations with regard to educational achievement and the amount of/quality of capital invested by the family (Coleman 1988). School, peer and familial pressure to attend a 'good' university was widely apparent, and evidence points to the salience of the concept of *habitus* (Bourdieu 1984) for capturing the totality of environmental and social influences (the multiple dimensions of privilege) coming together to make international education a viable, imaginable option for our participants. The biographies of students and graduates showed the importance of travel (as a child or young adult) – whether on family or school trips, as part of a 'gap year' or as a 'year abroad' within an undergraduate degree programme. Parents were almost always highly supportive, and would demonstrate this in material as well as less tangible ways, frequently offering to foot the bill for overseas study.

Strategy or the accidental accumulation of capital?

Given what we know already about both middle-class strategies around education and the apparent widespread strategising of international students, one of the most striking and unexpected findings to have emerged from our study was the ostensible *absence* of any explicit strategy underpinning many UK students' decisions around international education.[2] The lack of conspicuous strategising was evident from the data in a number of ways. Most notable, perhaps, is what individuals did *not* say with regards to their decision-making; only a handful of participants made any reference at all to employment and the economic advantages that would eventually accrue to them from pursuing an international education. This observation contrasts starkly with extant understandings of international students, where employability considerations (and particularly the assumed perceptions of employers) are of utmost importance (Waters 2008; Shepherd 2008). When asked why they were thinking, or had originally thought of studying overseas, the vast majority of individuals stressed 'excitement', 'glamour' and 'adventure'. Jamie, an undergraduate considering going overseas for postgraduate study, captures this sense of the absence of strategy. He said:

> I don't really see any of my education or academic studies or cultural enrichment or anything I partake in, in my life, as contributing to a final goal or career prospect; none whatsoever. It's purely to develop myself as a person so as to sort of have a more

objective understanding of the world and be able to perhaps contribute in a more positive way. Whereas as – this sounds very much like something a hippy would say, but you know, like – as opposed to sort of trying to use my academic studies for sort of monetary gain in the future, so to speak.

The lack of apparent strategy – particularly around career and monetary gain – was striking. Jamie's personal objectives when it comes to his educational decisions were not unique but, on the contrary, highly representative of the majority of views expressed by our research participants. Clearly, we need a different conception of 'strategy' in this instance – one not associated with highly rational and overtly calculating decision-making, but one that makes choices *appear* disinterested, even when they may ultimately result in the (same) reproduction of class privilege. For Pierre Bourdieu (1984), who has theorised extensively on the relationship between class strategies, social reproduction and education, 'strategy' amongst the most privileged individuals (particular the upper middle classes) has very different connotations than it does for working-class and lower-middle-class groups. He writes:

> To speak of strategies of reproduction is not to say that the strategies through which dominants manifest their tendency to maintain the status quo are the result of rational calculation or even strategic intent. It is merely to register that many practices that are phenomenally very different are objectively organised in such a way that they contribute to the reproduction of the capital at hand, *without having been explicitly designed and instituted with this end in mind.* (Bourdieu 1984, 272; emphasis added)

Bourdieu's theorisations – and particularly the concept of *habitus* – allow us to transcend the often-assumed dichotomy between rational and calculated action, on the one hand, and unconscious practices on the other. Consequently, educational strategies can be *both* conscious and unconscious, and should not therefore be always reduced to 'the economics of "human capital"' (Bourdieu 1984, 273) – in other words, to an overt concern with 'profitable outcomes' from investment in education (as much of the recent writing on the 'exclusionary tactics' of middle-class families in relation to education might imply; see Ball 2003). For the most privileged members of society, the pursuit of education can be seen as part of a more general 'aesthetic disposition':

> [a] capacity to neutralize ordinary urgencies and to bracket off practical ends, a durable inclination and aptitude for practice without a practical function, [which] can only be constituted within an experience of the world freed from urgency and through the practice of activities which are an end in themselves. (Bourdieu 1984, 54)

The ability to take such an 'un-instrumental' view of education depends, importantly, on an individual's 'past and present material conditions of existence' (Bourdieu 1984, 53–54) and the capacity to 'withdraw' from concerns over 'economic necessity'. Furthermore, this allows such privileged individuals the additional advantage of being seen (and of seeing themselves) 'as perfectly disinterested, unblemished by any cynical or mercenary use of culture' (Bourdieu 1984, 86).

This conception of 'strategy' has far more resonance with the motivations and objectives of our sample of UK students than does a more instrumental view of 'choice' around education (for example, Collins 1979; Ball et al. 1995; Waters 2006, 2008). Richard, who graduated from a university in Canada, epitomises the 'accidental' accumulation of valuable cultural capital. He was able to reflect upon the level of privilege he had experienced growing up and was open about his pursuit of 'aesthetic' (as opposed to overtly career-oriented) goals:

> I left school with five GCSEs, two Bs and three Cs – very, very poor. I didn't make any effort, I didn't try, I didn't study, I could not be bothered. I had no ... I was very lazy and unmotivated. I had no desire. I grew up in a very spoilt environment, so of course, why did I have to do anything, you know? The world was going to come to me.

After leaving school, he worked for two years in a video store, and during that time discovered his love of American football: '[For] someone who is easily bored, the thought of suddenly studying in America would be, you know, wow, amazing'. He had imagined studying abroad would be 'just one big juicy adventure [...] the adventure of it just swept me away, a big grand adventure you know'. When asked how he had envisaged an overseas education fitting into his 'future plans', he replied:

> I don't think I had a future plan, to be honest. My future plan was to avoid working and sleep late! And that fitted in well because of course it meant a guaranteed four year pass out of employment. At the time that was a massive motivation. I just didn't want to work and I wanted to find any way possible to avoid doing anything I didn't want to do.

Richard spent six years in Canada completing an undergraduate degree, funded by his parents, and now works as head of marketing at a large beauty chain based in the United Kingdom. Even he would freely admit to having 'fallen on his feet', almost despite his best efforts. His claim that he had 'no plan' for his future, when decisions around overseas study were being made, was not uncommon. Another participant, Idris, was considering studying for a master's degree in law somewhere in Europe. However, he claimed: 'I don't really have, like, any kind of great long-term career plan. I'd say I'm kind of, like, I want to do this and see, like, what avenues it opens up, and see where I go from there'. The vagueness of his plans undoubtedly reflect a confidence that he will similarly 'land on his feet' whatever his decision, perhaps born of his privileged experiences to date. When asked what advantages she had envisaged from studying abroad, another respondent replied:

> I didn't think it would offer me anything other than the ability to go abroad [...]. I didn't have any idea what I wanted to do for a career. I don't think I was that really focussed on it really, I just wanted to have an experience of living abroad. So I think, all it was was an ability to get me abroad [...]. I think I thought I'd worked really hard, I worked hard at school, I worked hard at university, and I just thought I wanted some time having some fun.

Numerous examples from our interviews demonstrate what Bourdieu described as 'an experience of the world freed from urgency' and 'the practice of activities which are an end in themselves' (1984, 54). Lillian went on to describe her overseas education as 'something I was doing purely for myself, for fun'; Shaun said 'to be perfectly honest, I wasn't very much thinking about advantage. I mean, I was quite interested in studying longer and I wanted to travel, and so it was an end in itself'; whereas Patrick said of his own aims 'I didn't think about mortgages and things like that [...]. I didn't have any future plans – everything was a lark'.

Opportunities to study overseas sometimes came along inadvertently. Tracy admitted that her failure to 'work hard' as an undergraduate had meant that she was unable, consequently, to secure a place on her preferred UK-based master's course. Then the option of studying in Canada 'appeared':

> I never really made the conscious decision to go, it had just been thrown at me, like – 'well why not try this?' […] Initially I thought, well, this is probably the only way I'm going to get further in to do graduate work […]. Now I look back I think there's a lot more advantages to, you know, having gone there.

Again, this example resonates strongly with Bourdieu's concept of *habitus,* wherein unconscious daily practices can lead inadvertently to social advantage for privileged individuals.

For some participants, far from representing a strategic long-term career move, overseas study offered an *alternative* to starting one's career – a way of forestalling the inevitable (i.e. the commitment associated with full-time employment). When asked what had prompted her thoughts about overseas study, Lillian replied: 'I didn't want to get a proper job! [*Interviewer: OK*] Didn't want to do the milk round[3] and didn't … really wanted to live abroad. It wasn't the study, it was living abroad'. Reflecting on his decision to spend two years pursuing a master's degree in Canada, Ralph said:

> Did I want to go straight to my career or did I want to buy some time really and go and study? And you know, in the end my decision was that it wouldn't hurt, you know, there will always be jobs out there, but you know there will only be this one, I could live to regret [missing] this opportunity to go and have someone pay me to study abroad, and go and live abroad, and go and have the luxury of being a student, you know, which is a luxury in many ways. To go and explore what you want to explore, research what you want to research, and someone is paying you to do it and paying you very nicely to do it […]. My decision was, if I don't do it I'll regret it, and that was it really. And do you know, it was a hard decision because, as I say, the company I had a job offer with clearly wanted me and were very, you know, it was amazing money and it was an amazing deal.

In this account, we see a decision being made between starting employment in a company with excellent monetary and other rewards and pursuing an 'adventure' abroad. Intriguingly, no association is drawn between the furthering of his education and improved employment prospects, challenging prevalent assumptions linking employability, individual responsibility and postgraduate learning (for example, Bowman 2005). His sense that 'there will always be jobs out there' reflects a lack of urgency associated with privileged individuals able to 'withdraw' from concerns over 'economic necessity' (Bourdieu 1984).

The pursuit of pleasure and 'experience for experience's sake' – evoking Bourdieu's (1984) 'aesthetic disposition' – was widely evident in the reasons individuals gave for undertaking study abroad. Ceri, for example, was asked what she thought she would 'get out of overseas study':

> Well, a different experience from a different country which, I mean you don't, if you travel to somewhere you usually see it and you see the sights, but you don't actually really get to know what a place is like unless you live there. […] I feel going to study abroad I can get the knowledge I want from a PhD but get a lot of other experiences as well….and meet different people, different lifestyles, different cultures.

Idris similarly said: 'I've always had, wanted to see different places and kind of seek out those experiences and try and get a greater understanding through seeing different places'. These extracts evoke Ulf Hannerz's (1996) notion of 'the cosmopolitan', forever searching for difference and yet, at the same time, always 'knowing where the exit is'. The spaces inhabited by the cosmopolitan are often 'bounded and elitist' and 'marked by a specialized and – paradoxically – rather homogeneous transnational culture, a limited interest in engaging 'the Other', and a rather restricted corridor of physical movement between defined spaces' (Vertovec and Cohen 2002, 7). The tendency for students to pursue 'difference' in the United States would seem to represent just that – a rather circumscribed engagement with 'the Other'. In fact, much of what students seemed to know about the United States – and the excitement and adventure they associated with it – came through exposure to films and television (Waters and Brooks forthcoming).

On the whole, undergraduate and postgraduate experiences of overseas study were almost uniformly positive, and articulated not in relation to any objective 'advantage' they bestowed, such as improved employment prospects, but in terms of a personally rewarding 'life experience'. Any 'career' advantages gained (and some were mentioned) were portrayed as incidental. The interviews, particularly those conducted with the most privileged individuals, display the 'playful seriousness' that Bourdieu invokes when he says:

> one has to belong to the ranks of those who have been able, not necessarily to make their whole existence a sort of children's game, but at least to maintain for a long time, sometimes a whole lifetime, a child's relation to the world. (1984, 54)

Our findings correspond with those of Brooks and Everett (2008) in their work on the incidence of 'life planning' amongst graduates in the United Kingdom. They review several studies about young adults' propensity to plan and note the differences that emerged 'by social position' (Brooks and Everett 2008, 326) – whereas privileged individuals would seem to design their lives in some detail, those from socially disadvantaged backgrounds would eschew such planning. In contrast, Brooks and Everett found a strong association between a *privileged* upbringing and a '*disinclination* to form detailed plans for the future' (2008, 335). In explanation, they suggest that socially advantaged young adults 'felt little need to plan because of a secure and highly advantaged family background' – they may have sensed that the 'carefree' nature of their present circumstances would not last, and so they would enjoy it whilst they could (Brooks and Everett 2008, 331). Amongst our sample, enjoyment was a strong motivator for overseas study, wherein individuals were able to 'bracket off practical ends' and seek pleasure as a goal in itself (Bourdieu 1984, 54). And yet, even if we accept that UK students' decisions regarding study overseas are usually unstrategic and made with only the vaguest conscious notion of accruing 'profit', we nevertheless have to confront the fact that the choices they make will often result in the reproduction of middle-class privilege.

Conclusion

This paper has provided an exploration of UK students' experiences of overseas study. It has argued that, in an intense period of higher education 'internationalisation', very little is still yet known about the experiences and motivations of international students – particularly those from English-speaking 'western' countries. An examination of recent work on the sociology of education indicates the importance of the concept of 'strategy' in relation to middle-class decision-making around schooling and higher education. In a purportedly saturated graduate labour market, gaining 'positional advantage' through educational choice is as important as ever. Similarly, a separate but related body of work on international students suggests the salience of the accumulation of cultural capital (such as linguistic skills) in motivating their decision to study abroad. The focus of this work, however, has generally been on students moving from non-English speaking *to* English-speaking western countries (or countries where the medium of educational instruction is English). To date, very little has been known about the motivations and objectives of students moving *from* English-speaking countries such as the United Kingdom. We have asked: how relevant is the concept of 'strategy' in this instance? The paper has drawn on a recent study of 85 UK students and graduates who have either completed or are seriously considering completing a degree course overseas. What we have found is that, contrary to expectations, these individuals displayed very little by way of 'strategic intent' when it came to decision-making around overseas study. In fact, any sense that an overseas education would confer some 'advantage' (over and above a home-based qualification) was noticeably absent. Instead, for many interviewees, international education seemed to represent an active shunning of 'life-planning' and the responsibilities associated with employment. Going overseas offered opportunities for 'excitement', 'glamour' and 'fun' and a way of deferring the inevitable encroachment of a 'career'. These findings go against what we know of international students more generally – that they are highly strategic and focussed primarily on subsequent careers, where their choice of institutions and subjects reflect explicit attempts to maximise their accumulation of 'cultural capital' (Bourdieu 1984), which can later be converted into economic capital in the labour market. In this paper, we have conceptualised our findings in terms of the 'accidental achievement' of UK students who, despite their claims of disinterestedness, nevertheless appear to be generally successful in everything they do.

The work of Bourdieu (1984, 1996) has been particularly helpful in allowing us to understand the apparent conflict between what we know of middle-class strategies around education (on which there is a substantial literature) and the findings uncovered in this research – an apparent tension between 'strategy' and the 'accidental' accumulation of capital. For the most privileged members of society, amongst which many of our research participants would count, practices of social reproduction are neither purely conscious nor unconscious, but are subsumed within a more general 'aesthetic disposition' within the *habitus*, wherein 'ordinary urgencies' and material concerns are put to one side and in their place can be found the tendency to pursue pleasure and experience for experience's sake.

And yet, the paper has also argued, the choices these individuals have made with regards to their education may nevertheless result in the reproduction of their privilege. This becomes clear when we examine the destinations of UK students. They are focused on 'world class' institutions abroad, and particularly Ivy League universities in the United States. The opportunities to study at these institutions presented themselves not by accident, but most usually in association with particular experiences of (private) schooling and parental involvement in education.

One of the main conclusions to be drawn from this work, then, is that – despite the fact that increasing numbers of individuals, globally, have access to higher education, and that opportunities for international study appear to be growing – educational opportunities (and the extent of 'achievement' that results from these) continue to be differentiated by social class background. It supports widespread claims that *real* 'choice' in education is often a myth, as are any remaining associations between this and positive outcomes for social mobility. There is a pressing need to examine further the uneven and often exclusive geographies of international student mobility.

Acknowledgements

The authors would like to thank the British Academy for funding this research and Helena Pimlott-Wilson for all her help with the data collection. Two referees provided helpful comments on a draft of this paper. The authors are also very grateful to all those that gave generously of their time to participate in this project.

Notes

1. Subject-based demand has a very particular geography – Western Europe and North American accounted for 60% of total demand for arts/humanities subjects in 2003, whereas the growing demand for business studies is driven largely by students from East Asia.
2. Brooks and Waters (2009) argue elsewhere that often, an international education represents for these students the 'next best thing', after they have failed to get into their first choice (invariably Oxbridge) institution.
3. The 'milk round' is an annual visit to universities in the United Kingdom, when recruiters from large commercial companies attempt to sign-up future employees.

References

Arthur, M.B., and D.M. Rousseau. 1996. Introduction: The boundaryless career as a new employment principle. In *The boundaryless career: A new employment principle for a new organizational era,* ed. M.B. Arthur and D.M. Rousseau, 3–20. New York: Oxford University Press.

Baas, M. 2006. Students of migration: Indian overseas students and the question of permanent residency. *People and Place* 14: 9–24.

Balaz, V., and A. Williams. 2004. 'Been there, done that': International student migration and human capital transfers from the UK to Slovakia. *Population, Space and Place* 10: 217–37.

Ball, S. 2003. *Class strategies and the education market: The middle classes and social advantage.* London: Routledge.

Ball, S.J., R. Bowe, and S. Gewirtz. 1995. Circuits of schooling: A sociological exploration of parental choice of school in social-class contexts. *Sociological Review* 43: 52–78.

Bourdieu, P. 1984. *Distinction; A social critique of the judgement of taste.* Cambridge, MA: Harvard University Press.

Bourdieu, P. 1986. The forms of capital. In *Handbook of theory and research for the sociology of education,* ed. J.G. Richardson, 241–58. New York: Greenwood Press.

Bourdieu, P. 1996. *The state nobility: Elite schools in the field of power.* Stanford, CA: Stanford University Press.

Bowman, H. 2005. 'It's a year and then that's me': Masters students' decision-making. *Journal of Further and Higher Education* 29: 233–49.

British Council. 2004. Vision 2020: Forecasting international student mobility. Report produced with Universities UK and IDP Education Australia.

Brooks, R., and G. Everett. 2008. The prevalence of 'life-planning': Evidence from UK graduates. *British Journal of Sociology of Education* 29: 325–37.

Brooks, R., and J. Waters. 2009. A second chance of 'success': UK students and global circuits of higher education. *Sociology* 43, no. 6: 1085–1102.

Brown, P. 1995. Cultural capital and social exclusion: Some observations on recent trends in education, employment, and the labour market. *Work, Employment and Society* 9: 29–51.

Brown, P., A.H. Halsey, H. Lauder, and A. Stuart Wells. 1997. The transformation of education and society: An introduction. In *Education: Culture, economy, society,* ed. A. Halsey, H. Lauder, P. Brown, and A.S. Wells, 1–44. Oxford: Oxford University Press.

Brown, P., and A. Hesketh. 2004. *The mismanagement of talent: Employability and jobs in the knowledge economy.* Oxford: Oxford University Press.

Brown, P., A. Hesketh, and S. Williams. 2003. Employability in a knowledge-driven economy. *Journal of Education and Work* 16: 107–26.

Brown, P., and H. Lauder. 2006. Globalisation, knowledge and the myth of the magnet economy. *Globalisation, Societies and Education* 4: 25–57.

Clark, T. 2006. A free lunch in Uppsala. *The Guardian,* October 24.

Coleman, J. 1988. Social capital in the creation of human capital. *American Journal of Sociology* 94: S95–120.

Collins, F.L. 2006. Making Asian students, making students Asian: The racialisation of export education in Auckland, New Zealand. *Asia Pacific Viewpoint* 47: 217–34.

Collins, R. 1979. *The credential society: An historical sociology of education and stratification.* New York: Academic Press.

Fielden, J. 2007. *Global horizons for UK students: A guide for universities.* London: The Council for Industry and Higher Education.

Findlay, A., R. King, A. Stam, and E. Ruiz-Gelices. 2006. Ever reluctant Europeans: The changing geographies of UK students studying and working abroad. *European Urban and Regional Studies* 13: 291–318.

Hannerz, U. 1996. *Transnational connections: Culture, people, places.* London: Routledge.

Institute of International Education. 2009. Record numbers of international students in US higher education. http://opendoors.iienetwork.org/?p=150649 (accessed January 28, 2010).

King, R., and E. Ruiz-Gelices. 2003. International student migration and the European 'year-abroad': Effects on European identity and subsequent migration behaviour. *International Journal of Population Geography* 9: 229–52.

Li, L., A. Findlay, A. Jowett, and R. Skeldon. 1996. Migrating to learn and learning to migrate. *International Journal of Population Geography* 2: 51–67.

Moreau, M.P., and C. Leathwood. 2006. Graduates' employment and the discourse of employability: A critical analysis. *Journal of Education and Work* 19: 305–324.

Ong, A. 1999. *Flexible citizenship: The cultural logics of transnationality.* Durham, NC: Duke University Press.

Open Doors. 2007. Report on international educational exchange. http://opendoors.iienetwork.org (accessed August 11, 2008).

Rivza, B., and Teichler, U. 2007. The changing role of student mobility. *Higher Education Policy* 20: 457–75.

Shepherd, J. 2006. UK students drawn to US for broad-based degrees. *Times Higher Education,* 4 August.

Shepherd, J. 2008. Why I chose the university of wherever. *Education Guardian,* Tuesday February 5, p. 14.

Vertovec, S., and R. Cohen. 2002. Introduction: Conceiving cosmopolitanism. In *Conceiving cosmopolitanism: Theory, context, and practice,* ed. S. Vertovec and R. Cohen, 1–24. Oxford: Oxford University Press.

Waters, J.L. 2006. Geographies of cultural capital: Education, international migration and family strategies between Hong Kong and Canada. *Transactions of the Institute of British Geographers* 31: 179–92.

Waters, J.L. 2008. *Education, migration and cultural capital in the Chinese Diaspora: Transnational students between Hong Kong and Canada.* New York: Cambria Press.

Waters, J.L. 2009. In pursuit of scarcity: transnational students, 'employability', and the MBA. *Environment and Planning A* 41, no. 8: 1865–83.

Waters, J., and R. Brooks. Forthcoming. 'Vive la difference'? The 'international' experiences of UK students overseas. *Population, Space and Place.*

Aspiration for global cultural capital in the stratified realm of global higher education: why do Korean students go to US graduate schools?

Jongyoung Kim

Department of Sociology, Kyung Hee University, Hoegi-Dong, Dongdaemun-Gu, Seoul 130-701, South Korea

This study aims to understand Korean students' motivations for studying in US graduate schools. For this purpose, I conducted in-depth interviews with 50 Korean graduate students who were enrolled in a research-centered US university at the time of the interview. In these interviews, I sought to understand how their motivations are connected not only with their family, school, and occupational backgrounds, but also with the stratification of global higher education. Theoretically, this paper attempts to combine the concept of global positional competition with Pierre Bourdieu's theory of cultural capital in the field of global education. By critically examining a push–pull model of transnational higher education choice-making, this study situates Korean students' aspirations in the contexts of global power and the hierarchy of knowledge-degree production and consumption. After analyzing the students' qualitative interviews, I classify their motivations for earning US degrees within four categories: enhancing their class positions and enlarging their job opportunities; pursuing learning in the global center of learning; escaping the undemocratic system and culture in Korean universities; and fulfilling desires to become cosmopolitan elites armed with English communication skills and connections within the global professional network. Based on this analysis, I argue that Korean students pursue advanced degrees in the United States in order to succeed in the global positional competition within Korea as well as in the global job marketplace. As they pursue advanced US degrees, Korean students internalize US hegemony as it reproduces the global hierarchy of higher education, but at the same time Korean students see US higher education as a means of liberation that resolves some of the inner contradictions of Korean higher education, including gender discrimination, a degree caste system, and an authoritarian learning culture. Therefore, this study links Korean students' aspiration for global cultural capital to complex and irregular structures and relations of class, gender, nationality, and higher education that extend across local, national, and global dimensions simultaneously.

Introduction

Early in 2005, Korean newspapers and broadcasts delivered the surprising news that Seoul National University, Korea's top university, was the top feeder school to US PhD recipients outside the United States (overall, it took second place, trailing only University of California – Berkeley). Two other major schools in Korea – Yonsei University and Korea University — were ranked fifth and eighth on the list (*Chosun Daily* 2005). While many Koreans may have noticed the clout that the US PhD carries in Korean society, few could have recognized the extent of Korean dependence on US higher education. Because of the strong US influence after the liberation and the Korean War (1950–1953), earning a degree from the United States became a main road to success and fame in Korean society. Statistics show that many Koreans still regard US higher education as superior, and in some contexts essential. For example, recent faculty recruitment in top universities overwhelmingly favors recipients of US doctorates over those from Korean and other foreign institutions. In 2005, 80% of new faculty members in the field of social sciences in the three top universities of Korea (Seoul National University, Yonsei University, and Korea University) received their doctorates from US institutions. In POSTEC and KAIST, the two leading science and engineering schools in Korea, 70–80% of the new faculty members held US degrees (*Kyosu Newspaper* 2005). The Institute of International Education reports that, next to India (94,563) and China (81,127), Korea (69,124) was ranked third in the leading places of origin for international students seeking US degrees in 2007/08 (Open Doors 2009). Considering national populations (India, 1.17 billion; China, 1.3 billion; and Korea, 49 million), the ratio of Korean students in the US higher education is 19 times that of India, and 25 times that of China. Koreans' enthusiasm for learning English and for workplace opportunities favoring those with US degrees have been well documented (Abelmann, Park, and Kim 2009; Park and Abelmann 2004; Song et al. 2007; Yoon 2007). It is therefore surprising that Korean students' extraordinary obsession with US higher education has rarely been studied in Korea or elsewhere.

This study explores why Korean students enter US graduate schools by analyzing in-depth interviews with 50 Korean graduate students who were enrolled in one US research university at the time of their interviews. Qualitative research provides the advantage of enabling us to understand the agent's complex strategies as well as the entire process and dynamics of the issue at hand (Berg 2007; Creswell 2007). Presenting their voices vividly, I intend to connect these students' experiences not only with their family, educational, and social backgrounds, but also with the domestic and global stratification of higher education.

Here, this study simultaneously incorporates and challenges existing literatures on transnational higher education choice-making, particularly amongst Asian students. Foreign students' decisions to study abroad typically have been analyzed in terms of 'a push and pull model' (Chen 2007; Mazzarol and Soutar 2002; Park 2009; Zikopoulos and Barber 1986). This model considers such factors as student characteristics (class, gender, and ethnicity), significant others (family, relatives, and professors), external 'push' factors (the home country's academic, economic, cultural, and political aspects), and external pull factors (the host country's academic quality, economic and political ties, geographic proximity, and immigration policy; the institution's reputation, financial aid, faculty, and location). To its credit, this model synthesizes individual backgrounds and environmental aspects to suggest multi-dimensional explanations of students' decisions. This study also aims to interweave students' background and membership with diverse environmental aspects in order to explain Korean students' decision to study in the United States. But the push–pull model pays little attention to geopolitics of knowledge-degree production and consumption. Most Asian students choose English-speaking countries for their destinations, and the global flow of foreign students is primarily uni-directional, as students travel from Asia to the United States and Europe, where most of the top-ranked research universities enjoying elite reputations are located. In other words, students' choices operate within the global stratification of higher education, and US hegemony exerts enormous influences on the production and consumption of academic capital. The push–pull model does not consider this global power and inequality in the field of higher education. Therefore, while this study encompasses various individual and environmental aspects to exploit the strengths of the push–pull model, it also locates Korean students' decision to study in the United States within the global stratification of higher education, and especially in the global hegemony of US universities.

Theoretically, this study expands Bourdieu's (1984, 1986, 1988) theory of cultural capital to the global field as it depicts studying abroad as a means of achieving 'global cultural capital.' Cultural capital means valued and exclusive cultural resources that enable one to signal, attain, or maintain a certain type of social status or position. We should note, however, that because Bourdieu and his followers have given insufficient attention to the constant global or transnational transformations of cultural capital, they tend to focus on one nation or society when they analyze how it is formed and how it operates. Therefore, I draw on conceptual frameworks developed by Phillip Brown and Simon Marginson, both of whom extended Bourdieusian insights to global positional competition in the field of higher education.

Drawing on neo-Weberian social closure theory (Hirsh 1977; Murphy 1988; Parkin 1979), Phillip Brown (1999, 2000) asserts that positional competition is becoming globalized as social groups and individuals mobilize their cultural, economic, and political powers and assets to attain higher social status beyond national boundaries. Hirsh (1977) argues that positional competition is a zero-sum game because one's status is relative to others' status. To gain a higher position, one must outsmart the other. On the one hand, the expansion of higher education within a nation makes position competition steeper, and fails to guarantee decent jobs to all degree holders. On the other hand, because global markets in every sector are expanding, new work opportunities arise beyond national boundaries. Korean students' motivations to study in the United States now operate in terms of positional competition and globalized work and educational environments. For one thing, given the fact that above 80% of high school graduates now enter tertiary education in Korea (C. Kim 2008, 34), gaining decent jobs and social status is becoming increasingly difficult. For another, the global market is also expanding rapidly, and Korea has emerged as a key global player in most sectors. For instance, around 50% of Korea's Gross Domestic Product is contributed by international trade. Within these structural conditions, Korean students attempt to outsmart others by earning US degrees, hoping thereby to gain more opportunities in the global job market.

Brown's model of global positional conflict is complemented by Marginson and his colleagues' serial analysis of how higher education is globally structured (Marginson 2006, 2008; Marginson and Sawir 2005). Recently, universities and national policy-makers in education around the world have been obsessed with the global rankings of universities (Horta 2009; Ishikawa 2009; Marginson and van der Wende 2006). The war for reputation and dominant position in higher education is now increasingly intense, begetting various effects. By using Bourdieu's (1993) concept of positioned/position-taking, Marginson (2006) distinguishes positional competition between producers (universities) from positional competition between consumers (students). In this process, as a global system of higher education emerges and each institution jockeys for a dominant position in the global hierarchy of universities, individuals also compete to enter elite universities. This global system is not unitary, but rather a complex and irregular combination among global, national and local contexts and interactions. Despite its imperfect, fragmented, and irregular stratification, Marginson (2008, 308) argues that the global system of higher education operates within the US hegemony, which is manifested in four aspects: 'research concentration and knowledge flows, the global role of English, US universities as people attractors and as exemplars of ideal practices.' Using global positional competition as its primary perspective, this article focuses on how Korean students compete for better position or status within the global hegemony of US universities. At the same time, this study shows how the contradictions of Korean higher education are revealed when Korean students choose to study in the United States, a collective decision that reinforces the global hegemony of US universities.

Combining the concepts of cultural capital and global positional competition, I interpret Korean students' aspirations to a US degree as the pursuit of global cultural capital to outsmart others in the stratified domain of global higher education. Global cultural capital means that degree attainment, knowledge, taste, and cosmopolitan attitude and lifestyle, understood as exclusive resources that designate one's class and status, globally operate, circulate, and exchange. The production and consumption of global cultural capital is stratified, but it is also diverse as it responds to various contexts. For example, Japanese students do not pursuit a PhD degree in the United States as often as Korean students because Japan has excellent world-class research universities, and the value difference between a Japanese degree and a degree from the United States is not perceived as significant. Consequently, despite the global stratification of higher education, various local and national contexts should be considered to understand the diverse ramifications of global cultural capital and global positional competition.

Therefore, to fully understand Korean students' motivations for studying in the United States, local and national contexts will be examined in connection with global cultural capital and a stratified global higher education system. From in-depth interviews, I found that the domestic stratification of Korean universities, the teaching and research systems at home and abroad, the relationship between occupation and academic credentials, and the undemocratic university cultures in Korea all influence Korean students' decisions to study in the United States. Ultimately, this study shows how these local and national contexts link with a stratified global higher education system multi-dimensionally, relationally, and simultaneously. This analysis helps us understand how local, national, and global forces and dimensions are interconnected in Korean students' aspirations to a US degree.

Method

Between 1999 and 2005, I conducted in-depth interviews with 50 Korean graduate students who were enrolled in MA or PhD programs in a US research university (pseudonym: Z University) at the time of the interview. All of them received their bachelor's or master's degrees in Korea, and then advanced to the US graduate school. Z University has several top-ranked graduate programs, and its overall ranking was highly positioned according to the two most-cited rankings invented by the *QS-Times* and Shanghai Jiao Tong University.[1] As I will explain later, the ranking of the university is highly important because Korean students consider it very critical when they choose the graduate school.

Interviewees[2] are selected to satisfy diverse backgrounds such as gender, major, age, and *alma mater* in Korea. I used snowball methods to collect interviewees. All interviews were frank and open as students explained in detail their motivations for study in the United States. The average interview lasted between one and two hours, and every interview was recorded and transcribed. The interview was relatively unstructured, relying on a few open-ended main questions. Because the qualitative interview is flexible, recursive, and dynamic in terms of interviewees' diverse backgrounds (Rubin and Rubin 2005), interview contents in this study continued and changed over time until a saturation point was achieved. The interview contents are mainly composed of two parts – the student's motivation to study in the US graduate school, and the subsequent adjustment process. Because the interviews are too large to describe completely, I will focus on students' motivation for studying in the United States.[3] When I asked about their motivations, interviewees linked them with their various family and educational backgrounds, learning experiences in universities, and job experiences. I used open coding and classified their motivations in four major categories: enhancing their class positions and enlarging their job opportunities; pursuing learning in the global center of learning; escaping the undemocratic system and culture in Korean universities; and fulfilling desires to become cosmopolitan elites armed with English communication skills and connections within the global professional network. I will explain those motivations in detail in the following section.

Korean students' motivations for studying in US graduate schools
Enhancing their class positions and enlarging their job opportunities
Most Korean students revealed that a US degree is a promising way to sustain or enhance their social position in Korean society. They linked this ambition to their family background and job experiences. A person's class or social position is mostly determined by parents' education and wealth and one's own occupation and income. The interviewees' parents are relatively well educated, possessing financial wealth that could support their sons' or daughters' studies in the United States. Those who are from less wealthy families are highly motivated, having excellent academic records. But regardless of their parents' background, interviewees' parents want them to become professionals or leading elites in Korea and beyond.

Without parents' financial support, it seems very difficult for Korean students to study in the United States. Hyuncheol (chemistry, male) said that his father owns a company and encouraged him to pursue a PhD degree in the United States. Because he is married with three children in the United States, he takes it for granted that his father should support his family as well as his study, even though he receives a research assistantship. Minhwa (social work, female) was also influenced by her father's view of the value of education. Her father was the Chief Executive Officer of a large company and traveled across the world. Minhwa agrees with her father's belief that economic wealth, education, and social status are positively circulated. 'It's almost impossible to overcome the environment you're born into these days. The rich get richer … especially in Korea. Economic power is a must. And to achieve economic power you need education ...' says Min-Hwa, agreeing with her father. Hye-In (music, female) admits she thought everyone studies abroad because her friends all came from economically privileged families: 'I never understood people who say they can't study abroad because they don't have enough money ...'

Also, parents' expectations and involvement in their children's education from an early age strongly influenced their offspring's aspirations for higher education. Miyoung's (social work, female) father, who is a professor in a leading university in Korea, told her from her childhood on that she should become a professor. When she accompanied him on his sabbatical year in the United States, Miyoung had a chance not only to improve her English, but also to meet her fathers' students in the United States, and these encounters motivated her to study there later. Minhwa (social work, female) and her parents travelled to the United States during her college years so that she could experience US culture, and this trip made up her mind to study in the United States. Kibeom's (sociology, male) father drove him to study English intensively from his childhood onwards, which led him to decide to study in the United States. Family background and parents' expectations naturally heightened their motivation. Interviewees did not conceal their belief that getting US graduate degrees has much to do with enhancing their class positions. To quote Nayeon (human resource development, female),

> I just thought I wanted to be a professor since I was a little kid. It just came to me. Both my parents weren't so highly educated, but my mom was very aggressive about my education. I have one brother and one sister. I know this may sound weird, but my mother called all three of us 'Doctor' ... I think to her being a 'Doctor' is a big deal. And I thought I should continue studying since I was a little kid ... when I was in college I never thought of getting a job after graduation ... My mother wanted us to be well-educated more than anything ... I think she wanted us to elevate our social class through education.

As most interviewees explain, the US PhD degree is a primary avenue to professional jobs in Korea. Professional positions are also stratified because of their credentials and qualifications, but the US PhD degree has been prerequisite to the core group of Korean professionals. For example, it is no secret that Korea's leading universities strongly favor PhD holders from US universities as their faculty members. Interviewees also experienced this reality in their daily lives.

> I'm going to get a Ph. D. anyway. The degrees in both Korea and US are the same, but the results are so different. They treat you differently. When you get a job, even if you both have PhDs, the one with the US Ph. D. receives better treatment. So if you're going to study anyway, why not do it in the US? ... I have lots of friends who studied in the US. There are so many seniors who acquired their degrees in other countries. Apparently, the ones with US degrees receive better treatment. But to be frank, I don't find them superior to people who studied

in Korea. So I thought, why should I feel inferior to these people just because of the nationality of my academic degree? (Hyunseop, civil engineering, male)

Many interviewees told me of personal job experiences demonstrating that US PhD holders are treated much better than others. The US degree is linked with initial job position, promotion, and income in workplaces. Professional trajectories in the workplace are strongly connected with US degrees. Because Korea is so dependent upon foreign countries' trade, the ability to speak English is also largely required for manager or director positions. Many other opportunities in the workplace also skew toward US PhD holders. Myungjin (economics, male), who worked for one of the most important government financial sectors in Korea, became thoroughly aware of this harsh reality as he observed how US degree holders dominate his prominent workplace:

Myungjin: Actually a doctor's degree just lets me insert the word 'PhD' in my name card ... it's just a title ... even my professor admitted that it has no other meaning than its name value. It's more worthwhile to just get a Master's degree and gain experience through working ... Korea, or the society (my workplace) forces us to value titles ... Everyone flies out these days to countries like England, the US, especially the US. The United States, Japan, Canada...

Interviewer: So as long as there's an opportunity, people want to fly out and gain experience.

Myungjin: Yeah ... of course you could study, but if you have a doctor's degree you can work in International Organizations. IBRD, IMF, World Bank [a conversation on degrees as discrimination factors in workplaces and related opportunities followed]

Interviewer: There must also be people with domestic degrees ...

Myungjin: Yes, but people with foreign degrees are almost always preferred over them...you have to speak English more than anything. You have to work in English when you work in international organizations ... the job requires English.

It is quite evident that earning a degree in the United States is the preferred way to gain a professional job and higher social status in Korea. Interviewees gave me endless stories recounting how people with similar qualifications are treated differently according to whether they held US degrees. In Korean society, the US degree signifies, in addition to the acquisition of English and its symbolic connotations, that the holder is entitled to become a professional. It is taken for granted that anyone in Korea who aspires to climb the social ladder should pursue the US degree, despite its expense, to acquire necessary cultural capital.

Pursuing learning in the global center of learning: the double stratification of higher education

Interviewees explained their choice of school by referring to its ranking, making statements such as 'My department ranks in the top 10 internationally,'

'You can't ignore college rankings,' 'Only a small number of mentally privileged people can enroll in our department,' 'This university ranks high in this field,' and so on. Overall, the global ranking is one of the most important considerations when Korean students decide to study in the United States.[4] The obvious stratification of higher education is recognized by Korean students when they study in Korean colleges and universities, where the curriculum is mostly based upon theories and methodologies created by US scholars and textbooks. From this experience, Korean students deduce that the United States is the most influential center of learning in the world. The US hegemony in the college classroom in Korean universities is manifested by several interviewees.

> All the professors in my department had US doctor's degrees. This affected the contents of the classes. Though the books were written in Korean, their contents were US-based. I sat and wondered why should I have to study second-hand rather than learning directly? I wanted to learn first-hand and teach someone in Korea. (Hyunyoung, social work, female)

Through their professors, seniors, and friends, interviewees internalize the beliefs that the United States is the center of learning and that they should get the US doctorate to join the mainstream. Before they apply for graduate school, they also search the Internet, which further confirms that US universities are far superior to Korean universities in terms of faculty members' excellence and fame, facilities such as laboratories and libraries, and financial support. Some interviewees visit US universities before they apply in order to gain more information for their decision to study in the United States. Yoonjung (music, female) told how her visit to a US university in her college years influenced her decision to advance to US graduate school:

> In the summer of my senior year, my friends and I came to visit the United States because I wanted to experience US universities. To see how American professors teach … after lessons with three professors and a tour of the university, I just stopped comparing it with the college I was in. It was impossible to compare. The practice rooms, the professors' abilities … The best part is that the professors here are so nice. They try to understand, and instead of scolding, they listen to what I have to say…With my last professor, I couldn't have my own music in Korea … I had to do what the professor told me to do … Here, I can do as I please. So the visit gave me a good impression. That's when I decided I should study in the United States.

Interviewees' experiences reflect the hierarchy of university rankings, where US universities are positioned at the top, but Korean universities are dominated by US ways of teaching and learning. This unequal position generates a structure of opportunity for Korean students, and they take advantage of the stratification of global higher education. However, there is another important dynamic that in-depth interviews revealed. The domestic hierarchy of Korean universities that forms the so-called 'Hakbeol' is so rigid that graduates of low-ranked colleges select US universities for their graduate degrees to overcome the stigma attached to their diploma.[5] In the Korean 'Hakbeol' system, people's abilities are evaluated in accordance with their *alma maters* (D. Lee 2007; K. Lee; 2008). People form networks based on their *alma maters*, and one's college diploma determines one's workplace, income, and even one's position in the marriage market. This 'degree caste system' and competition for entrance into top university is so severe in Korean society that many Korean parents send their children to foreign schools at an early age. Generally, Seoul National University ranks at the top, followed by Yonsei and Korea University. Many interviewees from low-ranked universities in Korea mentioned that the US diploma trumps their Korean 'Hakbeol.' Thus, ironically and interestingly, US higher education can act as an emancipatory tool that shatters the structures of the local hierarchy because of its global supremacy. The double stratification – global and domestic – of higher education operates when Korean students decide to study in the United States.

Escaping the undemocratic system and culture in Korean universities

Many interviewees revealed that they chose to study in the United States because they 'hate' the Korean academic system and culture. Females, in particular, confessed that they confronted many types of discrimination and believed that Korean universities are less than ideal for pursuit of a higher degree. The female ratio of faculty members reaches around 18% in Korea (C. Kim 2008, 234). When I called Haemin (leisure studies, female) for an interview, she gave me a direct and simple answer: 'I came to the US because I hate Korea.' When we met for the interview, she described how she experienced male-dominant academic culture as well as the low visibility of women in universities:

> My goal for studying was to become a professional in my field, but the Korean society fails to support this field. Frankly, I felt no matter how much I studied, I could never become a professor … I could never be recognized no matter how much I studied. The society made me think this way. This may be a personal experience, but once a male senior told me that he wouldn't support a woman as his follower … because he believed it to be a waste of time and energy. Once they get married, women give up studying and become less interested in the school. So what he does is support one male follower from each class. (Haemin)

The least likely candidate to earn a professor position in Korea is a female who has obtained her PhD from a Korean university. Kim and Kim (2003) describe how difficult it is for female doctorate holders to find faculty jobs in Korea due to the patriarchal academic system and culture. Even though females qualify through their ability and academic records, the male-dominant system and culture of Korea discourage them from studying in Korea. Jiyoung (biology, female), who received her master's degree in Korea, chose the United States as her destination because her advisor declared that he did not accept women as his PhD students. Her advisor told her that females who get a PhD degree in Korea have no chance to be hired in academic fields. Female interviewees revealed that the US academic culture is less biased against women than Korean culture, which led them to the United States.

Many interviewees also stated that they hate the undemocratic cultures in Korean universities and do not want to confront ugliness in their PhD years. Because of the influences of Confucianism, the teacher–student relationship in Korea is more rigid and authoritarian than in western culture. In Korean culture, students are more likely to be exploited by professors. Moreover, corruptions such as misuse of funds, bribery for degree, or violation of research ethics have plagued Korean universities. Interviewees confessed that the undemocratic cultures and corruptions of Korean academia caused them to favor US academia. For example, Donghwan (chemistry, male) expressed his resentment toward his advisor in Korea, who misappropriates research fund and students' RAship funds, and even called his advisor 'a son of a bitch.' Minseok (leisure studies, male) also said that he came to the United States in order to escape his advisor's exorbitant demands and authoritarian attitude:

Interviewer:	Why did you decide to study abroad after finishing graduate school? Was there a specific motive?
Minseok:	I hated my professor …
Interviewer:	In what way?
Minseok:	I couldn't stand him. I even took temporary absence from school … to quit permanently.
Interviewer:	Could you be more specific?
Minseok:	Up until I entered graduate school, I thought I should get my doctor's degree here as well … the professor was the kind of person who exploits students … he would make students work overtime without paying them … he didn't teach us anything … he just put us through hell. He would always scold us … because we would do something wrong … he would yell at us often … we …
Interviewer:	Dominating?
Minseok:	Very, very much!

Minseok compared the professor to a king, and students to slaves, in Korean academia. In addition to their stories about teacher–student relations, inter-viewees disclosed that they witnessed many instances of research misconduct in Korean universities. Those problems became known to the general public after the Hwang Affair. In 2006 and 2007, this affair revealed the undemo-cratic culture and system of Korean universities, in addition to widespread research misconduct (Kim 2009). Many Korean professors were caught in the midst of research misconduct, misuse of funds, and forged degrees. By study-ing in the United States, Korean students hope to escape the undemocratic culture, the authoritarianism, the corruption, and the research misconduct they associated with Korean universities.

Fulfilling desires to become cosmopolitan elites: English, professional networks, and cosmopolitan identity

Studying in the United States alters Korean students' identities, through which they interpret who they are, how they see the world, and how they make their lives. The interviews show that they did not regard studying in the United States as simply studying in another country, but instead regarded their experience as learning in a world-class center. Studying in Korea is often compared with being a 'babe in the woods' who encounters 'small waters,' or a single 'tree.' On the contrary, studying in the United States is often compared with a 'big ocean,' 'great waters,' and 'woods.' Interviewees attributed studying in the United States to their preferred lifestyle, cosmopolitan worldview, and larger network with foreigners. Haemin (leisure studies, female) describes how her study in the United States led her to cosmopolitan experience:

> I like traveling … so my future plans were to live a couple of years in Europe, then a couple more in Japan and so on all over the world…that's what I had in mind when I flew out of Korea … though I would return to Korea at some point … I wondered where it would be best to start my global journey. Europe? Japan? The United States? I decided starting in the US would be best. Everything revolves around the US anyway. I would start out in the big seas and move from there.

To Korean students, studying in the United States means encountering a bigger world with diverse people, while the smaller world of Korea is temporarily abandoned. Through this journey, they want to become both professionals and world citizens who can communicate and compete with foreigners, fulfilling their desires to be cosmopolitan elites. To Korean students, cosmopolitanism as a way of life is linked to studying in the United States, but it is also based on a perceived inequality within higher education. Realistically, they judge that studying in Korea is not sufficient to fulfill their dreams. They claim that it is necessary that cosmopolitan professionals should communicate with others in English. Learning and mastering English is a major part of their cosmopolitan identities.[6] For example, Myungseok's (civil engineering, male) reason to go to the United States shows his passion to learn this global language:

> In order to meet the bigger world, you have to know how to speak the global language [English]. That's why you have to go to the United States. My professor in graduate school in Korea recommended Japan, but I never thought of going to Japan. I didn't want to go there. You have to learn English to apply it to other places. I wanted to learn English. That was the only reason why I came to the US. Nothing else.

Just as obtaining the cultural capital signified by speaking English and earning a preferred degree is a major reason for Korean students to come to the United States, so is the opportunity to join professional networks. Interviewees revealed that they want to make connections with prominent scholars and scientists so that they will have multiple opportunities in various professional activities around the world. They expect that this professional network enables them not only to advance their research, but also to join the global professional network. Sanghyun (mathematics, male) emphasizes how important this professional network is to his research and development:

> The most important thing in research is to have access to the author when we have inquiries. However, prominent scholars, even my professor receives more than a hundred emails … laymen like myself, someone of absolutely no personal acquaintance are hardly recognized. If I don't have any personal acquaintance, my questions are unanswered. But questions on research problems consume a lot of time, making it hard to receive a quality reply. But here in this university, I have lots of chances to have personal acquaintance with great scholars. Then, I can email these people. This matters the most.

Sanghyun further explains that if he studied in Korea, he would never have the opportunities to meet great scholars and join globally recognized professional networks. All interviewees want to become cosmopolitan professionals equipped with English and membership in a globally renowned professional network. Here, their cosmopolitanism is aimed not toward equal partnership and common global good, but toward opportunities of becoming global elites. As a consequence, the US degree is pursued in order to gain privileged positions, within which Korean students expect to use their cosmopolitan attitude and lifestyle as the means of demarcation and access to exclusive cultural resources that others cannot easily enjoy. While idealized cosmopolitanism in higher education literatures emphasizes openness, plurality, and interconnectivity (Gunesch 2004; Sanderson 2008), my study shows that cosmopolitanism as a form of capital (Weenink 2008) is open but mostly pursued by the privileged, plural but US-centered, and interconnected but stratified. The privileged cosmopolitan identity and way of life pursued by Korean students exactly match the structure of stratified global higher education.

Discussion: global positional competition and global cultural capital

Global positional competition is the leading principle that drives Korean students to pursue US degrees. The US degree positively influences one's social class and status, functioning as a screening device to exclude other competitors. At the same time, US degree holders can extend their work opportunities in the global field beyond national boundaries. As a means to exclude others, global positional competition is strongly influenced by possession of global cultural capital, the symbolic and cultural resources to demarcate global elites from others. The question is how we conceptualize the structures of global positional competition. As my case studies show, it is structured by multiple power structures and relations – class, gender, nationality, global and national hierarchies of higher education, and hegemonic relationship between academic cultures.

First, the global positional competition among individuals (demand side) is increasingly and reciprocally intertwined with the global competition of global higher education institutions as suppliers of global positional goods (supply side). Competition among renowned universities has impelled higher education institutions to attempt to outsmart others. Current discourses on global university ranking reinforce this process. Global university ranking is mainly 'vectored' by research capability (Marginson 2006, 1). Because building a top research university is so expensive, enormous resources are necessary to build and maintain its position. The profound gap between top research universities and others generates the global hierarchy of higher education. If a nation has fewer top-ranked research universities, students seeking professional degrees are more likely to desert it in favor of those nations offering top universities: this is why Korean students pursue their master's and doctoral degrees in the United States. The global hierarchy structuring the relationship between US research universities and Korean universities encourages Korean students to study in a globally-recognized center of learning instead of staying in Korean graduate schools.[7] Consequently, the dependence on foreign top universities reflects the extent to which nations offer renowned research universities. For example, students in the United Kingdom, France, Germany, and Japan pursue US degrees much less often than Korean students. In the same way, economically privileged students from Asian nations other than Japan, from Africa, and from Latin America hope to attend US and European universities. The global hegemony of US universities is especially associated with the global market of positional competition. The role of English as a global professional communication tool leads non-English speakers to seek their degrees in the United States. Global professional networks, global stock of knowledge and technology, and research funds, all of which Korean students desire, are most concentrated in the United States. In this sense, US higher education is an 'obligatory passage point'[8] for Korean students who want to be global players in professional fields.

Second, class and status structures, as well as the job market, are increasingly associated with the global stratification of higher education. In my case, possession of a degree from the United States positively influences one's social class and status in Korea. Most Korean students in US graduate schools come from economically wealthy and culturally educated families in comparison with other Korean students. Less privileged students do not even dream of pursuing higher degrees in the United States. As the interviews reveal, Korean students want to enhance their class position by obtaining professional knowledge and an advanced degree through studying in the United States. Students' parents tend to support their aspirations, and even to persuade them to study in the United States. Parents also bequeath their cultural capital to their children through visiting the United States with them, imbuing vision and aspiration, and investing resources to teach English. At the same time, Korean students' job experiences in Korea confirm the conviction that the US degree is one of the best ways to attain elite status in Korean society. The US degree has exclusive value in the workplace, influencing one's rank and promotion. English fluency also opens possibilities to US degree holders who can extend their work activities in the global field.

Third, transnational gender relations and structures profoundly interact with global positional competition and the pursuit of global cultural capital. For example, female students especially hate the patriarchal system and culture of the Korean academy, where female faculty members are few, and academic activities are constructed around males. Possession of a degree from the United States cancels their previously unprivileged gender inequality in Korea. In this case, US graduate schools function to counter the rigid Korean patriarchy in higher education and the job market. Therefore, the global inequality of higher education ranking opens a new structure of opportunity for under-privileged females, who see the power of global cultural capital as a weapon to counter local male-centered hegemony.

Finally, global moral structures in higher education are also associated with the legitimacy of pursuing global cultural capital. The global positional goods have moral values, so to speak. Korean students see Korean universities as an immoral and undemocratic system, but regard US universities as an ideal place to do research. Interviewees repeatedly told me that the authoritarian relationship between professor and student is manipulated to exploit students' labor and time. Korean students also witness various types of research misconduct more frequently in the Korean academy than in US institutions. Because of those experiences, Korean students lose any sense of loyalty to Korean universities, and regard the US graduate school as a more democratic and gender-sensitive place. In other words, the absence of moral and cultural leadership in the Korean university system solidifies the global hegemony of US universities, to which Korean students succumb by their voluntary, and in fact active, consent and participation.

As I have shown, Korean students' pursuit of global cultural capital in the United States for a better global positional competition interacts with global, national, and local dimensions simultaneously and relationally. Bourdieu's concept of cultural capital is still relevant for understanding foreign students' global flows, but I have argued that more complex and dynamic relations among class, gender, nationality, and national education system should be taken into consideration to fully understand this phenomenon. While Bourdieu focuses on class reproduction through the education system, I have found that multiple power relations – class, gender, and nationality – operate and interact simultaneously, producing ironic results and new possibilities: Korean students' aspirations to US degrees succumb to US hegemony, reproducing the global hierarchy of higher education, even as Korean students see US higher education as a means of liberation that resolves or escapes from some of the inner contradictions of Korean higher education, such as gender discrimination, a degree caste system, and an authoritarian learning culture. This ironic picture denies any unified and single picture of a global education system, but instead requires more nuanced, multi-focal, and poli-centered perspectives. Further studies need to investigate how global cultural capital and global positional competition in global higher education across countries and contexts are differently produced, pursued, and circulated in complex and dynamic global, national, and local dimensions.

Acknowledgements

The author is very grateful to all interviewees for sharing their stories on studying abroad. Without their kindness and sincerity, this research would not be possible. The author also wishes to thank the sociology students in Kyung Hee University who helped transcribe all interviews in detail, and Gardner Rogers who edited this paper. Finally, the author thanks the anonymous referees for their valuable comments and criticisms. This paper draws on prior work published in Korea (J. Kim 2008).

Notes

1. For critical appraisal of the world ranking of universities, see Marginson and van der Wende (2006).
2. All students quoted in this article are given pseudonyms to protect their privacy.
3. I plan to discuss and analyze Korean students' adjustment process in another paper.
4. The relationship between Korean students' choice and global university ranking rarely has been studied. But Chen (2007, 769) and J. Lee (2008, 319) report that university ranking is one of the most important criteria for Asian student choice of foreign universities. Large-scale surveys and more qualitative research are necessary in the future to determine the degree to which global university ranking influences foreign students' destination choices.
5. For the classification of higher education in Korea in terms of research capability, see Shin (2009).
6. Yoon (2007) explores how English colonizes Koreans' consciousness and how Koreans feel deeply inferior due to the incursion of this global language into Korean society.
7. Recently, Asian countries have attempted to build research universities to compete with US and European universities (Altbach and Balan 2007). In particular, the Korean Government has implemented various educational policies to build high-quality research universities over the past 15 years (Kim and Nam 2007).
8. I have borrowed this term from Latour (1987, 245).

References

Abelmann, N., S.J. Park, and H. Kim. 2009. College rank and neoliberal subjectivity in South Korea. *Inter-Asia Cultural Studies* 10, no. 2: 229–47.
Altbach, P.G., and J. Balan, eds. 2007. *World class worldwide: Transforming research universities in Asia and Latin America.* Baltimore, MD: The Johns Hopkins University Press.

Berg, B. 2007. *Qualitative research methods for the social sciences.* 6th ed. Boston: Pearson Education.

Bourdieu, P. 1984. *Distinction: A social critique of the judgment of taste.* Trans. R. Nice. Cambridge, MA: Harvard University Press.

Bourdieu, P. 1986. The forms of capitals. In *Handbook of theory and research for the sociology of education,* ed. J. Richardson, 241–54. Westport, CT: Greenwood Press.

Bourdieu, P. 1988. *Homo academicus.* Trans. P. Collier. Stanford, CA: Stanford University Press.

Bourdieu, P. 1993. *The field of cultural production.* New York: Columbia University Press.

Brown, P. 1999. Globalization and the political economy of high skills. *Journal of Education and Work* 12, no. 3: 233–51.

Brown, P. 2000. The globalization of positional competition? *Sociology* 34, no. 4: 633–53.

Chen, L. 2007. Choosing Canadian graduate school from afar: East Asian students' perspectives. *Higher Education* 54, no. 5: 759–80.

Chosun Daily. 2005. Seoul National University at the second for feeder school to American Ph.D. recipients: UC Berkeley ranked top. January 11 (in Korean). www.chosun.com.

Creswell, J. 2007. *Qualitative inquiry and research design.* 2nd ed. London: Sage Publications.

Gunesch, K. 2004. Education for cosmopolitanism?: Cosmopolitanism as a person identity model for and within international education. *Journal of Research in International Education* 3, no. 3: 251–75.

Hirsh, E. 1977. *Social limits to growth.* London: Routledge and Kegan Paul.

Horta, H. 2009. Global and national prominent universities. *Higher Education* 58: 387–405.

Ishikawa, M. 2009. University rankings, global models, and emerging hegemony. *Journal of Studies in International Education* 13, no. 2: 159–73.

Kim, C. 2008. *Data analysis of educational statistics 2008.* Seoul: Korean Educational Development Institute (in Korean).

Kim, J. 2008. Global munwhajabonui chugu. *Korean Journal of Sociology* 42, no. 6: 68–105 (in Korean).

Kim, J. 2009. Public feeling for science: The Hwang affair and Hwang supporters. *Public Understanding of Science* 18, no. 6: 670–86.

Kim, J., and K. Kim. 2003. Experiences of female doctorate holders in the faculty job market and strategies to address the obstacles. *Korean Journal of Sociology of Education* 13, no. 3: 21–44 (in Korean).

Kim, K., and S. Nam. 2007. The making of a world-class university at the periphery. In *World class worldwide: Transforming research universities in Asia and Latin America,* ed. P.G. Altbach and J. Balan, 122–39. Baltimore, MD: The Johns Hopkins University Press.

Kyosu Newspaper. 2005. Ph.D.s from Korean universities count for only 10% among new faculty members in the national capital region. March 26. www.kyosu.net (in Korean).

Latour, B. 1987. *Science in action.* Cambridge, MA: Harvard University Press.

Lee, D. 2007. A study on the strategies for ending the fixed university ranking system. *Korean Journal of Sociology of Education* 17, no. 3: 131–57 (in Korean).

Lee, J. 2008. Beyond borders: International student pathways to the United States. *Journal of Studies in International Education* 12, no. 3: 308–27.

Lee, K. 2007. A study on 'Hakbeolism' and class conflict in Korean society: Toward a theorization of 'Hakbeol' capital. *Korean Journal of Sociology of Education* 17, no. 4: 63–85 (in Korean).

Marginson, S. 2006. Dynamics of national and global competition in higher education. *Higher Education* 52: 1–39.

Marginson, S. 2008. Global field and global imaging: Bourdieu and worldwide higher education. *British Journal of Sociology of Education* 29, no. 3: 303–15.

Marginson, S., and E. Sawir. 2005. Interrogating global flows in higher education. *Globalization, Societies, and Education* 3, no. 3: 281–310.

Marginson, S., and M. van der Wende. 2006. To rank or to be ranked: The impact of global ranking in higher education. *Journal of Studies in International Education* 11, nos 3/4: 306–29.

Mazzarol, T., and G. Soutar. 2002. 'Push-pull' factors influencing international student destination choice. *The International Journal of Educational Management* 16, no. 2: 82–90.

Murphy, R. 1988. *Social closure: The theory of monopolization and exclusion.* Oxford: Clarendon.

Open Doors. 2009. International students in the U.S.: Fast facts. http://opendoors.iienetwork.org.

Park, E. 2009. Analysis of Korean students' international mobility by 2-D model: Driving force factor and directional factor. *Higher Education* 57, no. 6: 741–55.

Park, S.J., and N. Abelmann. 2004. Class and cosmopolitanism: Mother's management of English education in South Korea. *Anthropological Quarterly* 77, no. 4: 645–72.

Parkin, F. 1979. *Marxism and class theory: A bourgeois critique.* London: Tavistock.

Rubin, H., and I. Rubin. 2005. *Qualitative interviewing: The art of hearing data.* London: Sage Publications.

Sanderson, G. 2008. A foundation for the internationalization of the academic self. *Journal of Studies in International Education* 12, no. 3: 276–307.

Shin, J. 2009. Classifying higher education institutions in Korea: A performance-based approach. *Higher Education* 57, no. 2: 247–66.

Song, C., M. Jin, H. Oh, H. Yoo, S. Lee, H. Yoon, and J. Park. 2007. *Survey of doctorate recipients.* Seoul: Korea Research Institute for Vocational Education and Training (in Korean).

Weenink, D. 2008. Cosmopolitanism as a form of capital: Parents preparing their children for a globalizing world. *Sociology* 42, no. 6: 1089–106.

Yoon, J. 2007. *English, the colonizer of my heart.* Seoul, Korea: Dangdae (in Korean).

Zikopoulos, M., and E.G. Barber. 1986. *Choosing schools from afar: The selections of colleges and universities in the United States by foreign students.* New York: Institute of International Education.

Higher education and linguistic dualism in the Arab Gulf

Sally Findlow

Keele University, UK

This paper examines the spread of English as a medium of higher education in the Arab world, addressing questions about the relationship between higher education, language shift and cultural (re)production through such post-colonial educational bilingualism. Drawing on exploratory ethnographic research, it documents how both Arabic and English have been implicated in the re-configuring of collective identities through mass higher education in one Arab Gulf country against a context of rapid modernisation with a regional undercurrent of recurrent pan-Arab and Islamist-tinged nationalism. It examines how far the resulting linguistic-cultural dualism amounts to a loss of linguistic–cultural diversity, and how far there is a linguistically-framed discourse of resistance to such a process. Theoretically, the paper engages with discourses relating to socio-cultural reproduction, collective identity, educational standardisation, change and cultural chauvinism, and markets. It offers insights into the potential for both language and higher education to act as tools or fields for cultural transformation and for resistance identity construction.

Introduction

The discursive starting point for the present paper was congruence between what appeared to be happening in higher education (HE) in the Arab Gulf immediately prior to the recent polarisation of Muslim and non-Muslim and more widespread concerns about the cultural–linguistic impacts of global convergence. In immigration contexts, these concerns are framed in terms such as 'language death', 'language loss', 'language decay' and even 'linguistic genocide' (Skutnabb-Kangas, 2000; Gogolin, 2002). They tend to produce arguments in *favour* of multilingualism or bilingualism— as a way of preserving indigenous language use inside the home while adopting the new 'national' language outside. Yet it is possible to see this bilingualism itself as contributing to cultural loss of the sort that prompted Joshua Fishman's (1991) calls for a halt to what he called 'language shift'. If language and culture (or languages and *specific* cultures) are connected so deeply that different languages embody different ways of seeing the world (Boas, 1940; Sapir, 1949; Whorf, 1956), then change in a given language, even in terms of a loss of range, logically produces a corresponding change-loss in the culture it embodies.

The question 'What do we mean by "culture"?' is already raising its head. To clarify, this article sets such concerns against a broad concept of 'culture'—one that *incorporates* its relative sense as a marker of geo-ethnic difference, but on a more general level denotes the realm of life concerned with meaning, identity, values, knowledge, belief, laws and custom (after Tyler, 1951); that is, the domain of symbolic interaction, of construction of communicable meaning (Willis, 2002) or that which links internal and external worlds. To the extent that all fields have a culture, business and economics as well as art and religion, it corresponds with some of the ideas incorporated into a reflexive notion of Bourdieu's '*habitus*'.

Dual linguistic cultures have also been detected, allegedly amounting to dual modes of consciousness, in many *non*-immigration contexts. Among countries whose political maps are being re-drawn, the language of the ruling political regime or colonial power is found to be used for business, with the indigenous language becoming the language of childhood, home, tradition, liturgy, nationalism and 'culture' in its narrow sense (high culture). In the Middle East, in Israel as well as Arab countries, descriptions have concentrated on the ways in which the native language has become symbolic of nostalgia and authenticity, with the colonial language (English or French) increasingly associated with 'status' in a modern, internationally oriented sense (Ben Rafael, 1994; Faiq, 1999; Gill, 1999). Anderson (1990) has described a similar scenario in post-colonial Indonesia. A similar picture is also starting to emerge in Europe, with discussions of how boundaries between indigenous and common European identities are negotiated via dualistic national language policies (Caviedes, 2003), and of the relative status and 'power' accorded to different languages in bilingual 'border' communities (Carli *et al.*, 2003). All discourses acknowledge the place of English as the 'language of globalisation' (Carli *et al.*, 2003, p. 865). Within the field of HE specifically, Walker's (2005) 'complicated picture' of South African HE change and fluid cultural identities shows how Afrikaans and indigenous African languages are seen as connoting, respectively, an occupied past and a form of authenticity, with English and HE institutional bilingualism (Afrikaans/English) representing the present state of transition.

One way in which such processes typically work is by the use of a shared language in creating and sustaining invented, constructed, imagined or willed 'nations' (Anderson, 1983; Gellner, 1983; Hobsbawm & Ranger, 1983, p. 4). On the other hand, non-native cultures are cast as 'other'—their languages embodying alien mind-sets and mentalities. This is the attitude that has underpinned the use of indigenous languages as nationalistic tools in post-colonial contexts, as repositories of the 'local' or forces for resistance against the recent tide of English-speaking convergence in places such as Wales and Quebec.

Language can thus be used as tool of symbolic violence in many ways (Bourdieu, 1991). In education, the scope for such violence is immense since the business of education—classifying and defining things, forming bodies of knowledge—relies on the interconnectedness of language and mindsets, medium and message. Perceptions of what constitutes teachable knowledge are either embedded in or determined by cultural circumstances that produce 'discourses' (Foucault, 1989) or curriculum (Bernstein, 1971). Deciding on a linguistic medium for a HE curriculum, therefore, is a decision not only about the availability of materials and staff and demands of the marketplace, but also about which society's values to transmit; language teachers are in fact 'teachers of culture' (Byram & Risager, 1999, p. 6). A historical line of persistent cultural chauvinism, deriving from colonial and neo-colonial heritages, has been traced behind the link between English-language teaching and the study of other societies (Pennycook, 1994).

It has also been suggested that particular languages socialise, or exert symbolic violence, by way of the methods in which they are conventionally learned and applied, which in turn reflect relative values, including what skills and types of knowledge are valued in the host culture (Gumpertz, 1986; Pennycook, 1989). Students can be either uncomfortable with or else adapt to and exhibit different kinds of behaviour in classes taught in either one or another language.

Bilingualism itself is generally seen as positive and enabling, a tool through which to negotiate the conflicting demands of external and internal realms (Jakobson, 1962), and as codeswitching (switching between languages in one speech act), a way of identifying with two cultures at once (Le Page, 1964). Codeswitching featured in Anderson's analysis of Indonesian cultural–linguistic dualism, and has been described as a tool for simultaneously asserting identity and communicating in modern South Africa (Finlayson *et al.*, 1998). Proponents of educational bilingualism argue that the acquisition of a second 'discourse' can help students to think better in metacognitive, critical and reflexive ways (Garcia & Jimenez, 1998). Yet such benefits do not mean it is acceptable to force students to study in a foreign language when so much is at stake competitively. Not only do non-native speakers have an additional workload, but the assessment playing field is hardly equal either. Discussing linguistic capital, Bourdieu and Passeron (1990, pp. 73, 76) cite the problem of judging language and not the thought it represents. If academic language in general can be used as a tool to obscure comprehension and thereby gain symbolic power, how much more so is this likely to be the case when that academic language is also a foreign language for the students?

The main conceptual tools providing insight into what appears to be happening in the United Arab Emirates (UAE) are linked with environment, agency and violence. The question drawing together culture change and political agency is: How far should the requirement for native Arabic speakers to pursue their higher studies in the English language be seen as an inevitable response to market needs, and how far a symptom of neo-colonialist power politics in which Arabic is relegated as non-useful, and Arab culture is cast as 'other'? The first reading feeds into a Marxian view of culture shift as organic, internal, evolutionary; the sort of analysis that has been applied to other studies of language shift (Brenzinger, 1992)—the socio-economically driven transformation of socio-cultural 'superstructure' that is nevertheless inevitable, a collective and organic response to change.

By contrast, the second political, strategic reading foregrounds the role of external agents in imposing 'culture' change by virtue of greater economic and political power. This is the reading against which the full meaning of the term 'linguistic genocide' becomes clear, in which the language used in education is not a straightforward cultural repository, but a tool for controlling how approved cultural norms are reflected, communicated and shaped.

The third possible interpretation is that such language–culture change happens only via the intersection of these forces. This interpretation would be grounded in a view of the language–culture relationship as fluid and dialogic, and would see the mourning of language–culture loss as false, since this implies particular language–culture relationships are fixed. Instead, people negotiate new modes and tools of communication in accordance with changing circumstances and purposes; in this way, culture is continually re-defined. Such linguistic dualism, enabling two identities and cultures to be claimed at once, can thus be seen as inevitable, even essential, for societies undergoing processes of acute global–local transition. The data explored here go some way to illuminating students' perceptions of the issue, and whether the way they use, and feel about, Arabic makes it the 'local' or 'regional' voice in an anti-colonial 'resistance' (Castells, 1997) discourse.

My questions around the role of HE in this process of linguistically framed (re)construction are conceived in Gellner's (1983) premise that education, promoting a shared literacy and framework and tools for abstract communication, is a pre-condition for nationalism. The questions are structural ones: Are the data consistent with the structural characterisation of HE as a 'field' within which cognitive construction and social change takes place through the dialogic use of symbols, or as the 'mediator'/'tool' itself of this process? Bourdieu and Passeron's (1990) characterisation of HE in these terms was inconsistent; and it may be, after Tapper (1976), that the structural–functional flexibility of HE is its most definitive characteristic.

The United Arab Emirates

The exploratory study drawn on here into the role of HE in UAE nation-state development and identity construction over the final quarter of the twentieth century (from 1971 to 2000) was conducted between 1997 and 2000. It provided a snapshot view of current HE policy and practice, and students' feelings about their place within the HE system and society as a whole. I interviewed and corresponded with 65 students, teachers and educational administrators, and administered (with the help of staff working in the three main state HE institutions) a mainly open-ended questionnaire survey in both Arabic and English to 500 students, of which I selected 340 for analysis. Relatively proficient in Arabic, I was able to administer the questionnaires and when necessary conduct interviews in Arabic as well as English. Some of the questions were factual, or immediately quantifiable, and in other cases I was able to code and quantify open-ended answers. But, overall, analysis was qualitative and interpretive—survey results were contextualised and triangulated, and particular attention was paid to nuances in the actual words used. My experience living, study-ing and working for 10 years in the Arab world and Gulf states in a range of HE and non-compulsory education sectors helped this process. The 'snapshot' was set within a historical context established via analysis of institutional documents/planning archives, newspaper archives and interviews (some by telephone, fax or email) with key players in the evolution of the system. For reasons of economy, few of these sources are listed here.

The present discussion focuses on findings from one-half of the total 24 survey questions:

i.   Where are you from?
ii.   What do you want to get from your university or HE?'
iii.   Why?
iv.   What do you want to do when you have finished college/university?
v.   Why is it important that young Emiratis are educated, in your opinion?
vi.   Which is the best HE institution in the UAE?
vii. Why?
viii. Why did you choose this institution?
ix.   Why did you choose this area of specialisation?
x.   What kind of jobs do you think graduates from this institution can get after they graduate?
xi.   Do you prefer to be taught in English? Or Arabic?
xii. Why?

The picture that emerged from this study, of fluid cultural identities amid rapid social and educational change, echoes Walker's 'complicated picture' of South African student identity in some ways. Similarly, this is not a context of immigration, but one where the country itself is changing, people (especially young people at university) are exposed to 'otherness' in a way that their parents were not, local heritage is steeped in political struggle, official discourse endeavours to be eclectic and reconcile. The particulars of the UAE's complicated picture are the status of Arabic as a national language, Islam as the state religion, its broadly post-colonial mindset and close ideo-logical and political links with other Arab countries, a small indigenous and tradition-ally conservative population and much larger expatriate communities (approximately 90% of the workforce), and the recent and rapid modernisation accompanying the acquisition of oil wealth and independence from British 'protection' in the late 1960s, and federal statehood in 1971. Over the final quarter of the twentieth century, the UAE was transformed from a collection of materially poor and sparsely populated tribal homelands with no formal education system to a politically, economically and technologically sophisticated federation of seven states. The UAE's wealth, combined with its newness and consequent need for a process of 'national' construction, means that the state's regional reputation for openness and entrepreneurship is tempered by conformity in many ways to the *'rentier'* or distributive state paradigm (Delacroix, 1980; Beblawi, 1987)— in which governments obtain the loyalty of citizens through what they give rather than through shared endeavour.

HE has from the start been central to the UAE's search for a 'national' identity. This centrality was initially due to some immediate needs: to train an indigenous skilled workforce, and to create a national university that would provide appropriate nation-state symbolism. But in the longer term, its impact lies in the manner in which an outward-looking, diverse and largely foreign-staffed state HE system has socialised the academically able younger generation (Findlow, 2005). With more than 30 universities and HE colleges, the three state HE institutions (UAE University, the Higher Colleges of Technology and Zayed University) together cater for over 23,000 students, about 60% of the country's total student population.

The UAE government has been careful to co-opt this HE system, including its symbolism—possibly mindful of the century-old Arab tradition for universities (Cairo, Beirut, as well as rumblings closer to home in the Gulf) to be hotbeds of radicalism (Said, 1991). This Arab tradition of HE-linked radicalism has many of the defining characteristics of what has been called 'anti-colonial' nationalism—'both imitative and hostile' (Breuilly, 1982, p. 125), divided between the drive to modernise and the drive to emphasise national traditions (Plamenatz, 1976). Traditions of political dissent to have impacted on the UAE psyche variously idealise change and continuity, localism and internationalism (Findlow, 2005).

The role of Arabic is also of unique importance to UAE (what has the basis of a claim to be called) 'nation-statehood' and collective identities. Language has been implicated symbolically, albeit loosely and inconsistently, in these traditions of ambiguous dissent. In one sense, Arabic is a singularly political and ideological language; the shared Arabic language has underpinned successive Arab nationalist movements (Suliman, 1987), and the adoption of Arabic as a national tongue makes a country nominally and politically 'Arab' (permitting membership, for instance, of the Arab League).

At the same time, Arabic has been identified as the 'culturally weaker' partner (Asad, 1986) within the widespread Arabic–English, or Arabic–French, dual-language infrastructures that exist around the world, and limited in its role as a tool for positive linguistic nationalism—in terms of either cultural unification, what Geertz defined as the 'second stage' of anti-colonial or post-colonial nationalism (1975, pp. 239–240), or even coherent resistance. This can be attributed at least in part to decades of marginalisation, particularly in education, where modernisation has been achieved through imitation of foreign models—mainly British and French. Several modern Middle Eastern scholars, such as Said and Asad, have grounded much of their work in an identified cultural chauvinism in the English-speaking world's relations with Arab societies. And conviction of the non-neutrality and basic Eurocentrism of epistemological–educational models applied in Muslim countries has informed the missions of 'Arabisation' academies around the Arab world, following the Arab League's Educational, Cultural and Scientific Organisation cultural treaty declaration of 1946. Others have pointed out intrinsic limitations, such as its division between different dialects, and thus ownerships, which Benrabah (1999), for instance (pointing to problems in national infrastructure-building in post-French colonial Maghreb), suggests has instead lent Arabic the propensity to be used as a tool for exclusion.

These considerations, then, make up the UAE's Arab identity, and are implicit in the importance the Arabic language holds in the national psyche. In historically deep-rooted ways, the status of Arabic is tied to the role of Islam; and more recently proponents of 'Islamisation', many of them non-Arab, have combined a devotional perspective to their support for the anti-Orientalist thesis (Sardar, 1982; Karmani, 1995). Indeed, the belief that command of Arabic is *the* way to understand the meaning of the Qur'an is widely shared by Muslims worldwide, and the theme appears consistently in the curriculum literature of 'Islamic' universities, colleges and departments around the Gulf. The combined Arab–Islamic cultural basis of the nation is accordingly emphasised in the UAE provisional Constitution, drawn up at a time when Nasserist pan-Arabism was still a significant influence and Islamist resurgence was just beginning in neighbouring countries:

> The Union (the UAE) is a part of the great Arab Nation, attached to it by the ties of religion, language, history and common destiny. The people of the Union are one people, and one part of the Arab Nation. ... Islam is the official religion of the Union. The Islamic Shari'a shall be a main source of legislation in the Union. The official language of the Union shall be Arabic. (Article 7, Provisional Constitution, 1972, subsequently ratified as permanent)

Summary of exploratory findings

Rapid language shift in one generation, caused by the revolutionary, externally fuelled, socio-economic change already described, appeared to have lead to the present existence of distinct worldviews, both impacting on the HE system, linguistically embodied/represented as follows:

- Arabic—'cultural authenticity', localism, tradition, emotions, religion.
- English—modernity, internationalism, business, material status, secularism.

This dualism is contextually demarcated within several different systems: public/private, childhood/adulthood and according to academic subject. In the UAE economy, public sectors associated with local concerns and with the maintenance of systems, such as municipality offices, operate mainly in Arabic. The private sector, particularly commerce and information technology, associated with modernism, internationalism and materialism, operates largely in English. And the education system as a whole is bifurcated both vertically and horizontally. In education, Arabic is the language used in state primary and secondary schools, while the majority of private schools teach in English with compulsory Arabic lessons (although even in state schools the use of English appears to be increasing overall). At the tertiary level, a divided epistemological (subject-related) paradigm sees 'cultural' or locally focused subjects such as *Shari'a*, Islamic studies, arts/humanities, social sciences and education taught mostly in Arabic, while subjects with a global orientation, especially technologically or commercially oriented ones, or applied sciences, are taught in English.

The bifurcation is embodied in institutions in so far as each has had to take language policy decisions. To a large degree, each institution's position is determined by the subjects taught there, which in turn reflect its mission in the new state. UAE

University, founded in 1976 as a national flagship, with deep-rooted religious and traditionalist Egyptian influences, has tended to be the institution of choice for traditionally minded students and their families. UAE University's original published intention was to teach almost entirely in Arabic and, although this has had to be revised since, it retains links with the Arabisation ideal; for instance, playing host to the Movement for the Arabisation of University Education in 1992 (UAE University, 1999). In contrast, Arab–Islamic traditionalist considerations have been felt as little more than constraints for the Higher Colleges of Technology, a federal system of technical colleges established in 1988 with the aid of the Canadian firm Educansult. These colleges work around what are perceived as local cultural 'constraints' to fill national manpower needs identified with the help of the World Bank. With mostly non-Arab expatriate instructors, the colleges teach almost exclusively in English, Arabic only being used for Arabic and Islamic Studies. Zayed University, the newest of the three state HE institutions, founded in 1998, was mandated to combine local manpower provision with '… advancing the UAE as a participant in a modern, global society' (Zayed University, 1998). Its curriculum emphasises applied science and technology, and it operates a hybrid US–Canadian–British academic and administrative model. Initial reported plans to teach in equal proportions of Arabic and English were soon shelved and only a minority of subjects are now taught in Arabic.

The student survey provided insight into some of the feelings of UAE national students about this divide, suggesting ways in which Arabic and English are tied up with identity and personal agendas. Overall, 22% stated that they preferred to be taught in Arabic, 50% in English and a significant 28% ignored the rubric of the answer sheet and inserted 'both'. In order of frequency, the reasons given for Arabic preference were:

(1) 'my mother tongue'
(2) 'easy'
(3) 'We are an Arab country'
(4) 'language of the Qur'an'.

English language preference was due to:

(1) *'lughat al-'asr'* or 'world language'
(2) 'good to study a second language' or 'to communicate with outsiders'
(3) 'for work'
(4) 'to help with my study'.

These responses broadly replicated the reasons given by interviewed faculty members, such as 'English is the world language/the language of the world market' and 'We are training UAE youth for this world market'. There were mixed feelings among both students and academics about the fact that learning in English was required, and some correlation between support for more instruction in Arabic and romantic nationalist-type sentiments. But there was little evidence of overt politicisation of this, and the cause of neither political Islamism nor cultural Islamisation appeared to have any real impact on how respondents felt about the language issue.

Analysis

The nature of this educational linguistic–cultural dualism

The linguistic bifurcation of educational stages is coterminous with that between localism–authenticity and globalism–pragmatism. State policy can be read to imply that, throughout childhood, Arabic supplies all or most communication needs, while the transition at age 18 to learning in English requires a substantially changed cultural mindset. In the UAE, the traditionalist, largely Egyptian-run, 'Ministry of Education and Youth' (in Arabic: *'tarbiyya wa ta'lim'* ['upbringing and education']) produces most of its literature in Arabic, and emphasises the importance of fostering Islamic and Arab culture. The distinct 'Ministry of Higher Education and Scientific Research', which oversees tertiary education, research, the licensing of institutions and professions, and supervision of awards for study outside the UAE, operates in English. The symbolic naming of the two ministries evokes dual constructions of prestige: tradition and Arab–Islamic correctness versus high socio-economic status, modernism and internationalism.

A given subject is placed in either realm partly according to the language in which course material is found, as this determines the associated cultural context. There is pervasive feeling that subjects dealing explicitly with values, ideas and 'culture' *should* be taught according to traditional Arab–Islamic models, and in Arabic, despite the availability of international frameworks—particularly among the Islamisation lobby. At UAE University, the relatively un-theorised (in other than traditional, religious and prescriptive terms) subjects of Social Work, Family Studies, and *Shari'a* are taught in preference to Sociology. There is disagreement over whether relying on international models for scientific subjects is problematic, acknowledgement of the need for global competitiveness balanced by concern that this simply highlights a shortcoming of current Arabisation or Islamisation epistemologies.

This subject-related linguistic dualism reflects competing constructions of prestige in the sense that each language was ascribed importance for distinct reasons. Respondents (both students and faculty) expressing a preference for Arabic as he educational medium felt they were making an ideological stand for a cause rooted in heritage, while those supporting English were responding to the 'ideology' of pragmatism (in this case modernism–globalism). The reasons given in Arabic and English for pursuing tertiary education, while apparently equivalent, were also connotatively distinct. The literal equivalence of 'status in society' (in Arabic) and 'to reach the top' (in English) masks connotative distinctions in the sense that the former connotes a social, traditional and local idea of status, and in the survey typically correlated with other answers containing ideas of appropriacy, and service—either to the family or, most often, to the country. For instance, the phrase, *'al-husul 'ala wadhifa munasiba'* ('manage to get a fitting position') was accompanied, often in the same phrase, with *'takhaddum al-watan'* ('and serve the country'). The prevailing English-language notion of 'reaching the top', on the other hand, appeared to imply status in economic and business/entrepreneurial terms—in a modern, borderless world.

Further evidence of the extent to which these distinct worldviews are implicit in the two languages lies in so far as the content of some answers appeared to be determined by the language in which a student answered. For instance, the motifs 'service', 'dreams' and 'country' ('*al-watan*', '*al-bilad*', '*al-dawla*', '*baladi*' and '*dawlati*' were all used), with their patriotic, idealistic connotations, were strikingly more prevalent in Arabic-language than English-language response papers, and the reasons given in Arabic for why it was important for Emirati youths to be educated connotatively or metaphorically more nationalistic. 'What do you want to get from your university or higher education?' produced in English (in order of frequency) the responses 'education'/'knowledge', 'a degree', 'work', 'to reach the top' and 'to be active in society', while Arabic answers to the same question produced the responses 'information'/'skills', 'a degree', 'to fulfil personal dreams', 'status in society', 'a job' and 'to serve the country'. That is, the Arabic answers were marked by the presence of the following themes: status, dreams, service.

Another reading would see a *cognitive*, not merely associative, aspect to such divergence, supporting the idea that such dual consciousness is cognitively hardwired, and underlining the impossibility of method being non-neutral in these terms (Gumpertz, 1986; Pennycook, 1989, 1994). It is in this respect that connotative differences between superficially equivalent terminology in the two languages become significant. The Arabic word '*asr* (*lughat al-'asr*), translated as 'age' or 'epoch', is more culturally–historically evocative than the pragmatic connotations of the English 'world language'. Then again, correlating answers to this question with others in the same questionnaire papers suggested further distinct constructions of 'society': the Arabic version connoted prestige, status, position; the English version connoted business and activity.

Conversations with teachers about the language in which they taught reinforced the point. Who teaches a given subject also partly determines its language of instruction (linked to the choices these teachers made about the place to go to for their own studies). Religious or cultural subjects have tended to be taught by Egyptian and/or Egypt-educated personnel, while 'modern', technically oriented subjects are taught by western or western-educated Arab expatriates—in much the same way that epistemological bilingualism in post-colonial Maghreb saw 'essential subjects' (Gill, 1999, p. 125) taught in French. When I interviewed them, teachers explained that the language in which they studied their subject played a large part in the language in which they were able to teach. A US-educated Arab teacher of natural sciences, for instance, said he would have been completely unable to teach his subject in Arabic as he possessed neither the requisite content terminology nor (most significantly for this discussion) the instructional thought processes—which he could summon only in English.

And its causes—symbolic violence?

What, then, in terms of the evolution–agency debate, is the main cause of such dualism? 'Habit' (how *accustomed* individuals are to thinking and talking about subjects in particular languages) is clearly implicated, whether we cast this as mainly an associative or cognitive process. To this extent, it is worth considering Bourdieu's concept of *habitus* as a tool for making sense of both the dualism itself and the shift towards it. The concept has been used effectively elsewhere for analysis of Arab academia (Sabour, 1988).

A usefully reflexive reading of *habitus* casts language as a tool used to reproduce a culture that is constantly changing and redefining itself, in the process refining and redirecting that language (Bourdieu, 1991, esp. chapt. 1). But Bourdieu's overall paradigm sees changed practice as the combined product of *habitus* and field; *habitus* evolving, but largely constant within one generation. In the UAE's case, external agencies—via sudden wealth, the cash-enticed involvement of outsiders and external (regional and global) political considerations—have had a major contribution in defining the line that is maintained via this dualistic national culture. The externally driven nature of both the change and the precise framing of the dual worldviews, together with its (*non*-evolving) rapidity, suggest that the key might lie outside this paradigm.

Instead of *habitus* and 'field' together determining 'practice', what seems to be happening here is that new 'practice' is feeding back into *habitus* and 'field', all three evolving reciprocally. Such a dialogic reading, more reminiscent of Althusser's 'structural causality', shifts scrutiny away from the old mechanistic question preoccupying Sapir and Whorf—whether language is means of *imparting* culture, a *product* of it or actually *determines* its characteristics—to one where the focus is instead on the field or context.

In the present such context—the UAE HE system, currently a melting-pot of different interests and agendas—agency through symbolic violence offers more insights than *habitus*. In Bourdieu's (1991) own discussions of language as a shared code for exerting control, such violence works by the giving of gifts that produce indebtedness, which then extends to each of the rhetorical images and themes evoked in the gift. The method is familiar to the Arab world: the exclusive Arabic dialects in post-independence Maghreb; the pervasiveness of the *rentier* state model; Said's description of the regional (Arab) currency of repetition in the establishment of national identity—repeating something and linking it to Palestine, 'in order to make it Palestinian ...', and thereby reaffirming the existence of Palestine itself (Said, 1995, p.111). These examples all emphasise that English does not have exclusive use of language as a tool of symbolic violence.

Bourdieu and Bernstein have each argued persuasively that such violence is intrinsic to education in relation to curriculum decisions. But a more explicit manifestation of 'the almost magical power of ... bringing into existence by virtue of naming ...' (Bourdieu, 1991, p. 236) can be seen in the extent to which UAE free state HE is, still, self-consciously thought of as a gift that previous generations, before statehood, did not enjoy. Attaching the dual Arab–Islamic motif to this gift illustrates the political nature of cultural construction in the country (as throughout much of the region)—important in the ongoing quest for legitimacy in a context where 'indigenous' needs to be defined.

Students' feelings—resistance?

The effectiveness of the government's *rentier* hold via these assorted symbols over the surveyed student population can be gauged by the unelicited frequent occurrence of the following sort of declaration (answering the question 'Which institution is the best?'): 'Our government would not build something not good'. A range of answers established an association between government generosity, HE, duty to the smaller (UAE) and wider (Arab) nation, and being religiously dutiful.

Given that Arabic does appear to work imaginatively in the UAE, as around the Arab and Muslim worlds, as a repository of the local (Castells, 1997), logic would suggest some disjunction between such blanket acceptance and the government's and the HE system's use of English as described. Is there an undercurrent of post-colonial nationalist resistance to the tide of English-speaking convergence and all that represents? Indeed, the survey found a broad correlation between support for Arabic and 'nationalist' (UAE, pan-Arab or religious) type sentiments, and the ideal of 'Emiratisation' (making the country self-reliant through training an indigenous workforce) was not lost on HE students. When asked in the survey what they as individuals wanted to get from their studies and why it was important that young Emiratis were educated (with no optional answers provided), the most frequent responses were 'To help my country' and 'To overcome reliance on foreign labour'. Response papers also contained a number of key terms that might suggest a perception of the world incorporating readiness for revolutionary nationalism (however narrowly or widely constructed). And the fact that these evocative terms appeared only in the Arabic answers underlines the potential of Arabic to be used as a tool for such an ideology. Among these were '*nahda*' (rebirth), as in:

> *Inna nahda ayyi dawla la taqumu illa 'ala nahdati shababaha, w'al-ta'lim sabab ayyi nahda.*
> [The rebirth of any state/nation cannot take place without the rebirth/revival of its youth, and education is the foundation of any rebirth/revival.]

This term has strong nationalistic and idealistic overtones in Arab–Islamic tradition, underlining the general currency among students of joint Arab–Islamic imagery, but it also highlights one way in which nation-*(re)*building is conceptualised within a post-colonial framework—through higher education and training.

On the whole, resistance was expressed in idealistic or 'civilisational', rather than actively political, terms: 'It is my language/my mother tongue/the language of the UAE', 'The UAE is an Arab country' and 'English assaults Arab culture' were accompanied by emphatic disassociations—between love of Arabic because it is 'our language' and any commitment to *political* pan-Arabism. Arabic was described as important for either personal or *UAE* 'national' reasons. Objections from faculty I interviewed were couched in 'logical' terms, such as 'I have never seen a(nother) country that teaches in a foreign language!', rather than in direct condemnation of neo-colonial attitudes (although respondents' reluctance to cause personal offence may have had something to do with this).

Any identification with either national or individual *religious* identity appeared in only 23% of the response papers, and was presented almost as an afterthought—

surprising given the country's religiously conservative heritage combined with the recent (even in the late 1990s) religio-political climate. Students for whom preserving 'traditional culture' was their main reason for wanting to maintain Arabic-medium instruction mostly labelled this culture 'Arab', and personnel (Emirati and expatriate Arab) felt imported English educational models were a greater threat to 'Arab' than to Islamic culture. Interviews revealed very little awareness of or interest in the (cultural) Islamisation cause. These expressed views of individuals were also quite different from public rhetoric, where concern for the preservation of indigenous culture even before the post 9/11 re-polarisation was cited in terms of 'Islamic correctness'.

A combined range of circumstances may explain why awareness of the political nature of the language–culture policy did not at the time of this research amount to focused or political resistance—in whichever terms. Luck, and government strategy, plays a large part. Loyalty towards the government (facilitated by favourable socio-economic conditions and the absence of real political instability) has helped to prevent resistance that is anti-government in focus. The government's careful, eclectic, use of symbols may also partly account for why Arabic is not, nonetheless, being mobilised as tool for anti-colonial reassertion of the merely 'local'. Appropriating all available cultural tools as part of a new distinctly 'Emirati' identity—as opposed to pan-Arab, with Egyptian connotations (Findlow, 2005)—incorporates and assigns indispensable roles to both 'traditional' Arabic and 'modern' English. This leaves little space for ideological resistance expressed in linguistic terms. Multiple stakeholdership in favourable political and socio-economic conditions means that there is no clear-cut opponent—nothing to rebel against, not even the tide of globalisation represented by compulsory English language.

Another insight may lie in the non-ideological ways English is presented. A total 40.3% of students who preferred to be taught in Arabic said this was because it was easier. Their comments 'We have to understand the content' and 'English language doesn't differentiate between good and bad students, but only between good and bad English language level' suggested that awareness of this point is not limited to theorists (Bourdieu & Passeron, 1994) or Islamisation proponents, who also cite non-religious issues such as additional workload in support of Arabisation (Husain, 1985), but is shared by the students themselves. Yet frustration was combined with declarations such as 'It is good to learn a second language'—in the context of other answers, suggesting that this 'good' was conceived in both collective and individual terms. That is, good for the country and good for them.

Transitional inevitability?

So English appears to be implicated in the sort of ambivalence that underpins 'anti (or post)-colonial nationalism'—simultaneously imitative and resistant. Interviewees and survey respondents spoke of difficulties in negotiating what can seem like contradictory societal expectations. Grumbles about the requirement to learn English often accompanied expressed frustration at having to be conventionally dutiful at home, while making the most of internationalist aspects of modern life outside, including being a student and speaking English.

There are ways in which this ambivalence is linked to the overall state of rapid and great change in the country, to revised values and alternative notions of prestige that were shown earlier to underpin preference for one language or the other. Codeswitching theory (Le Page, 1964) points to a way in which the UAE's linguistic–cultural dualism can be seen as inevitable, even enabling, in such transitional times: a strategy for dealing with the essential dualistic nature of consciousness and society, and for laying claim to two identities and 'cultures' at once. Such a strategy can be seen behind the phrase that appeared most often in the student surveys (expressed in similar terms by almost all of those who argued that Arabic and English were equally necessary):

> English is the language of the world, Arabic is the language of my country.

Changes in popular constructions of prestige are reflected in the following typology of subject status:

1. Medicine/Engineering (at UAE University, or Zayed University): traditional but secular, thought of as globally prestigious, flexible—public or private sector (the first wave of subjects to be taught in English around the Middle East, in English).
2. Modern technological, business or service-related subjects (at the Higher Colleges, or Zayed University): outward-looking, entrepreneurial (recent additions to the curriculum, taught in English).
3. Education/*Shari'a* and law: concerned with the conservation, guardianship of traditions, of local society, public sector (taught in Arabic).

This typology reflects changes in the prestige of jobs. While the sorts of jobs envisaged (and deemed to be 'good') by respondents from UAE University were the traditional ones of teaching, public administration, engineering and medicine, Higher Colleges of Technology and Zayed University students anticipated careers in banking, business, information technology, management and accountancy, associating these with high salaries, and also deeming them on this basis to be 'good'. This is in a context where, 20 years ago, public sector and traditional professions would have won across the board.

Language was implicated in an additional way. While 80% of students who expressed a preference for instruction in English cited motivation in terms of a specific career goal, or a specific academic field, and there was a broad qualitative correlation between English-language preference and well-articulated career goals, Arabic-language preference tended to correlate with holistic, 'doing well', type goals. Only 20% of Arabic supporters cited a specific career goal as their reason, and in all of these cases the specific career in question was teaching—further illustration of the persistence of an underlying framework of genuinely competing values, namely between community service (represented by Arabic) and individualism (English).

But it is not necessarily a matter of straightforward competition. The reasons given for choosing to study at a particular institution suggest flexibility within such constructions. Modernist, skills-focused institutions were selected as the 'best' on account of the quality of English-language teaching and the modern facilities offered. At the same time, UAE University was equally deemed to be 'good' on account of its size/the range of subjects offered. its fame/national flagship status. the currency, and perceived quality, of its 'degree' (UAE University was depicted by those students who favoured it as representing traditional academia, difficulty and selection), and its traditionalism.

This is consistent with the ways in which HE policy appears either to have been revised continually in relation to changing constructions of prestige or to have attempted simultaneous inclusiveness. For instance, the distinct symbolic codes embodied in the names of the two educational ministries appeals to distinct, but clearly intended as complementary, value sets. And pragmatic flexibility can be seen in policy changes such as UAE University's and Zayed University's decisions to discard plans for the promotion of Arabic as instructional media, or in the ways the socialisation packages of 'Arabic–Islam-state-HE provision', and 'internationalism-state-HE provision' have been according to immediate need. Thus, UAE University was characterised from the start as a *jami'a Arabiyya Islamiyya* ('Arab–Islamic university'), affirming the UAE's credentials in a regional context. While symbolism at the Higher Colleges of Technology has been modernist and internationalist, Zayed University in its turn was named after the country's first President, symbolising the agenda of the time for a new, UAE-specific (rather than generically Arab–Islamic), culturally eclectic way forward.

Conclusions

This analysis has presented a linguistic–cultural dualism that is intrinsic to UAE collective identity as both a tool and a product of social change. To the extent that this change is agency and agenda-driven rather than evolving, it can be seen in 'symbolic violence' terms, with both English and Arabic used as tools in the establishment of a new nation-state (UAE) identity. The process amounts to the post-colonial 'relegation' of Arabic only if that realm (of home/tradition/culture) is considered inferior itself. Its relative status appears to depend on the market and varying priorities or contexts.

Although politics have been implicit in the processes that have brought about such a current state of affairs, and a sustained undercurrent of 'loss' is related to imaginative commitment to Arab–Islamic heritage, Arabic has not so far been mobilised as a tool in any political resistance discourse. This appears to be because the anthropological perspective of 'loss' is quite remote from the socio-economic or pragmatic concerns of the average UAE citizen. Feelings of HE stakeholders appear to be governed by resignation to inevitability, rather than questions over ethics. There may be underlying ideological conflict between two value sets (community and heritage versus individualism and opportunity). But the present climate (modernist, global, a buoyant economy, no evident material need for resistance) has facilitated a cognitively dissonant cultural flexibility that is actually 'enabling'. The ability to tap into bilingual resources, to use language (after Finlayson *et al.*, 1998, p. 395) as both an 'index of identity and a tool of communication' is what has enabled citizens to negotiate rapid socio-political, cultural and economic change in the creation of appropriately hybrid, transitional collective identities.

Structurally, this is an example of socio-economically driven change, a matter of markets, with 'culture' in its broad sense continually re-producing, confirming, this change. In its narrower sense (traditional, indigenous), culture is active as a resister to such change only in the context of a very limited resistance discourse. But changed political or socio-economic circumstances could at any time threaten this balance and bring about a rather different set of feelings about the prevalence of English. Illustrating a way, then, in which *habitus* can be both 'structuree' (with speed, and from outside!), as well as 'structurante' (Bourdieu, 1979, p. 191), the case highlights some potential limits to the culturally generative potential of (slowly evolving) *habitus*.

Tapping in, at least, to questions about the mechanistic role of language, language here is most accurately cast as a reflexive tool—reproducing changing cultures that then feed back into and change language and its use. Reminiscent of other cases, such as the South African example cited, this case underlines how this reflexive function, and the link between shift and dualism, is, moreover, intrinsic to language itself.

The structural role of HE in this case of socio-cultural and cultural–linguistic change is seen to be highly analytically flexible: 'field', 'tool' or 'agency', according to the question being asked, suggesting a relative appropriation of such structural terms themselves. In the UAE case, HE via a range of communicative tools has contributed to defining new national identities and agendas, and has been a major influence on Emirati youth's apparent ability to assimilate conflicting cultural influences as represented by Arabic and English. This flexibility in turn is seen as a *de facto* tool in the creation and self-definition of the UAE as a new 'nation-state' (Findlow, 2000)—challenging both the old definitional link between 'nationhood' and sole use of one single language, and some of the more established grounds for distinguishing 'nationhood' from 'statehood'. Whether or not the requirement for students to learn English constitutes an infringement or enrichment of human rights comes back both to how we define these rights and to what is considered a more valid higher educational ideal: providing equality of educational opportunity, subsequent career opportunities, collective cultural heritage or collective capability to take part in a global economy.

References

Anderson, B. (1983) *Imagined communities* (2nd edn, 1991) (London, Verso).

Anderson, B. (1990) *Language and power: exploring political cultures in Indonesia* (Cornell, NY, Cornell University Press).

Asad, T. (1986) The concept of cultural translation in British social anthropology, in: J. Clifford & G. E. Marcus (Eds) *Writing cultures: the poetics and politics of ethnography* (Berkely, University of California Press).

Beblawi, H. (1987) The rentier state in the Arab world, in: H. Beblawi & G. Luciani (Eds) *The rentier state* (London, Croom Helm), chapter 2.

Ben Rafael, E. (1994) *Language, identity and social division* (Oxford, Clarendon Press).

Benrabah, M. (1999) *Langue et pouvoir en Algerie: histoire d'un traumatisme linguistique* (Paris, Seguier).

Bernstein, B. (1971) On the classification and framing of educational knowledge, in: M. F. D. Young (Ed.) *Knowledge and control* (London, Collier-Macmillan).

Boas, F. (1940) *Race, language and culture*, 199–239 (Original work published 1917, '*Introduction*' to American linguistics (vol. 1)) (New York, Macmillan).

Bourdieu, P. (1979) *La distinction* (Paris, Minuit).

Bourdieu, P. (1991) *Language and symbolic power* (Cambridge, Polity).

Bourdieu, P. & Passeron, J.-C. (1990) *Reproduction: education, society and culture* (2nd edn) (London, Sage) (Original work published 1970).

Bourdieu, P., Passeron, J.-C. & de Saint Martin, M. (1994) *Academic discourse: linguistic misunderstanding and professorial power* (Cambridge, Polity).

Brenzinger, M. (1992) *Language death: factual and theoretical explorations with special reference to East Africa* (Berlin, Mouton de Gruyter).

Breuilly, J. (1982) *Nationalism and the state* (Manchester, Manchester University Press).

Byram, M. & Risager, K. (1999) *Language teachers, politics and cultures* (Clevedon, Multilingual Matters).

Carli, A., Guardiano, C., Kaucic-Basa, M., Sussi, E., Tessarolo, M. and Ussai, M. (2003) Asserting ethnic identity and power through language, *Journal of Ethnic and Migration Studies*, 29(5), 865–883.

Castells, M. (1997) *The information age: economy, society and culture. Vol II, The power of identity* (Oxford, Blackwell).

Caviedes, A. (2003) The role of language in nation-building within the European Union, *Dialectical Anthropology*, 27(3–4), 249–268.

Delacroix, J. (1980) The distributive state in the world system, *Studies in Comparative International Development*, 15(3), 9–17.

Faiq, S. (1999) The Status of Berber: a permanent challenge to language policy in Morocco, in: Y. Suleiman (Ed.) *Language and society in the Middle East and North Africa* (Richmond, UK, Curzon), chapter 7.

Findlow, S. (2000) *The United Arab Emirates: nationalism and Arab-Islamic identity* (Abu Dhabi, Emirates Centre for Strategic Studies and Research).

Findlow, S. (2005) International networking in the United Arab Emirates higher education: global–local tensions, *Compare*, 35(3), 285–302.

Finlayson, R., Calteaux, K. & Myers-Scotton, C. (1998) Orderly mixing and accommodation in South African codeswitching, *Journal of Sociolinguistics*, 2(3).

Fishman, J. (1991) *Reversing language shift* (Clevedon, Multilingual Matters).

Foucault, M. (1989) *The archaeology of knowledge* (London, Routledge) (Original work published 1969).

Garcia & Jimenez (1998) in: D. J. Hacker, J. Dunlosky & A. C. Graesser (Eds) *Metacognition in educational theory and practice* (London, Lawrence Erlbaum Associates).

Geertz, C. (1975) *The interpretation of cultures* (London, Fontana) (Original work published 1973).

Gellner, E. (1983) *Nations and nationalism* (Oxford, Basil & Blackwell), 35–38.

Gill, H. (1999) Language choice, language policy and the tradition-modernity debate in culturally mixed postcolonial communities: France and the Francophone Maghreb as a case study, in: Y. Suleiman (Ed.) *Language and society in the Middle East and North Africa* (Richmond, UK, Curzon), chapter 6.

Gogolin, I. (2002) Linguistic and cultural diversity in Europe: a challenge for educational research and practice, *European Educational Research Journal*, 1(1), 123–138.

Gumpertz, J. J. (1986) Interactional sociolinguistics in the study of schooling, in: J. Cook-Gumpertz (Ed.) *The social construction of literacy* (Cambridge, Cambridge University Press), chapter 3, 45–68.

Hobsbawm, E. & Ranger, T. (1983) *The invention of tradition* (Cambridge, Cambridge University Press).

Husain, S. S. (1985) The teaching of English poetry in Saudi Arabian universities: the problem and the solution, *Muslim Education Quarterly*, 3(1), 30–42.

Jakobson, R. (1962) *Selected writings* (vol. 1) (The Hague, Mouton).

Karmani, S. (1995) Islam, politics and English language teaching, *Muslim Education Quarterly*, 13(1), 12–33.

Le Page, R. (1964) *The national language question: linguistic problems of newly independent states* (London, Oxford University Press).

Pennycook, A. (1989) The concept of method, interested knowledge, and the politics of English language teaching, *TESOL Quarterly*, 32(4), 589–617.

Pennycook, A. (1994) *The cultural politics of English as an international language* (London, Longman).

Plamenatz, J. (1976) Two types of nationalism, in: E. Kamenka (Ed.) *Nationalism: the nature and evolution of an idea* (London, Edward Arnold).

Sabour, M. (1988) *Homo academicus rabicus*. Publications in Social Sciences, University of Joensuu.

Said, E. (1991) Identity, authority and freedom: the potentate and the traveller, presented *TB Davie academic freedom lecture* (T. B. Davie, Ed.), University of Cape Town, 22 May.

Said, E., (1995) *The politics of dispossession: the struggle for Palestinian self-determination 1969–1994* (London, Vintage).

Sapir, E. (1949) *Selected Writings of Edward Sapir in language, culture and personality* (D. G. Mandelbaum, Ed.) (Berkeley, University of California Press).

Sardar, Z. (1982) Why Islam needs Islamic science, *New Scientist*, 1 April, 25–28.

Skutnabb-Kangas, T. (2000) *Linguistic genocide in education – or worldwide diversity and human rights?* (Mahwah, NJ, Lawrence Erlbaum Associates).

Suliman, H. (1987) *The nationalist movements in the Maghrib: a comparative approach* (Uppsala, Scandinavian Institute of African Studies).

Tapper, T. (1976) *Political education and stability: elite responses to political conflict* (London, John Wiley & Sons).

Tyler, E. B. (1951) *Primitive culture* (London, John Murray) (Original work published 1871).

UAE University (1999) *bayan yudhah mawa'id wa mawadi' al-mu'tamarat w'al-nadawat w'al-halaqt al-'ilmiyya alathi nadhamatha UAEU, 3/81–5/98*. UAE University, Vice Chancellor's Office.

Walker, M. (2005) Race is nowhere and race is everywhere: narratives from black and white South African university students in post-apartheid South Africa, *British Journal of Sociology of Education*, 26(1), 41–54.

Whorf, B. L. (1956) *Language, thought and reality: selected writings of B. L. Whorf*, edited and with an introduction by John B. Carroll etc (New York, John Wiley and sons).

Zayed University (1998) *ta'lim mutawattir fi 'alam mutaghayyir*. Draft Plans, March.

Qualitative research as a method for making just comparisons of pedagogic quality in higher education: a pilot study

Andrea Abbas[a] and Monica McLean[b]

[a]University of Teesside, UK; [b]University of Nottingham, UK

Systems designed to ensure that teaching and student learning are of a suitable quality are a feature of universities globally. Quality assurance systems are central to attempts to internationalise higher education, motivated in part by a concern for greater global equality. Yet, if such systems incorporate comparisons, the tendency is to reflect and reproduce inequalities in higher education. Highlighting the European context, we argue that, if higher education is to play a part in tackling social inequalities, we must seek alternative methods to explore pedagogic quality in institutional settings. The sociologist Basil Bernstein's concepts of *classification* and *framing* provide an illustration of the potential of sociologically informed, qualitative approaches for exploring and improving higher education pedagogy and also for addressing social justice issues: these two concepts are used to analyse documentation about undergraduate sociology in two universities that have quite different reputations within the English and Northern Irish higher education system.

Introduction

Quality assurance is at the centre of policy debates about the internationalisation of higher education. The inclusion of education in the World Trade Organisation's General Agreement on Trade in Services causes concern even though the opening up of trade is purportedly designed to promote economic equality (Knight, 2003).[1] Although academic and student unions support internationalisation, they appear largely opposed to the inclusion of higher education under the General Agreement on Trade in Services because they see it as a right and social good to be provided by welfare states rather than by international trade. So, while there is broad agreement across a range of organisations and interest groups that a global education system could promote greater economic and social equality, there is no such agreement about the means of achieving it. A compromise is suggested by the International Association of Universities, made up of management representatives of higher education institutions from across the globe: it accepts that the market will drive a global higher education sector and proposes that quality systems are put in place to 'ensure that a cross-border education contributes to the public good' (International Association of Universities, 2005, p. 1). However, there is sociological criticism of current quality systems because the value and worth attached to different universities and the qualifications they award are strongly tied to economic power and social and cultural status. The International Association of Universities expects quality systems to play a role in challenging inequalities between nations, institutions and students by specifying and attempting to impose high standards.

The new European Higher Education Area (EHEA) aims to harmonise higher education across the European Union by 2010, and 45 nations have agreed to participate. The process of 'harmonisation' or 'convergence' is known as the Bologna Process and it is introduced here because those involved also view quality assurance as key to its success. Academic staff (Education International, 2005), students (National Union of Students in Europe, 2003) and ministers (Bergen Communiqué, 2005) all state that quality reviews should include the views of students, academic staff and employers, and should encompass quality enhancement as well as evaluation. All groups also want higher education in Europe to address social inequality. However, the proposed quality systems appear to be based largely upon those currently in use across the EHEA that do not challenge inequality.

The rhetoric in EHEA documentation about 'quality' seems convincing: under instruction from ministers, quality assurance agencies in Europe are developing guidelines claiming to have:

> A widely shared set of underpinning values, expectations and good practice in relation to quality and its assurance, by institutions and agencies across the European Higher Education Area. (European Association for Quality Assurance in Higher Education, 2005, p. 3)

Such a statement appears as a rational attempt to maintain comparative standards in a cooperative system. But Hahn (2003) makes the point that there is a conflict between the apparent cooperation of the Bologna Process and the competitive ideology underpinning the development of EHEA in an 'international higher education market'. Our argument rests on the premise that there has been an economising of education (Jones, 2004) with global capitalism driving forward a managerial and marketised quality agenda that, although associated with some positive changes, does not incorporate the redistributive principals necessary to address inequality (Morley, 2003, 2005). The opportunity is being missed to develop alternative quality systems that would reveal what Bernstein (1996) calls 'biases' and to provide education with a basis for tackling distributive injustices.

Quality systems and the facilitation of social justice

The market ideology of quality systems

In order to clarify the problems (and possibilities) of contemporary quality systems we must trace their history and identify the national and international social, economic and political processes that shape them and are embedded within their discourses (Bottery, 2000; McCarthy & Dimitriadis, 2000; Vidovich, 2004). In Australia, Western Europe, New Zealand and the United States, the form and focus of quality systems is linked to declining resources and a different relationship to the state. Ainley (2004) argues that states should now be called 'market-states' to signify the movement in their obligations from providing welfare to citizens to facilitating 'opportunity' through multinational companies that offer services globally for which the individual is responsible for taking up. Higher education's part in this trend is seen in its diminishing role in creating and perpetuating national cultures and in its links to new forms of employment and a global economic agenda, which, in turn, signals the changing contract between the state and universities (Readings, 1996; Delanty, 2001). Although there is no clear agreement among commentators about whether politically motivated, capital hungry states or disinterested markets are the key drivers of change, suspicions abound that the actual quality of learning and teaching, as well as equity and social justice, are low on the agenda (Middleton, 2000; Morley, 2003; Brunetto & Farr-Wharton, 2005).

Historical evidence suggests that the adoption of quality systems is closely aligned to a perceived need to compete in a global market mainly in Europe, Australia and New Zealand (Rhoades & Sporn, 2002; Vidovich, 2004), but also in the developing countries (Lemaitre, 2002). So, although in many countries the growth of quality systems is associated with widening access, it is also associated with increasing government control, declining state resources and internal pseudo markets (Morley, 2003). At the same time, the influences of quality systems are undoubtedly complex and specific: different local circumstances throw up different configurations, contradictory trends and alternative interpretations (Brennan & Shah, 2000a, b; van Damme, 2001; Rhoades & Sporn, 2002; Billing, 2004; Jones, 2004). For example, Vidovich and Slee (2001) contrast Australia and the United Kingdom by noting how, in the United Kingdom, universities have been more complicit in developing a punitive audit culture because the 1992 abolition of the divide between polytechnics and universities aroused fears about standards. Scotland, however, boasts a system that emphasises quality enhancement and cooperation with institutions. Notwithstanding differences, we need to be wary of all quality systems: in Europe the expansion of higher education is represented as aiming for both economic growth and greater economic and social equality both within and between nations; however, as Jones (2004) points out, when social democratic concerns are raised it is within the framework of the new neo-liberal, marketised discourse.

Quality and the justification of hierarchies

Generally students from poorer backgrounds go to universities with reputations of being less good (Forsyth & Furlong, 2000; Archer et al., 2003; Archer, 2005); quality systems do nothing to alleviate this inequality. Ashworth et al. (2004) reveal how universities reproduce stratification according to wealth and class: those that excel in league tables have a small proportion of working-class students; and working-class students typically do not go to highly rated universities. In England and Northern Ireland, quality systems do not of themselves reinforce the status of universities: under the current system most universities are judged to be satisfactory, and many departments in less prestigious universities attained the highest score for teaching quality when they were inspected. However, in the public arena the lengthy public documents about the quality of teaching in individual universities do not make news, and it is league tables that are influential. League tables combine indicators of pedagogic quality with other indicators that depend on institutional status and wealth (e.g. the entry qualifications of students and the staff–student ratio); thus the tables become 'status measures' (Ashworth *et al.*, 2004, p. 6) and their validation and persuasiveness resides in 'their conformity to a general supposition about the status hierarchy of universities' (p. 6).

Underpinning debates about higher education quality systems are notions of accepted differences between institutions. Perry's (1994) assertion that 'It would be wholly inappropriate to expect the models of Oxford and Cambridge to determine our expectations' (p. 31) is echoed in everyday debates about quality in a diverse national system. Nevertheless, there are attempts to define 'equivalence' as illustrated by a seminar entitled 'The End of Quality?', at which was discussed:

> [...] diversity of institutions, providing different student experiences and having different missions and subject focuses, but at the same time ensuring that student in any institution has an equivalent experience and that the outcomes are the same. (Harvey, 2002, p. 14)

Yet, it is difficult to ascertain the meaning of equivalence when the consequences of engaging in higher education are different for different groups of students, and when the system itself is hierarchical.

Hierarchy plays out in the global arena. The draft proposals for quality assurance for the EHEA (European Association for Quality Assurance in Higher Education, 2005) delineate systems similar to those currently used in England and Northern Ireland. It is likely that market-driven comparisons will be published in league tables and will most benefit countries and institutions with more established reputations and economic advantages. As with the national UK league tables, the international ranking of universities appears to divide according to economic and social status:

> The world's top 200 universities are in 31 countries. All but two are in Europe, Australasia, the US or Canada. The exceptions are the National Autonomous University of Mexico and Sao Paulo in Brazil. No African university made the top 200, and only two Russian universities feature from Eastern Europe. (Ince, 2005)

If quality procedures are to play a role in challenging global inequality, a starting point is to reveal biases in our current understanding of quality. From our perspective, institutions and nations should be thought of in terms of their contributions to social justice. Developing methodologies to judge these contributions will require critical exploration of the factors that influence our views about what constitutes good university pedagogy. In particular, we should challenge the nature and role of league tables.

Exploring constructions of quality: an example.

Sociological perspectives can help us generate accounts of quality systems that are sensitive to complexities and to how they construct academic and student identities (Pels, 2000; Morley, 2003); they can also suggest alternative ways of thinking about pedagogic quality (McLean, 2006). In the remainder of this paper, we illustrate these claims by making qualitative comparisons of undergraduate sociology courses in two English universities that appear in quite different positions in the league tables. We draw on the work of the sociologist Bernstein, who explains why conceptions of pedagogic quality are closely connected to hierarchical structures in society and also why hope for the future should be based on investigating the 'social biases' in education:

> Education is central to the knowledge base of society, groups and individuals. Yet, education, like health, is a public institution, central to the production and reproduction of distributive injustices. Biases in the form, content, access and opportunities of education have consequences not only for the economy; these biases can reach down to drain the very springs of affirmation, motivation and imagination. In this way such biases can become, and often are, an economic and cultural threat to democracy. Education can have a crucial role in creating tomorrow's optimism in the context of today's pessimism. But if it is to do this then we must have an analysis of the social biases in education. These biases lie deep within the very structure of the educational system's processes of transmission and acquisition and their social assumptions. (Bernstein, 1996, p. xix)

Our application of Bernstein's concepts aims to demonstrate how social biases in higher education can be revealed and how debate could include the relationship between pedagogic quality and social justice. Bernstein's sociological theory allows a comparative analysis of the way an understanding of quality is enacted within different institutional contexts so that the relationship between hierarchical social processes and what counts as quality might be mapped (McLean & Abbas, 2004). Broadly, the discursive practices of quality systems can be seen as forming part of what Bernstein (1996) calls a 'mythologising discourse', which functions to make university and student hierarchies appear unconnected to broader social relations influenced by such factors as class, age, gender and ethnicity. We use Bernstein's concepts to attempt to penetrate the mythologising discourse.

A methodological note

We want to explore the foundations of the contradictory claims that are operating in the United Kingdom today: on the one hand, academics acting as external examiners endorse the view that standards are comparable across the system; on the other, the informal discourses of academics and the press convey the notion that different standards are operating; and league tables reflect the latter view.

The two departments that permitted us to evaluate their documentation are in sharply contrasting institutions: Syringa is an elite university, and Lilacsville a former polytechnic. We have aimed to preserve anonymity throughout even though this means that, at times, the data presented cannot be as specific as we would like. Using a critical discourse analysis (Wooffitt, 2005) informed by Bernstein's (1996) theoretical concepts, we analysed the websites advertising the degrees, course documentation and handbooks, and official statistics about the two institutions. Lilacsville students read sociology within a single honours degree, while the students in Syringa take sociology as part of a degree that combines two other subjects; we have disregarded this difference to explore some of the key findings.

Conceptual framework

According to Bernstein, 'Curriculum defines what counts as valid knowledge, pedagogy defines what counts as valid transmission of knowledge, and evaluation[2] defines what counts as valid realization of the knowledge on the part of the taught' (Sadovnik, 1995, p.169). For our purposes we define 'what counts as valid' as 'what counts as good quality'. Some forms of transmission and evaluation come to be seen as more valid than others, so, even when quality systems appear to make neutral statements about curricula and pedagogy, they are confounded by judgements made by academia and the press. Symbols of value trigger automatic reactions to particular degrees and universities: for example, a module that had 'Beckham' in the title attracted negative media attention, despite its compliance with externally imposed quality standards and its being scrutinised through validation and external examiners' processes. The derogatory publicity is legitimised by the hierarchically low status of the university in which it is located.

For Bernstein (1996), education bestows particular rights: to the means of critical understanding, to seeing new possibilities, and to the capacity to participate actively in the political process. He evaluates whether there is equal distribution of these rights by comparing the images and resources of different institutions, what knowledge is transmitted and how knowledge is acquired. According to Bernstein, acquisition of knowledge should not be evaluated in isolation from considering how it facilitates participation in society. In our example, whatever knowledge each set of students acquires, students from Syringa leave university with more labour-market value, power and potential than students from Lilacsville. As a challenge to convention, we are interested in exploring whether the life advantages enjoyed by the students in the more prestigious universities are justified by the quality of their knowledge and understanding of the discipline studied.

The two concepts that we use for our analysis are *classification* and *framing* (Bernstein, 1996). Classification refers to the way boundaries are created and maintained between categories, which can be agencies, practices or discourses; and it acts to translate power and power relations. A relevant example is the way institutions are classified within England and Northern Ireland, which is expressed in several different ways—old/new, pre-1992/post-1992, elite/local, Russell group/others, research/teaching universities; each of these binaries is hierarchical, and, by and large, the former of each binary enjoys more wealth and prestige than the latter. The insulation between them, while by no means complete, is high and it appears as if the government would like it to be higher (e.g. by separating teaching and research; DfES, 2003). The classification comes to have the force of natural order. We seek to reveal the 'contradictions, cleavages and dilemmas' (Bernstein, 1996) that are usually suppressed.

Framing, on the other hand, operates to control relations and practices *within* a category. In terms of curriculum it refers to how it is transmitted. This includes organisation, selection, sequence, pacing and timing, as well as student/staff relations. It also includes the evaluation of whether the 'acquirer' recognises and can 'realise' in the form of written and spoken acts the messages that are being transmitted.

Classification, league table indicators and student progress

First we show how league tables contribute to a classification that ignores whether or not students make progress: official statistics do not take into account the differences involved in teaching students with begin university with lower qualifications and no familiarity with higher education (Forsyth & Furlong, 2003). In England and Northern Ireland, institutions accept students with A-level qualifications (or qualifications deemed equivalent) for which points are allocated for different grades. Many students apply for each place in Syringa, which is then in a position to select students with the highest points (30 points); while Lilacsville competes for students with similar institutions to itself and often struggles to fill places. The difference between the average A-level points of students attending Lilacsville and Syringa to study sociology is 15.6 points (Higher Education Statistic Agency, 2003). So, once accepted onto the degree at Lilacsville, students must improve academically at a far greater rate to achieve an equivalent degree to their counterparts at Syringa.

Students studying at the two universities are also classified by social backgrounds. Each year the Higher Education Funding Council for England sets benchmarks for the percentage of students from lower socio-economic classes each university is expected to admit. Lilacsville's benchmark is more than double that of Syringa and it exceeded it by over five per cent in 2003, whereas Syringa was over five per cent short. This pattern is repeated if we look at statistics about students from geographical areas where participation in higher education is low: the benchmarks were almost seven per cent apart, with Lilacsville achieving over 10% more than its high benchmark and Syringa achieving considerably below its much lower benchmark. A similar pattern emerges if we look at the percentages of students who have been educated at state and private school. In short, Lilacsville's students compared with Syringa's have low economic and cultural capital: they are more likely to be from poorer backgrounds, to take on employment to finance their studies, to have personal or financial problems that might impinge on their studies, and to have parents who have not been to university (Archer & Leathwood, 2003; Hutchings, 2003).

Approximately 50% of students at both Lilacsville and Syringa leave university with an upper second degree.[3] But in Lilacsville most of the rest receive a lower second, while in Syringa most of the rest receive a first-class degree. If we accept that degree classifications have a similar meaning within the system, it could be argued that it is more difficult for Lilacsville to assist poorly qualified students to gain upper second degrees than it is for Syringa to assist some of the most highly selected and privileged students in the country to gain a first-class degree. Nevertheless, Syringa is portrayed in league tables and in the public imagination as a better teaching institution. Furthermore, a discourse of commonsense insists that a second-class degree at Syringa is of a better quality than a second-class degree from Lilacsville, even though this assertion challenges both the traditional acceptance that the quality of degrees can be compared in different institutions and the judgements of quality assurance systems. While the progress made by students at Lilacsville might represent more work on the part of students and teachers, and might also be of the same quality, the possibility should be acknowledged in league tables in order to improve the labour-market chances for the students.

In the reputation stakes, Lilacsville is doubly disadvantaged: on the one hand, entry qualifications are an indicator of quality contributing to a place in the league tables; on the other, meeting or not meeting benchmarks intended to encourage students such as those attending Lilacsville is not. Universities' images are damaged by attracting students from lower socio-economic backgrounds with lower A-level points; and they are unable to overcome the disadvantage because league tables do not consider progression within the university context as a major indicator of quality. Although some funds have been targeted to acknowledge the greater resources that are required to teach students like those from Lilacsville, it is viewed by commentators as insufficient and is sometimes targeted at the wrong universities (Archer & Leathwood, 2003).

Bernstein's concept of classification can also be seen in differential resources, images and access. Syringa is substantially richer than Lilacsville (its annual income is over £400 million greater[4]); the difference in wealth creates different images as well as different material conditions for learning and teaching. Syringa has vast estates of historical buildings, significant art works and has symbolic and actual association with figures at the core of national and international intellectual and political history. These factors contribute to its image as an 'Ivory Tower' institution, representations of which are encountered in English literature and film and are associated with the British upper and upper-middle classes. Lilacsville's more contemporary and functional looking buildings, its location in the heart of a post-industrial city, its association with locally known public figures, its local student body and its former polytechnic status bestow a much less prestigious and less widely known public image.

Lilacsville and Syringa are probably as well insulated from each other as it is possible to be within the higher education system in England and Northern Ireland, certainly as an elite and distinctive university. Certainly, Syringa can only maintain its identity if it can effectively insulate itself from any other university, even those with league table positions closer to its own. However, as we have indicated, being prestigious tells us nothing about actual pedagogic quality. We can speculate, too, that prestige and the mythologising discourse will influence judgements about quality: relations between quality assessors and powerful and less powerful institutions will be different.

Classifying sociology as a discipline in Syringa and Lilacsville

The issue of pedagogic quality should not be addressed without answering questions about whether understanding of and engagement with a discipline differs from university to university. Is a first-class degree of the same quality in all universities? Or, in Bernstein's words, are 'different knowledges and their possibilities differentially distributed to different social groups?' (1996, p. xxi).

In terms of curriculum, classification refers to what counts as 'good quality' knowledge and to what it is legitimate to incorporate. Boundary maintenance between the discipline of sociology in the two institutions is evident in how it is presented to prospective students and the public. On its website, Syringa's sociology department refers to its 'distinguished history' and lists the 'illustrious names' of those who work or worked in the department (some dead), giving the titles of their books; links with international scholars are also noted. The website mentions a particular type of sociology for which the department is renowned and a study claimed to be a 'masterpiece' in its field. Claims, too, are made to expertise in theory that has worldwide relevance and to superiority to all other sociology departments nationally. The message conveyed to potential students is that the discipline of sociology resides in exemplary form in named academics who are associated with this particular department. In these ways, sociology at Syringa is presented as a 'leading brand' that is rooted in tradition and continuities. The student is not visible but, by implication, is constructed as an acolyte or an apprentice.

Lilacsville's publicity refers to its comparatively short history as 'long' and emphasises the contemporary vocational relevance of sociology and the lively way it is taught within a research culture. Although it is emphasised that the teachers are also researchers, nationally and internationally well-known scholars of the past or present department are not named (although they could have been). The claim is that sociology is a changing discipline and that national and international developments are incorporated into the curriculum, which focuses on contemporary social issues. The discipline is portrayed as constantly evolving; and students are constructed as individuals who will find the discipline personally rewarding and as future employees who will find it useful. While Syringa's publicity is likely to alienate a young person from a disadvantaged background (Forsyth & Furling, 2003), Lilacsville's will not be attractive to a typical Syringa applicant.

Classification of curriculum content

Boundary maintenance is also achieved through curriculum content. The core courses in both universities cover a similar range of theories and methods that are generally regarded as central to the discipline. However, the real difference can be found in the options offered: at Lilacsville topics include unemployment, health, sport, leisure, tourism, drugs, cities and human relationships; at Syringa they are at a high level of abstraction—for example, the sociology of urban industrial societies, political sociology and statistical methods in social science. Bernstein (1996) helps us understand the significance of this with his concepts of 'vertical' and 'horizontal' discourses. Vertical discourse, in this context, is the specialised language of academic disciplines that carries a sense of the 'sacred or esoteric'; whereas horizontal discourse is the everyday, mundane discourse of students outside academia. So we can argue that Syringa is holding the discipline within the boundaries of vertical discourse, while Lilacsville is engaging with the 'profanity' of everyday life of the students. Although Syringa claims to deal with 'real world' problems, they are other peoples' problems; global and abstracted from the students' lives and course titles draw only upon disciplinary terms. At Lilacsville, course documentation links sociology students to local community issues. This is how the students in the two institutions are differentially and hierarchically situated in the social world: Syringa students' arena is the whole world, while Lilacsville students are directed towards the local, imminent community. In Bernstein's terms, Syringa's sociology is strongly classified, which he associates with high status; nevertheless, for us the question remains open of whether we are seeing genuine differences in quality in what or how students learn. A critical evaluation of pedagogy (beyond our scope for the present) could examine the different interplay between core and options in terms of how it develops disciplinary knowledge and analytic ability.

Framing the sociology curriculum in Lilacsville and Syringa

Differences might reside in how sociology is taught and in the work that students are asked to do. In Bernstein's terms, the stronger the framing of curriculum and pedagogy, the less control teachers and students have over what and how content is taught and learned. In terms of quality, there is not a straightforward relationship between weak and strong framing and pedagogic quality, and a mix is often the best option. For example, Morais (2002) suggests that, in schools, better pedagogy includes weak pacing, the flexibility to allow individuals to progress at their own pace, combined with strong framing of assessment criteria, which conveys clear messages about what learning is expected. An area of future research would be to explore the effectiveness of strong and weak framing for different aspects of university pedagogy.

Framing at Syringa. Students at Syringa take eight courses in their last two years[5] for each of which students attend a compulsory weekly or bi-weekly one-hour tutorial of up to three students; they are generally expected to write an essay on the tutorial on which they receive feedback (sometimes written, sometimes verbal, depending on the tutor—usually not a mark). This amounts to eight essays for each course. Tutors have a great deal of autonomy within tutorials in terms of both content and process. Students may or may not have other organised classes; each course has a series of 16 lectures that are optional and the connection between lecture and tutorials is not specified. The degree result rests on final examinations over which tutors have no control, although some contribute questions. In the last two years of their combined degree, students will write altogether between 32 and 64 essays that are formatively assessed and take eight summative examinations for each of which they must answer three of 14 questions. The amount of detail in written information provided for students varies considerably for each course.

Framing at Lilacsville. Sociology students at Lilacsville take nine courses in their final two years. Attendance throughout is between two and four hours each week. Teachers decide how to organise the sessions, but they almost always have weekly lectures and seminar activities that have been pre-specified in a handbook. Seminar groups are between 15 and 40 students, except for dissertation supervision or additional personal tutoring. Although teachers are given guidelines on the amount of work they can require of students (in terms of credits and level of work), it is difficult to ascertain exactly how much work students undertake. All courses have some, usually one, form of formative assessment and also summative assessments that vary in form and number but are deemed to have equivalence to other courses in terms of demands on students (e.g. essays, critical reviews, portfolios, presentations, media analysis). There are examinations in a few of the courses, all students must write a dissertation in their final year and the overall degree result is calculated on the basis of a small percentage of second-year work and a larger percentage of third-year work. Guidance for Lilacsville students is written, explicit and standardised.

Analytic comparison of the framing of the sociology curriculum at Lilacsville and Syringa. In certain respects, both universities' organisation of teaching appears to be strongly framed for students. Enshrined at the organisational level are the number of teaching events that students must attend and teachers must teach; and the structure of the degree and the number of assessments that students must complete and that tutors must mark is largely not the decision of individual teachers (in Lilacsville, course design must be validated by a university panel and then cannot be changed). Students in both universities will therefore take the same number of topics as one another, and the mode of delivery (from the outside at least) will be similar.

In Syringa the weekly essay can be seen in Bernstein's terms as a 'realisation' that attracts constant evaluation from the tutor of what counts as valid knowledge. In theory, the space for discussion is open (weak framing) and guidance through reading and subject matter is given verbally, and so will vary by tutor, which reflects the classification of individual tutors as incumbents of the discipline. If students choose not to attend lectures, they might have one or two hours contact with a tutor each week, which assumes a good deal of autonomy for the students. However, Syringa's final examinations are a strong frame, a highly regulated mechanism for evaluation of the acquired knowledge.

A good deal of Lilacsville students' experience is strongly framed. They meet their tutors for longer and in much larger groups than at Syringa for teaching sessions that are highly structured. In sharp contrast to Syringa, Lilacsville's students have more summative than formative assessment; for example, the core second-year course requires one piece of formative work and four pieces of summative work with no examination. Yet the final-year dissertation is a weak frame allowing independence other than meeting tutors on a one-to-one basis for approximately one half-hour session every two weeks.

It is evident that the pedagogic framing in each university is quite different. At Syringa, students' pedagogic activities are relatively limited in type, they enjoy a good deal of individual attention and feedback, which they receive frequently, and their experience of the curriculum varies according to tutors. It is costly teaching and can be characterised as 'elite' framing. At Lilacsville, pedagogic activities are varied, students are required to adopt a wider variety of ways communicating and engaging with the discipline, but it is standardised and feedback comes more slowly. Teaching here is comparatively cheap and can be thought of as 'mass' framing.

Our pilot study is limited, we are not yet in a position to evaluate the significance of our findings in terms of pedagogic quality. Nevertheless, our analysis does not support the common perception that the curriculum and pedagogy in prestigious universities is of a better quality than in less prestigious universities. In order to explore fully the issues we have raised we must compare many more qualitative dimensions of pedagogy, most of which are not visible in documentation. Further research will include interviews with staff and students, comparisons of student work and more ethnographic approaches to ascertain, for example, comparative 'time on task' preparing for seminars and writing essays, the formal and informal opportunities for knowledge realisation and feedback, and the effects of the balance of formative and summative assessment. We need, also, to examine the actual products and outcomes of learning. Simultaneously, we shall challenge existing biases about what constitutes a good university education. For example, is there any foundation to the commonly held view that engaging with the 'profanity' of everyday life through empirically focused courses actually relates to a reduction in the quality of learning?

Biases can be revealed using social science research methods. Our documentary analysis shows how power and wealth become enshrined in curriculum and pedagogy. Syringa's discursive practices are much more highly valued by society, but such an evaluation is not yet supported by investigation. It is worth noting here that the hierarchy we have been discussing might itself make further study difficult because it could expose false boundaries that would potentially threaten the position of elite universities.

Concluding comments

We have argued that quality systems used to compare institutions are biased and contribute to reproducing social hierarchies. The hierarchy appears to be neutral on the basis of 'ability' (merit), and the difference in entry qualifications between, for example, Syringa and Lilacsville makes this appear incontrovertible; but it is, as Bernstein puts, it a 'pretence [that] the hierarchy within [the system] is created by different principles from those of the hierarchy outside the university' (2000, p. xxii). Future European and global hierarchies are even more complex and biases are likely to be more difficult to uncover. It is our view that an examination of pedagogic quality could play a role in promoting social justice.

A critical analysis of the components that, implicitly and explicitly, underpin judgements about quality would be an important first step. The academy itself should challenge inequitable components and include them in public debate about pedagogic quality. Information to the public could be provided using the qualitative methods we suggest and might help students and others to understand how the biases within the system impact upon their choices and life chances. Descriptions of students' progression rates and identification of the attributes they leave university with might raise public consciousness of institutional similarities and differences as well as improve pedagogic practice. But altering current hierarchies requires national and international commitment to an understanding of what kind of pedagogy contributes to social justice.

Notes

1. There are of course a plethora of economic problems in developing countries that cannot be addressed through higher education, as Ntshoe (2003) argues in relation to South Africa.
2. Usually known as 'assessment' in the United Kingdom.
3. In the UK system, honours degree classifications, starting from the top award, are: first class (1st), upper second (2.1), lower second (2.2).
4. Source withheld to maintain confidentiality.
5. We have analysed the last two years because the structures of the two degrees differ considerably in the first year.

References

Ainley, P. (2004) The new market state and education, *Journal of Education Policy*, 19(4), 497–514.

Archer, L. (2005) Diversity, inclusion and equality: revisiting critical issues for the widening participation agenda, in: C. Rust (Ed.) *Improving student learning: diversity and inclusivity* (Oxford, The Oxford Centre for Staff and Learning Development), 21–34.

Archer, L. & Leathwood, C. (2003) Identities, inequality and higher education, in: L, Archer, A. Ross & M. Hutchings (Eds) *Higher education and social class: issues of inclusion and exclusion* (London, RoutledgeFalmer), 176–191.

Archer, L., Hutchings, M. & Ross, A. (2003) *Higher education and social class: issues of exclusion and inclusion* (London, RoutledgeFalmer).

Ashworth, P., Clegg, S. & Nixon, J. (2004) The redistribution of excellence: reclaiming widening participation for a just society, paper presented at the *12th Improving Student Learning Symposium, Inclusivity and Difference*, Birmingham, 6–8 September.

Bergen Communique (2005) *The European Higher Education Area – achieving the goals*, Communiqué of the Conference of European Ministers Responsible for Higher Education, Bergen, 19–20 May 2005. Available online at: http://www.bologna-bergen2005.no/Docs/00-Main_doc/050520_Bergen_Communique.pdf (accessed 14 September 2007).

Bernstein, B. (1996) *Pedagogy, symbolic control and identity: theory, research, critique* (London, Taylor Francis).

Bernstein, B. (2000) *Pedagogy, symbolic control and identity*, revised edn (New York, Rowman & Littlefield).

Billing, D. (2004) International comparisons and trends in external quality assurance of higher education: Commonality or diversity?, *Higher Education*, 47, 113–137.

Bottery, M. (2000) *Education, policy and ethics* (London, Continuum).

Brennan, J. & Shah, T. (2000a) Quality assessment and institutional change: experiences from 14 countries, *Higher Education*, 40, 331–349.

Brennan, J. & Shah, T. (2000b) *Managing quality in higher education: an international perspective on institutional assessment and change* (Buckingham, Society for Research into Higher Education and Open University Press).

Brunetto, Y. & Farr-Wharton, R. (2005) Academics' responses to the implementation of the quality agenda, *Quality in Higher Education*, 11(2), 162–180.

Delanty, G. (2001) *Challenging knowledge: the university in the knowledge society* (Buckingham, Society for Research into Higher Education and Open University Press).

DfES (2003) *The future of higher education* (London, Department for Education and Skills).

Education International (2005) *Bologna Process: academics are on track with it.* Available online at: http://www.ei-ie.org/highereducation/file/(2005)%20Bologna%20Process%20en.pdf (accessed 14 September 2007).

European Association for Quality Assurance in Higher Education (2005) *Standards and guidelines for quality assurance in the European Higher Education Area* (Helsinki, European Association for Quality Assurance in Higher Education).

Forsyth, A. & Furlong, F. (2000) *Socioeconomic disadvantage and access to higher education* (Bristol, The Policy Press)

Forsyth, A. & Furlong, F. (2003) *Losing out? Socioeconomic disadvantage and experience in further and higher education* (Bristol, The Policy Press)

Hahn, K. (2003) The changing *Zeitgeist* of German higher education and the role of GATS, *Higher Education in Europe*, XXVIII(2), 199–215.

Harvey, L. (2002) The end of quality?, *Quality in Higher Education*, 8(1), 5–22.

Higher Education Statistic Agency (2003) *Higher education statistics for the UK 2001/02* (Cheltenham, UK, Higher Education Statistics Agency).

Hutchings, M. (2003) Information and advice and cultural discourses of higher education, in: L. Archer, A. Ross & M. Hutchings (Eds) *Higher education and social class: issues of inclusion and exclusion* (London, RoutledgeFalmer).

Ince, M. (2005) UK leaps to global success, *Times Higher*, 28 October. Available online at: http://www.thes.co.uk/story.aspx?story_id=2025650 (accessed September 14 2007).

International Association of Universities (2005) *Sharing quality higher education across borders: a statement on behalf of higher education institutions worldwide.* Available online at: http://www.unesco.org/iau/p_statements/index.html (accessed 14 September 2007).

Jones, K. (2004) Higher education in crisis: the English experience, contribution to *SIPTU Seminar, Irish Universities and the Threat of Privatisation*, Liberty Hall, Dublin, 22 May.

Knight, J. (2003) *GATS, trade and higher education: perspective 2003—where are we?* Report for the Observatory on Borderless Higher Education. Available online at: http://www.obhe.ac.uk/products/reports/archived.html?year=2003 (accessed 14 September 2007).

Lemaitre, M. J. (2002) Quality as politics, *Quality in Higher Education*, 8(1), 29–37.

McCarthy, C. & Dimitriadis, G. (2000) Governmentality and the sociology of education: media, educational policy and the politics of resentment, *British Journal of Sociology of Education*, 21(2), 169–184.

McLean, M. (2006) *Pedagogy and the university: critical theory and practice* (London, Continuum International).

McLean, M. & Abbas, A. (2004) Towards alternative methods of evaluating the 'quality' of courses in different universities, paper presented to the *Annual Conference of the Society for Research into Higher Education, Whose Higher Education?: Public and Private values and the Knowledge Economy*, Bristol, 14–16 December.

Middleton, C. (2000) Models of state and market in the modernisation of higher education, *British Journal of Sociology of Education*, 21(4), 537–554.

Morais, A. M. (2002) Basil Bernstein at the micro level of the classroom, *British Journal of Sociology of Education*, 23(4), 559–570.

Morley, L. (2003) *Quality and power in higher education* (Buckingham, Society for Research into Higher Education and Open University Press).

Morley, L. (2005) Opportunity or Exploitation? Women and quality assurance in higher education, *Gender and Education,* 17(4), 411–429.

National Union of Students in Europe (2007) *Bologna with students' eyes,* 2007 edn. Available online at: http://www.esib.org/index.php?option=com_content&task=section&id=4&Itemid=241 (accessed 14 September 2007).

Ntshoe, I. M. (2003) The political economy of access and equitable allocation of resources to higher education, *International Journal of Educational Development,* 23(4), 381–398.

Pels, P. (2000), The trickster's dilemma: ethics and the technologies of the anthropological self, in: M. Strathern (Ed.) *Audit cultures: anthropological studies in accountability, ethics and the academy* (London, Routledge).

Perry, Baroness P., (1994) Defining and measuring the quality of teaching, in: D. Green (Ed.) *What is quality in higher education?* (Buckingham, Society for Research in higher Education and Open University Press).

Readings, B. (1996) *The university in ruins* (London, Harvard University Press).

Rhoades, G. & Sporn, B. (2002) Quality assurance in Europe and the U.S.: professional and political economic framing of higher education policy, *Higher Education,* 43, 355–390.

Sadovnik, A. R. (Ed.) (1995), *Knowledge and pedagogy: the sociology of Basil Bernstein* (Westport, CT, Ablex Publishing).

van Damme, D. (2001) Quality issues in the internationalisation of higher education, *Higher Education,* 41, 415–441.

Vidovich, L. (2004) Global–national–local dynamics in policy processes: a case of 'quality' policy in higher education, *British Journal of Sociology of Education,* 25(3), 341–354.

Vidovich, L. & Slee, R. (2001) Bringing universities to account? Exploring some global and local policy tensions, *Journal of Education Policy,* 16(5), 431–453.

Wooffitt, R. (2005) *Conversation analysis and discourse analysis: a comparative and critical introduction* (London, Sage).

Research assessment as a pedagogical device: Bernstein, professional identity and Education[1] in New Zealand

Sue Middleton

Department of Policy, Culture & Social Studies in Education, School of Education, University of Waikato, Hamilton, New Zealand

Recent restructuring of research funding for New Zealand's higher education institutions is 'outputs-driven'. Under the Performance Based Research Fund, units of assessment of research quality are individuals, every degree teacher receiving a confidential score of A, B or C (if deemed 'research active') or 'R' ('Research Inactive'). Despite its relatively high number of A and B rated individuals, Education's collective ranking was low. I interviewed staff and draw on Bernstein to explore how this process affects professional identity formation, a process involving engagement with changing 'official' external identities. I overview Bernsteinian concepts, historicise Education's changing official identities and illustrate how these enabled and constrained participants' self-definitions before, during, and immediately after, the quality evaluation. The imposition of audit culture reproduces old theory/practice binaries.

As in Britain and Australia, recent restructuring of research funding for New Zealand's higher education institutions is 'outputs-driven'. The research component in equivalent full-time student (EFTS) enrolment funding is being replaced by a contestable Performance-Based Research Fund (PBRF) to increase 'the quality of research through peer assessment and performance indicators' (Ministry of Education 2002, 17). Responsible for PBRF's design, implementation and oversight, the Tertiary Education Commission (TEC) introduced:

> A mixed model combining both peer review and performance indicators preferable to the prevailing alternatives, namely a model based solely on peer review, like the British Research Assessment Exercise (RAE), or a model based solely on performance indicators, such as the Australian Research Quantum. (Boston 2004, 1)

Research funding would be allocated on the basis of three, differentially weighted 'elements' of each Tertiary Education Organisation's (TEO) research performance over a six-year period: 20% for its external research income, 20% for research degree completions, and 60% for 'the research quality of its staff, based on peer review' by 12 panels of experts in a subject, or group of subjects (Tertiary Education Commission 2003, 11). Units of assessment of research quality would not be departments, but individuals.

Accordingly, in 2002, every degree-level teacher submitted a personal Evidence Portfolio (EP) listing all quality assured research outputs, evidence of peer esteem, contributions to the research environment, and brief descriptions of four nominated best research 'outputs'. Institutions awarded each EP a provisional grade, confidentially communicating these to staff. Provisionally graded

EPs were sent to the TEC's 12 subject panels for final evaluation. Months later, participants received their confidential personal grades – a 'mark' of A, B or C (if deemed 'research active') or 'R' ('research inactive'). Collective grades and rankings of subjects and institutions were made public (Performance Based Research Fund 2004). Despite its relatively high number of A and B rated individuals, as a subject Education's collective ranking was amongst the lowest. Institutions and media berated Education's 'huge research inactive tail' urging remedial action to help it catch up with high scoring subjects like philosophy or physics.

Policy-makers often 'know what they do; they frequently know why they do what they do; but what they don't know is what what they do does' (Foucault, as cited in Dreyfus and Rabinow 1982, 187). What is it that this quality evaluation process *does* to Education as a field of inquiry, and to its individual participants? Following Bernstein (2000), sociologists have described Britain's RAE as a 'restructuring not merely of the external conditions of academic and professional practice, but even more fundamentally of the core elements of academic and professional identity' (Beck and Young 2005, 184; see also Croll 2003). Under RAE, institutions chose whose research to submit, and there was 'no assumption that all academic staff engage in research' (Morgan 2004, 463). The individualisation, and compulsion, of the PBRF suggest that its 'consequences for academic identity are likely to be greater than is the case with the RAE' (Codd 2006, 226).

Bernstein combines 'sociological analysis of identity within institutional levels ... and the analysis of projected official identities at the level of the state' (Bernstein 2000, 204). 'Official identities' are projected via statutes, regulations, handbooks, templates, contracts and job descriptions. Professional identity formation is 'a continuous and reflexive process, a synthesis of (internal) self definition and the (external) definition of oneself offered by others' (Henkel 2005, 157). My study of policy documents identified the official (external) identities 'teacher', 'researcher' and 'manager/administrator/leader'. I wrote these on flash cards and used these in interviews with 36 volunteers from seven TEOs. Of the 35 who disclosed their PBRF scores, two were rated A, 10 as B, 12 as C and 11 in the R category (see Middleton 2005). Did these categorisations affect their sense of identity? How did they see themselves and their work before, during and after the quality assurance process? After a brief introduction to Bernsteinian concepts (1), I outline Education's history of changing official (projected external) identities (2) and illustrate how these enabled and constrained participants' (internal) self-definitions before, during, and immediately after the 2003 quality evaluation (3). I argue that the requirement for all degree teaching staff to 'be researchers' could undermine Education's 'other' mandate to produce intellectually independent professional practitioners (4).

1. Bernsteinian concepts

A sociologist of knowledge, Bernstein studied the social organisation and status hierarchies of subjects or disciplines and their participants (students, teachers, researchers, etc.). His foundational concepts are classification and framing. Classification refers to boundaries between, and within, disciplines or subjects, encompassing 'relations between categories, whether these categories are between agencies, between discourses, between practices' (Bernstein 2000, 6). The PBRF delineated subjects, or groups of subjects, and appointed 12 panels of subject experts to examine individuals' Evidence Portfolios. Education had its own panel. Identifying with subjects 'other' than Education, some staff located administratively in Education chose to send their EPs to other subject panels. The panels also referred EPs elsewhere (Education Panel 2004, 10). The quality evaluation process projected new classifications within and across disciplinary boundaries, inscribing new collective (institutional and subject-wide) and personal identities: 'research active/inactive', and 'A, B or C' rated research activity.

Framing refers to 'the locus of control over pedagogic communication and its context' (Bernstein 2000, 6). Pedagogic communication is any 'sustained process whereby somebody(s) acquires new forms or develops existing forms of conduct, knowledge, practice and criteria from somebody(s) or something deemed to be an appropriate provider and evaluator (Bernstein 2000, 78). As teachers, supervisors, reviewers, examiners etc, academics are 'providers and evaluators'. When we write theses, submit articles for review, learn new technologies, or submit Evidence Portfolios to a PBRF panel we are also acquirers of new forms of conduct, knowledge, practice and criteria. Framing is strong when the locus of control is towards the transmitter and weak when the locus of control is toward the acquirer. The PBRF requirement that individuals produce and submit an Evidence Portfolio is an example of strong framing, its format, content, length and style being strictly prescribed by the transmitter. Designed to be *formative* in the sense of raising institutional (and personal) levels of research productivity, the PBRF can usefully be seen in Bernstein's sense of a *pedagogic device*.

Professional identities are constructed *by* us and *for* us. Academics locate or position our work and ourselves in relation to epistemological classifications of disciplines or fields. A sense of belonging is nurtured in allegiances to learned societies, conferences, and journals: professional identity formation involves intellectual, inter-personal and psychological processes of identification. We *identify* as educational psychologists, science educators, etc. Such personal affinities intersect in complex, and sometimes contradictory, ways with the financial and administrative categories whereby institutions allocate students to programs, distribute resources to departments, and locate bodies in buildings. Bernstein refers to identifications as *sacred or profane* – sacred describing inward (introjected) relations to knowledge, and profane an outward (projected) orientation towards economic, political or institutional imperatives.

As an academic subject, Education did not emerge until the twentieth century. However, the earlier social sciences and humanities disciplines (particularly history, philosophy, psychology and, later, sociology) would later form its foundations. In the Western world, the nineteenth century saw the development and classification of knowledge into distinct scientific or humanities subjects, and their organisation into self-regulating communities. Bernstein termed these *singulars*: 'A discourse as a singular is a discourse which has appropriated a space to give itself a unique name … And the structure of knowledge in the 19th century was, in fact, the birth and development of singulars' (Bernstein 2000, 9). The epistemological, professional, administrative and social cohesion of singulars was tight (strong classification): 'Organisationally and politically, singulars construct strong boundary maintenance' (Bernstein 2000, 54). Culturally (in professional associations, networks and writing) and psychologically (in students, teachers, researchers), 'singulars develop strong autonomous self-sealing and narcissistic identities. These identities are constructed by procedures of *introjection*' (Bernstein 2000, 54).

Each singular (physics, history, psychology, etc.) functioned as a *pedagogic device,* regulating the transmission, and criteria for access to, and evaluation of, its knowledge base. Membership of disciplines requires mastery of 'three interrelated rules: distributive rules, recontextualising rules and evaluative rules' (Bernstein 2000, 114). The *distributive rules* 'specialise access to *fields* where the production of new knowledge may legitimately take place' (Bernstein 2000, 114). Distributive rules determine whose, or what, research counts as legitimate, who qualifies for degrees, which articles are relevant to journals. They also 'mark and distribute who may transmit what to whom and under what conditions' (Bernstein 2000, 31) – who may supervise or examine, review, edit, or be on a panel. In short, distributive rules 'specialise forms of knowledge, forms of consciousness and forms of practice to social groups' (Bernstein 2000, 28).

Recontextualising rules regulate the work of the discipline's teachers – those who constitute its *Pedagogic Recontextualising Field* (PRF). The pedagogic recontextualising field produces textbooks, curricula, examination criteria and standards. The knowledge produced by researchers and theorists 'passes through ideological screens as it becomes its new form, pedagogic discourse' (Bernstein 2000, 115). Recontextualising knowledge for teaching involves selection, translation, and filtering: emerging as a syllabus for 'physics 101' or 'sociology 300' etc. In the late nineteenth century, the establishment of state funded and regulated education systems established *Official Pedagogic Recontextualising Fields (ORF)* 'created and dominated by the state for the construction and surveillance of state pedagogic discourse' (Bernstein 2000, 115). Emanating from the *ORF,* the PBRF rewards contributions to the knowledge base (laboratory science, field work, theoretical writing), but not the production of its teaching texts, especially those used in schools. The recontextualising activities needed to reproduce and advance a discipline are devalued.

As a pedagogic device, the PBRF recontextualises government policies: they are summarised, translated, and operationalised in handbooks, manuals, pro-forma, and seminars. Like any pedagogic practice, these are 'there for one purpose: to transmit criteria' (Bernstein 2000, 28). They define the system's *evaluative rules* and 'provide for acquirers the principles for the production of what counts as the legitimate text. The legitimate text is *any* realisation on the part of the acquirer which attracts evaluation' (Bernstein 2000, xiv). The production of legitimate texts is a hallmark of academic life – essays, theses, journal articles, curriculum vitae, or promotion applications require mastery of recognition, realisation and evaluation rules. Recognition rules help identify contexts – a sociology class, faculty meeting, psychology journal, Evidence Portfolio, etc. Realisation rules enable textual production – written, spoken, visual etc. It is possible to recognise a context, but lack the realisation rule needed to speak or write its texts.

Bernstein argues that those working in a field of knowledge may feel 'threatened by a change in its classificatory relation, or by an unfavourable change in the economic context' (Bernstein 2000, 203). From the mid- to late twentieth century, Educationists experienced continual shifts in the classification and framing of their subject/s, and these reconfigured the constraints and possibilities for collective and individual identity formation.

2. The subject/s of Education: a brief history

The twentieth century saw the formation of interdisciplinary, or applied, fields situated at 'the interface between the field of the production of knowledge and any field of practice' (Bernstein 2000, 9). Bernstein termed these *regions*. In its formative years as a university subject, Education exemplified a region. A region 'is created by a recontextualising of singulars' according to a 'recontextualising principle as to which singulars are to be selected, what knowledge within the singular is to be introduced and related' (Bernstein 2000, 9). Culturally (in professional associations, networks and writing) and psychologically (in students, teachers, researchers), 'identities produced by the new regions are more likely to face outwards to fields of practice and thus their contents are likely to be dependent on the requirements of those fields' (Bernstein 2000, 54).

The classification and framing of Education as a region in New Zealand was influenced by American and British trends and, well into the 1970s and 1980s, Education staff often gained higher degrees in those countries (Middleton 1989; Philips et al. 1989). By the 1960s and 1970s, Education in universities was strongly influenced by the British pattern. There the nature of Education as a subject had been negotiated by a group of senior Education Professors (the pedagogic recontextualising field) and Ministry officials (official pedagogic recontextualising field) (McCulloch 2002; Richardson 2002). In British universities there were to be four core Education disciplines: sociology of education, philosophy of education, history of education and educational psychology each rooted in its 'parent' discipline (singular), establishing its own journals, conferences and networks (McCulloch 2002). Staff and students sometimes identified with the parent discipline, writing for its conferences and journals rather than for its educational derivative. This encouraged 'inward' looking, narcissistic, or introjected, collective and personal identities.

Education's story is one of ambiguity as a (sometimes low status) university subject and as part of a non-degree teachers' college qualification. As in Britain, 'two types of mud would stick: university teacher training is too academic and it is not academic enough' (Richardson 2002, 40). Education's academic components (sub-disciplines) were intended as complementary components of 'a pluralist vision of educational studies that sought to draw on a wide range of human knowledge and experience' (McCulloch 2002, 103). While the foundation Education disciplines were taught in universities, teacher education's professional dimensions were relegated to the 'methods' components taught in teachers' colleges. The opportunity was lost to 'bridge the academic concerns of the universities and professional concerns of the colleges as well as to diminish the artificial separation of "theory" and "practice", widespread in the outlook of teachers' (Richardson 2002, 19). The epistemological split between academic (discipline-based) and applied (professional/practicum) components was configured by a segmentation of courses taught in university Education departments and courses developed for teaching diplomas in colleges. College curriculum departments focused on the learning and teaching of specific school curriculum subjects. Colleges also had their own Education Departments. College students were not always qualified to take university Education courses, but those who were often did degree units in Education concurrently with college diploma courses. While research was a requirement for university Education staff, it was not for those in colleges of Education, although a few college staff voluntarily engaged in such activities (Middleton 2007).

From the early 1960s, the introduction of Bachelor of Education degrees in universities involved some college staff in degree teaching. College and university staff taught in teams; college staff enrolled in qualifications supervised by university colleagues. Joint research projects emerged. It was usually staff in colleges' Education (rather than curriculum) departments who were in such close relationships. An interviewee noted, 'That still persists. The Education people have more contact with the university'.

The interface of university-based Education with college-based teacher education encouraged porous boundaries between its sub-disciplines: 'a weakening of the strength of the classification of discourses and their entailed narcissistic identities and so a change or orientation of identity towards greater external dependency: a change from introjected to projected identities' (Bernstein 2000, 115). This reorientation became increasingly evident during the unrest of the 1970s when new socio-political movements challenged dominant classifications of knowledge and the emergence of trans-disciplinary fields: curriculum theory, comparative education, Māori education, women's and gender studies. National associations for *educational* research, with generic journals and conferences, were established in Britain (BERA) (Furlong 2004), Australia (AARE) (Yates 2005) and New Zealand (NZARE). Encouraged by funding opportunities from governments, 'educational research was increasingly advanced as a unitary and autonomous kind of study in its own right' (McCulloch 2002, 101).

During the 1990s, government zeal for market-driven tertiary education (Devine 2005; Peters 1997) saw degrees introduced in polytechnics, colleges of education and the new Māori institutions, wānanga. The 1989 Education Act (New Zealand Government 1989) defined the characteristics of the various types of TEO and established a New Zealand Qualifications Authority (NZQA) responsible for approval and monitoring of degrees outside the university sector. Colleges of education and polytechnics, quick to take this opportunity, set up three-year Bachelor of Teaching degrees, which undercut the more expensive four-year university-approved qualifications taught jointly by university and college staff. With government now refusing to fund a fourth year, universities shortened their qualifications. Teacher education's theoretical components were drastically reduced and falling enrolments in social science and humanities faculties threatened the viability of Education as a major for these students. The dominance of the 'disciplines of education' classification (regions) was over.

The Education Act ruled that NZQA could award degree status only to qualifications 'taught mainly by people engaged in research' (section 254(3)(a)). College and polytechnic degree teachers, not previously required to be research-active, were pressured to re-invent themselves as researchers (Fergusson 1999): 'NZQA pointed their finger at me at the degree approval process and said, "you have to get a doctorate"'. The Act defined colleges of education as 'characterised by teaching and research required for the pre-school, compulsory and post-compulsory sectors of education, and for associated social and service roles' (section 162(4)(b)(ii)). College staff's service roles included contributions to pedagogic recontextualising fields in the teaching profession – writing national curricula or textbooks for schools. Would these 'count' as research? Many 'felt vulnerable in the presence of people who already had their masters or their doctorates and wanted to validate their classroom experience'. The reclassification of college staff as researchers challenged Education's distribution rules: 'after individuals outside the field of production create new knowledge, the field's principles will operate as to whether such knowledge is incorporated into the field' (Bernstein 2000, 115). As with its Australian counterpart (AARE), the NZARE 'focussed more on processes of support and development ... than on setting hurdles and sanctions for who can be an education researcher and what can count as education research' (Yates 2005, 3).

From the 1990s, amalgamations of teachers' colleges with universities intensified pressures towards research activity. Unlike the college degrees, university degrees were not subject to NZQA's authority. The Education Act characterised universities as 'primarily concerned with more advanced learning, the principal aim being to develop intellectual independence' (Section 162(4)(a)(i)). Universities' academic freedom was mandatory: they 'accept a role as critic and conscience of society' (Section 162(4)(a)(v)). Universities' 'research and teaching are closely interdependent and most of their teaching is done by people who are active in advancing knowledge' (Section 162(4)(a)(ii)). Once a former college was amalgamated into a university to form a School/Faculty of Education, would 'advancing knowledge' include the former college service roles?

Amalgamations required geographical shifts of staff. University Education department staff moved out of social science or humanities blocks in their universities and into former college buildings. For both groups, these physical, organisational, and interpersonal changes provoked insecurity and anxiety: 'Status or lack of status became an extremely important personal feeling. We would feel like we didn't have the status that the people from the [university] Education Department had'. A curriculum specialist said: 'It was very fraught. The academics who had to come across, I didn't know who they were. They didn't resonate with my department. I was always aware that I was not one of the academics'. Another had been employed as 'a good curriculum practitioner' and experienced 'a big tension between who I am and what I do as a good subject specialist and the other profile we have to have in the university, which is to publish'. Conversely, a lecturer with a doctorate was marginalised by her new curriculum department's lack of research culture: 'research was something that was done by certain august persons, but the people on the ground floor just taught'.

As a pedagogical device, the PBRF's research assessment exercise is a site of 'struggle to produce and institutionalise particular identities' (Bernstein 2000, 66). Before its introduction, some self-identified as 'researchers', but others chose: 'curriculum leader', 'intellectual', 'activist-writer', 'poet and literary critic', 'musical director/conductor' etc., illustrating Bernstein's claim that 'the analysis of identity within institutional levels' may conflict with 'the analysis of projected official identities at the level of the state' (2000, 52). Interviewees' 'internal' professional identities fell into three main categories. 'The academics' were familiar with, and comfortable in, a university research culture. 'Curriculum staff' were former college of education staff whose contracts had not previously required research and who had prioritised 'service roles' to the teaching profession. 'Researching professionals' were those whose identities bridged boundaries between academic and curriculum. They had usually worked in college Education departments, and regarded new imperatives to research as an opportunity to upgrade qualifications, teach degree courses, and identify as researchers. The academics, the curriculum staff and the researching professionals were affected by the PBRF in different ways.

3. Producing the legitimate text: the PBRF experience

As a pedagogic device, research assessment acts as: 'a symbolic ruler, ruling consciousness, in the sense of having power over it, and ruling in the sense of measuring the legitimacy of the realisations of consciousness' (Bernstein 2000, 114). Citing the Education Act's requirement that NZQA-authorised degrees be taught mainly by those engaged in research (Boston 2006), it projected the identity 'researcher'. It classified research (by subjects) and researchers (as research active or inactive; and as of A, B or C quality) and ranked collective performances of subjects and institutions. It transmitted criteria for the production of the legitimate text (Evidence Portfolio). To produce a legitimate EP 'acquirers' must internalise the category's recognition rules (what counts as research) and realisation rules (to have carried out the research and published). They must recontextualise outputs in the mandated format, positioning themselves in 'internal command economies of disciplinary repute, professional prestige, and administrative allocation' (Luke 1997, 54).

Internal self-definitions of academics rated 'A' or 'B' were consistent with the projected (external) identity 'researcher'. Having published in high status journals, supervised and examined theses, and been cited in the works of peers, they experienced PBRF's requirements as affirming existing internal identities: 'I felt fairly relaxed about what they were asking. I had more than fifty publications. I didn't have a problem selecting my best four pieces and writing about my influences on the field'. A 'B-rated' researcher, whose publications received little departmental acknowledgement, 'was very pleased they did the PBRF because that was the first time that people focused on that aspect of my work and valued it'.

Some used the exercise as a career scaffold: 'I've begun to realise what you had to do to get through the hoops and this exercise makes it even more transparent. They have laid out in three categories the sorts of things you should be doing in research, which is what's being valued in terms of promotion'. Compiling an EP helped them acquire recognition and realisation rules: 'I was aware that there were agreed benchmarks or categories in terms of which I could reflect on my progress. So I found it a valuable exercise in terms of where I might project myself in future'. Reporting 'contributions to the research environment' (CRE) and 'evidence of peer esteem' (PE) was reassuring:

> When I first looked at the peer esteem section I thought, 'My God, what goes in there? What on earth does that mean?' Not having ever won any medals! Then I started to say, 'Well, I could put this in and that in.' By the time I had finished I had quite a list. That was quite satisfying.

The experience helped them decode the mysteries of academic culture, as in a department 'where there weren't a lot of conversations going on about where we stood in respect to one another. We often just don't know where we stand'. It offered: 'an abstract set of benchmarks ... something that had been agreed nationally to think about'. A former college Education department lecturer found her EP:

> quite affirming because the funny thing about where we work is you don't really know how you are getting on. It is individualistic; it is competitive. We might work in research teams, but our promotions are individual and you don't know how you match up with anyone else.

It helped some participants identify the recognition rules for the quality categories and to pitch EPs accordingly: 'Because they had the descriptors of the C and B and A there, I actually kept those in mind, and I tried to write it above what it was'. The criteria for 'A-ness' offered another informant an indication of 'what professors actually do'.

But those who had not 'done research', but may have proud records of advancing knowledge through 'service roles', inevitably fared poorly. A curriculum specialist 'felt that we shouldn't have been involved. I felt bad about the time I spent doing it when I knew I wasn't going to have any effect at all and when I knew there was no research as part of my contract. I felt I was bringing down the grades of the School of Education through no fault of my own'. She grasped the recognition rule and knew that, to continue working in what had been reclassified as a university, (no longer a college), position, she needed to develop research expertise. Accordingly, she had completed her masters, which 'did not count'. Through no fault of her own, she was unable to 'speak the required legitimate text' (Bernstein 2000, 17).

The quality evaluation classified, ranked and ordered individuals' 'research outputs' on a scale that 'echoes everyone's experiences of schooling' (Web Research 2004, 203). One academic said: 'The way it's scaled A, B, C means that most people are going to come out looking mediocre, even though they may be very active researchers'. A curriculum expert felt 'very belittled by that whole process. I feel I came in as a good banana and now I am a half pie apple… I've had a lot of depression, feeling not good enough anymore for this place'. A curriculum leader said, 'When you've got a score like "research inactive", it suggests that you're not doing anything. And you've been socialised to have a strong work ethic'. A senior lecturer with a record of successful Ministry curriculum contracts resented the fact that: 'that's not counted as research, all the masses of writing and stuff in the exemplars I've put together!'.

The workforce in Education is largely middle-aged (Crothers 2005). The reclassification of experienced and successful practitioners as 'inactive' meant that many 'experienced what is, to some a sense of crisis and loss. Cherished identities and commitments have been undermined and, for some, this has been experienced as an assault on their professionalism' (Beck and Young 2005, 184). Changing classifications of knowledge, and knowledge-workers, have psychological consequences for the formation and maintenance of professional identities. Maintaining one's self-identification might involve resisting official reclassification:

> Within the individual, the insulation becomes a system of psychic defences against the possibility of the weakening of the insulation, which would then reveal the suppressed contradictions, cleavages and dilemmas. So the internal reality of insulation is a system of psychic defences, to maintain the integrity of the category. (Bernstein 2000, 17)

Some older ex-college staff were emotionally unaffected by their new labels. A curriculum leader completed his doctorate just before retirement and held on to his self-identification as a researcher despite PBRF's rating of him as Research Inactive: 'it didn't matter whether they thought I was a researcher or not. I was a researcher'. Others continued to prioritise teacher-education's 'social and service roles':

> In curriculum, many of us regard the national network as the people we need to reach in our research. And that's who we write articles for, and that's who we do workshops with, and that's why we 'be the University moderator' for bursary exams. They're big jobs. And it just doesn't count, but it's *what we do* in professional education.

Personal (internal), as well as official (external), professional identities are highly volatile: these 'identifications are never fully made; they are incessantly reconstituted and, as such, are subject to the volatile logic of iterability' (Butler 1993, 105). Waiting to see if the provisional scores allocated by employing TEOs would be confirmed by the PBRF panel was worrying: 'I became very anxious as to whether I was going to retain the C that I'd gone in as, so there was a period of anxiety wondering whether my EP was good enough'. Some experienced a raise in grade. One former college staff member, whose provisional C was raised to a B, said: 'Because I got a good result, it's boosted my confidence, made me feel, "Yes I can do this"'. Another expressed 'anger that my own University had underestimated me and that it had taken outsiders to fix it up'. Some experienced downgrading. Identifying herself as a 'curriculum leader', one teacher-educator's 'service roles' had included chief examiner of a senior high school examination, writer of a national curriculum, and editor of a professional journal for teachers. Her TEO rated her: 'C, research active. I was happy with that. I thought, "I'm on the continuum, coming along quite nicely". And then, when I found that I was adjudged research inactive, I was very hurt and I felt very disempowered'.

Interviews were done at a time when Education's low subject ranking was attracting negative publicity, and institutional and individual identities and priorities realigned. In historically teaching-only institutions, novice researchers found themselves charged with research leadership: 'I am a C, but I am seen as a person that's going to assist in driving a research culture'. In another TEO, management organised meetings where staff felt 'beaten around the head to get started on research! They were telling everybody to go out and be researchers. But the people giving the message themselves aren't researchers'.

The imperative to research for *all* degree teachers was described as counter-productive for teacher education: 'My appraisals were reinforcing initially the service component to go out to schools and conferences. They are now very clearly saying, "Stop doing that, start doing more formal work with what you're thinking and writing". It's a big change and partly that's PBRF driven'. The PBRF was described as: 'an uncomfortable sort of reminder at the back of most things now, around the university. There's pressure to do things that are "PBRF-able"'. Some spoke of a new self-consciousness, 'which occasionally takes the form of self parody like, "Gee, that could earn you a few brownie points"'. Taking on institutional service roles (head of department etc.) might get in the way of research productivity (Ministry of Education 2005); 'The PBRF creates quite selfish careers. If you're going to be successful in that exercise then it's for yourself – not having a commitment to the department'. There was a more calculating attitude to publication: 'it has sharpened my focus to be smart and strategic about both where I publish, how I choose, and who I choose to publish with'. A young academic, aspiring for an A, would no longer consider local journals: 'I went to the Web of Science, looked up the journals that had the highest rating or ranking in terms of Education, and thought, "Right. The next article that I submit, I am going to submit it to this highest ranking journal"'. Although confidentiality of individuals' scores is protected in policy it was not always in fact (Web Research 2004). Positioning recipients as commodities of economic value, good scores are being used in promotion, job and grant applications (Ashcroft 2005); as currency in the 'accumulation of a symbolic capital of external renown' (Bourdieu 1988, 98).

4. What PBRF 'does' to Education

At the time of writing (November 2006), research assessment in Britain and Australia is under review (Adams and Smith 2006; Sheehan 2006) and New Zealand's PBRF concluding its second (but partial) round (allowing exemption for those who scored well in 2003 and who wish to retain their grade until its regular six-year cycle completes in 2012). A new category for beginning researchers has been added. All degree staff are still required to participate and this will perpetuate the systemic bias against Education and similar professional credentialing subjects (nursing, social work, etc.). As with Britain's RAE, it 'preserves structural relations between social groups but changes structural relations between individuals' (Bernstein 2000, xxiv).

Historically, university Education staff identified 'inwards' to foundation disciplines (e.g. sociology or history of education), to interdisciplinary curriculum subject communities (e.g. science education), or, later, as educational researchers more generically. The classification and framing of the four-year degrees jointly taught by university and college staff (but granted by universities) in the 1960s–90s was based on epistemological, administrative and institutional divisions of labour between Education, curriculum and practicum staff, encouraging advancement of knowledge in multiple forms – theoretical, empirical, professional and practical. Policy-makers' enthusiasm for market-forces in the 1990s led to a proliferation of shorter, cheaper NZQA-accredited teaching degrees outside universities, the reduction of theoretical/disciplinary Education studies, dispersion of the research funding 'top-up' that accompanied degree enrolments under the EFTS model, and reclassification of polytechnic and college staff as researchers. Policy-makers and university managers hoped that the PBRF would offer 'a means of securing additional public resources for New Zealand's universities and in a manner that would help protect, if not increase, the degree of institutional and sectoral differentiation' (Boston 2006, 6).

This drives a wedge through professional subjects previously spread across different types of TEO, but now university degree programmes in their own right. Education's dissonance between the identities 'teacher-educator' and 'researcher', evident before the PBRF, remains and is intensifying. The PBRF projects onto all degree staff the external identity 'researcher', citing the Education Act's benchmark for NZQA-approved degrees (section 254(3)(a); see also Boston 2006). However, the Act also contains a broader definition of university teachers as 'active in advancing knowledge' (Section 162(4)(a)(ii)), a description that better accommodates the 'service roles' mandated for colleges of education (section 162(4)(b)(ii)), and now a requirement for University-based teacher education. If the system allowed honourable exemptions for clinical/practicum teachers (alternative identities), and if these were reported as 'exempt' (rather than 'failures') in league tables, Education's status would be raised.

As a pedagogical device, the PBRF is politically charged, and 'the group who appropriates the device has access to a ruler and distributor of consciousness, identity and desire' (Bernstein 2000, 202). The peer review systems of pedagogic recontextualising fields are harnessed to the state's official recontextualising field: 'Today the state is attempting to weaken the PRF through its ORF, and thus attempting to reduce relative autonomy over the construction of pedagogic discourse and over its social contexts' (Bernstein 2000, 33). Official recontextualising fields are 'arenas for the construction, distribution, reproduction and change of pedagogic identities … A pedagogic identity, then, is the embedding of a career in a social base' (Bernstein 2000, 62). Projected official identities are internalised as career aspirations: 'I can aspire towards the A research category. It is personal ambition. It has become something I can aim for'. Numerical scores signify, or reify, identity: 'Getting the Cs to Bs' or 'I'm an A'.

This has implications for academic freedom. New Zealand's Education Act requires universities, and their staff, to develop intellectual independence and to 'accept a role as critic and conscience of society' (section 162(4)(a)(v)). Determining academic priorities according to an external agenda, in order to 'get an A' or 'be classified as research active' marks a shift away from intellectual autonomy. Summarising Bernstein, Beck and Young (2005, 184) write:

> For generations, such identities had centred, he suggested, in a particular kind of humane relationship to *knowledge* – a relationship that was centred in what he termed 'inwardness' and 'inner dedication.' And it was this that was now most profoundly threatened by the rising tide of marketisation, external regulation, and an 'audit culture.'

And this is what the first quality evaluation round of New Zealand's PBRF 'did' to the subject/s of Education.

Notes

1. A capital E is used when referring to Education as a field of study in order to avoid confusion with education as a system or process.

References

Adams, J., and D. Smith. 2006. Evaluation of the British Research Assessment Exercise. In *Evaluation of the Performance Based Research Fund,* ed. J. Bakker, J. Boston, L. Campbell, and R. Smyth, 109–17. Wellington: Institute of Policy Studies, Victoria University of Wellington.
Ashcroft, C. 2005. Performance Based Research Funding: A mechanism to allocate funds or a tool for academic promotion? *New Zealand Journal of Educational Studies* 40, nos. 1 & 2: 113–29.
Beck, J., and M.F.D. Young. 2005. The assault on the professions and the restructuring of academic and professional identities: A Bernsteinian analysis. *British Journal of Sociology of Education* 26, no. 2: 183–97.
Bernstein, B. 2000. *Pedagogy, symbolic control and identity: Theory, research, critique.* Lanham, MA: Rowman and Littlefield.
Boston, J. 2004. *The future of the Performance-based Research Fund: Issues and options.* Paper presented at the PBRF Forum, Royal Society of New Zealand, May 21, in Wellington.
Boston, J. 2006. Rationale for the Performance-Based Research Fund: Personal reflections. In *Evaluating the Performance-Based Research Fund: Framing the debate,* ed. J. Bakker, J. Boston, L. Campbell, and R. Smyth, 5–31. Wellington: Institute of Policy Studies, Victoria University of Wellington.
Bourdieu, P. 1988. *Homo academicus.* Trans. P. Collier. Cambridge: Polity Press.
Butler, J. 1993. *Bodies that matter.* New York and London: Routledge.
Codd, J. 2006. The Performance-Based Research Fund and the production and commodification of knowledge. In *Evaluating the Performance-Based Research Fund: Framing the debate,* ed. J. Bakker, J. Boston, L. Campbell, and R. Smyth, 215-30. Wellington: Institute of Policy Studies, Victoria University of Wellington.
Croll, P. 2003. Editorial: The Roberts review and the RAE. *British Journal of Educational Studies* 51, no. 3: 199–201.
Crothers, C. 2005. 'Inside' education: An assessment of this discipline under the PBRF. In *Punishing the disciplines - the PBRF regime: Evaluating the position of Education – where to from here?,* ed. R. Smith and J. Jesson, 124–61. Wellington: New Zealand Association for Research in Education and New Zealand Council for Educational Research.
Devine, N. 2005. *Education and public choice.* Westport, CT: Praeger.
Dreyfus, H.L., and P. Rabinow. 1982. *Michel Foucault: Beyond structuralism and hermeneutics.* Chicago: Harvester.
Education Panel, P.B.R.F. 2004. *Report of the Education Panel.* Wellington: Tertiary Education Commission.
Fergusson, P.B. 1999. *Developing a research culture in a polytechnic: An action research case study.* Unpublished Ph. D., University of Waikato, Hamilton, New Zealand.
Furlong, J. 2004. BERA at 30: Have we come of age? *British Educational Research Journal* 30, no. 3: 343–58.
Henkel, M. 2005. Academic identity and autonomy in a changing policy environment. *Higher Education* 49: 155–76.
Luke, T. 1997. Thinking about cultural politics in the university. In *Cultural politics in the university in Aotearoa/ New Zealand,* ed. M. Peters, 51–65. Palmerston North: The Dunmore Press.
McCulloch, G. 2002. Disciplines contributing to education? Educational studies and the disciplines. *British Journal of Educational Studies* 50, no. 1: 100–19.
Middleton, S. 1989. American influences in the sociology of New Zealand education 1944-1988. In *The impact of American ideas on New Zealand's educational policy, practice and thinking,* ed. D. Philips, G. Lealand, and G. McDonald, 50–69. Wellington: The NZ–US Educational Foundation in association with the New Zealand Council for Educational Research.
———. 2005. Disciplining the subject: The impact of PBRF on Education academics. *New Zealand Journal of Educational Studies* 40, nos. 1–2: 131-55.
———. 2007. The place of theory: Locating the New Zealand 'Education' PhD experience. *British Journal of Sociology of Education* 28, no. 1: 69–87.
Ministry of Education. 2002. *Tertiary Education Strategy 2002-07.* Wellington: New Zealand Ministry of Education.

Ministry of Education. 2005. *What determines the research performance of staff in New Zealand's tertiary education sector? An analysis of the Performance-Based Research Fund Quality Evaluation.* Wellington: New Zealand Ministry of Education.

Morgan, K.J. 2004. The research assessment exercise in English universities, 2001. *Higher Education* 48: 461-82.

New Zealand Government. 1989. *Education Act.* Wellington: New Zealand Government.

Performance Based Research Fund. 2004. *Evaluating Research Excellence: The 2003 Assessment.* Wellington: Tertiary Education Commission.

Peters, M., ed. (1997). *Cultural politics and the university.* Palmerston North: The Dunmore Press.

Philips, D., G. Lealand, and G. McDonald, eds. 1989. *The impact of American ideas on New Zealand's educational policy, practice and thinking.* Wellington: The NZ–US Educational Foundation in association with the New Zealand Council for Educational Research.

Richardson, W. 2002. Educational studies in the United Kingdom, 1940–2002. *British Journal of Educational Studies,* 50, no. 1: 3–56.

Sheehan, P. 2006. A perspective on the proposed Australian Research Quality Framework. In *Evaluating the Performance-Based Research Fund: Framing the debate,* ed. J. Bakker, J. Boston, L. Campbell, and R. Smyth, 109–17. Wellington: Institute of Policy Studies, Victoria University of Wellington.

Tertiary Education Commission. 2003. *Performance-Based Research Fund: A guide for 2003.* Wellington: Tertiary Education Commission.

Web Research. 2004. *Phase 1 evaluation of the implementation of the PBRF and the conduct of the 2003 quality evaluation.* Wellington: Centre for Research on Work, Education and Business Ltd.

Yates, L. 2005. Is impact a measure of quality? Producing quality research and producing quality indicators of research in Australia, Keynote address to the Australian Association for Research in Education Focus Conference on 'Quality in educational research: Directions and practice', July 5–6, in Cairns.

Kindness in pedagogical practice and academic life

Sue Clegg[a] and Stephen Rowland[b]

[a]Centre for Research into Higher Education, Carnegie Research Institute, Leeds Metropolitan University, Cavendish Hall, Leeds LS6 3QS, UK; [b]Higher Education, University College London and Institute of Education, London University, London, UK

The paper presents the argument that kindness in teaching is both commonplace yet unremarked and that, moreover, it is subversive of neo-liberal values. In arguing for the value of attending to kindness, we reject the dichotomy between emotion and reason and the associated gendered binaries. We distinguish kindness from 'due care' and acts that are required of professionals, and instead locate it philosophically in personal values and with a concern for lay normativity. We illustrate our claims for the pervasiveness of kindness through a re-reading of student data from an earlier study. These data are used to elaborate the concept. We conclude by suggesting that what is subversive in thinking about higher education practice through the lens of kindness is that it cannot be regulated or prescribed.

On kindness

Writing about kindness in pedagogical settings, particularly in higher education, which tends to be conceptualised in overly cognitive terms, might seem perverse. As Lynch, Baker, and Lyons (2009) argue, in their work on affective equality, education is a paradigm case of the celebration of a narrow conceptualisation of reason to the exclusion of other human qualities. The impact of Cartesian rationalism runs deep (Grummell, Devine, and Lynch 2009) not only in the practice of education that privileges mathematical and linguistic reasoning and technical rationality, but also in academic and in particular sociological accounts of education. Sayer (2005) argues that the splitting of the 'positive' in social theory from the 'normative', which has historically been the preserve of moral philosophy, results in sociology sidestepping what he calls lay normativity. He argues:

Lay normativity should be taken seriously precisely because it matters to people, and it matters to them because it is about things that seriously affect their well being. The struggles of the social field, between different groups, classes, genders and ethnicities, certainly involve habitual action and the pursuit of power, but they also have a range of normative rationales, which matter greatly to actors, as they are implicated in their commitments, identities and ways of life (Sayer 2005, 6)

The sociology of higher education has been quick to analyse the struggles of the field – audit, mass education, academic capitalism – but this has tended to bracket out normative matters such as kindness. We want to argue, however, that although kindness is a commonplace in pedagogical encounters, easily recognisable by its presence or absence, attending to it can be subversive of neo-liberal assumptions that place value on utility and cost above other human values. Our paper then connects sociological and philosophical arguments and explores what might count as a good – contra to most sociological accounts, which have a penchant for talking about the bad (Sayer 2005, 10).

Students readily see kindness as a mark of the good teacher and yet the concept of kindness is singularly silent in accounts of teaching 'excellence' (Skelton 2007), student satisfaction (NSS 2010) or professional values (HEA 2010). We are not claiming that this is a new way of theorising about teaching. Rather, we are seeking to elucidate a quality that is already there in good teaching, but is unremarked and under threat in the contemporary conditions of higher education. There are good reasons for understanding kindness to be a natural predisposition, part of what counts in being human (Archer 2000). The word 'kind' has the same etymological roots as 'kin', 'kindred' (family) and 'kind' ('type'). This is suggestive of a natural relationship of kindness between members of the same family, group or species. The *Shorter Oxford English Dictionary* (2007 edition) gives the first definition of 'kindly' as 'existing or occurring according to the laws of nature', thus implying that kindness is natural capacity. Stoic philosophy celebrated the natural order as a basis of its ethics. Thus the Roman Emperor Marcus Aurelius, a leading Stoic philosopher, speaks of kindness as 'mankind's [*sic*] greatest delight' (Philips and Taylor 2009, 18). There are a number of closely related conceptualisations such as 'respect', as understood by Richard Sennett (2002), and a rich tradition of feminist thinking about ethics stretching back to Carol Gilligan's (1982) pioneering work 'in a different voice', which challenged research on moral reasoning based on male as norm. She controversially argued that women's forms of moral argumentation relied more on the relational and contextual. In education, Noddings (2005a, 2005b, 2010) has developed an extensive analysis of caring and argued for the practice of a phenomenology of care that embodies a relational view of care containing both the carer and the cared-for, which she characterises as an 'ethic of relation'. Such an ethic, she argues, is not anti-intellectual but is as much a mark of personhood as rationality. Lynch, Baker, and Lyons (2009) have similarly developed a highly elaborated concept of nurturing capital and the importance of 'love, care, solidarity' for human flourishing and equality. While Lynch, Baker, and Lyons (2009) have concentrated largely on the multi-dimensional work involved in 'love, care, solidarity', including the sorts of physical care that are usually associated with the notion of care, our context concentrates on the relationship of care, or what we are calling kindness, to distinguish it from the broader contexts of caring. Kindness, care and respect are interrelated terms but we have found it productive to think about kindness as a way of traversing public and private concerns, and as a term particularly appropriate in thinking about teaching and academic life (Rowland, 2009). While Noddings argues 'It is sometimes said that "all teachers care". It is because they care that people go into teaching' (2010, 1), the same could not be claimed for university teachers – whose attachment to discipline have been widely documented (Henkel 2000). The challenge is to talk about kindness in university teaching without reducing the epistemological and knowledge dimensions (Young 2008) of learning simply to process, or to collapse, the distinction between the institution of the university and the school.

There are good reasons why it is timely to think about kindness. In their recent book *On Kindness*, psychoanalyst Adam Philips and feminist historian Barbara Taylor give an historical account of how we have come to under-value kindness in a social context in which people are fundamentally antagonistic towards each other (Philips and Taylor 2009). Moreover, many people have come to identify the financial 'crash' as a consequence of narrow competitive self-interest in the economic world, whose values have extended well beyond the world of finance. Writing in the *London Review of Books*, John Lanchester shows how the 'economic metaphor', which has come to apply to every aspect of modern life, including education, has failed. As a consequence, he says, 'we need to rediscover other sources of value' (Lanchester 2009, 13). Stephen Ball is among many writers identifying the general malaise of the audit culture and governmentality. Ball, drawing on Lyotard's (1984) 'report on knowledge' with its concept of the 'terrors of performativity', has analysed how a culture of surveillance and audit have led practitioners to 'find their values challenged or displaced by the terrors of performativity' (Ball 2003, 216). Kindness is one such displaced value. A love of knowledge and a concern for social justice are others.

Lynch, Baker, and Lyons (2009) have particularly remarked on the care-less-ness of academic life with its assumption that successful academics are 'care commanders' able to off-load their care needs and demands on others, mostly women, while they have time to write, network, engage in care-free travel and so on, a highly gendered but seemingly neutral set of work practices that ensure the continued male domination of the university hierarchy. It is unsurprising, therefore, that speaking (or writing) about kindness in the context of higher education brings about embarrassment. Such embarrassment signifies a transgression of accepted boundaries: what Mary Douglas (1966) calls 'matter out of place'. 'Kindness' is 'out of place' in talk about higher education, and higher education pedagogy. It can suggest a sentimental and unrigorous approach taking us into fields better addressed by therapy and as indicative of being focused on the relational at the expense of ideas. Work that considers higher education from anything other than a rationalist perspective is controversial (see Beard, Clegg, and Smith 2007; Leathwood and Hey 2009). Mortiboys (2002) notes that some commentators regard any recognition of emotions in learning as 'inappropriate territory'. Furedi (2004), in particular, has identified what he characterises as a 'therapy culture'. The subtitle of his book is 'cultivating vulnerability in an uncertain age' and his main argument is that therapeutic discourse creates dependencies. To talk of kindness, therefore, might seem to be vulnerable to this critique (see Clegg, Bradley, and Smith 2006). Ecclestone (2004a, 2004b) has used Furedi's ideas to caution against the adoption of ideas of a 'diminished-self' in education. Ecclestone, in particular, has argued that some feminist and radical critics (for example, Griffiths 2003; Hey 2003), by drawing on the themes of identity and self-esteem, are creating new ideas about pedagogy that create a therapeutic sensibility, replacing older humanist models of pedagogy. Ecclestone and Hayes' (2009) and Furedi's critiques, however, rest on a series of dualisms that place the emotions and values such as kindness on one side of the dualism and the intellect and ideas on the other, and depends on a philosophically thin account of what it means to be human, which ignores the primacy of practice and the emergent nature of both the intellect and affect (Archer 2000). These dualisms are of course inscribed in the gendered dualism of male and female that feminists have sought to deconstruct (for example, Paechter 2006) not, as Ecclestone assumes, reinscribe. Our intention in thinking about kindness in pedagogy and in academic life involves resisting these dualisms and entails a view of intellectual development which does not see cognitive capacity in opposition to the embodied and experiential (Ashworth 2004). Thus, as with Rowland's use of the concept of 'intellectual love' (Rowland 2008), kindness has as much to do with the cognitive as with the effective aspects of social action.

It is not surprising that kindness, as a virtue, has became associated with safety of domestic rather than working life, and thus feminised. Philips and Taylor demonstrate that kindness, which had previously played a central role in public morality, was displaced and downgraded as a consequence of industrialisation and the rise of Protestantism. By the early nineteenth century, it had become the prerogative of specific constituencies, such as clergymen, romantic poets and women (Philips and Taylor 2009, 41). A Victorian stereotype comes to mind of the middle-class father earning the income from the cut and thrust of industrial employment, while his wife keeps an atmosphere of kindness and safety in the home where children play (and learn) and to which the father returns for refreshment (Ehrenreich and English 1979). The nostalgic paintings of William Powell Frith (1819–1909) celebrate such domesticated kindness and its contrast with industrial energy. The relegation of the care to the private domain has profound consequences for understanding of law, citizenship and the economy, and thus in turn for education, which is understood as the preparation of students for the public life of work (Lynch, Baker, and Lyons 2009).

Such a gendered version of kindness underpins institutional ideals of teaching. In a study of the relationships between teaching and research, heads of department in a research-led university were asked what qualities they associated with successful teachers and researchers (Rowland 1996). Respondents typically mentioned 'drive', 'self-motivation', 'stickability', 'confidence' and the ability to 'go out into the world and get it' as typical of the successful researcher. Good teachers, in contrast, were represented by the more 'feminine' qualities of 'openness', 'care' and 'concern for students'. The distinction is redolent of the industrial and domestic worlds portrayed by Frith's paintings. Since 1996, when this study was reported, quality assurance systems have further transformed the 'domestic' space of teaching into the public space of work (Morley 2003). What has not changed is the denigration those very qualities associated with teaching, as Lynch, Lyons, and Cantillon argue in their paper *Breaking Silence*: 'the teachers role as an affective caring person is not attributed much significance, not least because the teacher is largely seen as a midwife for delivering student performance' (2007, 14), which is in turn subjugated to the needs of employment.

Kindness, however, extends beyond the private domestic sphere and is not limited to public performative function. There was nothing soft or domesticated about Aurelius's celebration of kindness as 'mankind's greatest delight'. In his Stoic philosophy, justice was natural and a consequence of the exercise of reason. As such it was the primary virtue to which kindness and the other virtues naturally contributed (Aurelius Antonius 167, para. IX). Kindness as a public virtue, built upon a commitment to social justice, embraces critique. In educational research the term 'critical friend' is used by action researchers to describe the relationship between co-enquirers (be they researchers or students) who share a commitment to social justice. It combines the kindness of friendship with the critique of the educator. Developed in relation to practitioner research in schools, by such writers as Elliott (1985), Carr and Kemmis (1986), its theoretical roots are traced back to the Frankfurt School of critical theory. Just as intellectual love can be seen to underlie the relationship between learner and subject matter (Rowland 2008), so might the opportunity for kindness be a significant dimension of educational relationships.

There is risk involved in not only writing about kindness, but in the kind act itself. The paradox of kindness is that it can lead to acts that by intention are kind but may involve misjudgement and harm to the others, paradoxically kindness therefore may involve regulation. Feeling kind is not enough. Intellectual judgements are involved and not just empathy. Empathy, understood as an affective interpersonal capacity, would limit acts of kindness to particular sorts of imaginary others. Kindness is not simply the projection of one's own needs and desires onto people who are in fact not like us and/or do not share our values, considerable rigour is entailed in working out what would be kind in relation to the realisation of the projects of others. Kindness shares an emphasis on the relational that Noddings (2005a) developed in her analysis of care. Kindness, therefore, requires the recognition of differential power and positionality, and a recognition of the projects of other people not just our own (Archer 2007). It also involves an understanding of the pain and difficulty that may be involved in realising projects particularly where the project under consideration here is pedagogical and involves learning and the mastery of new ways of understanding. Kindness does not dissolve the demands of knowledge. Meeting the needs of someone else is not at all straightforward. The kind teacher is not necessarily the one who receives the highest satisfaction ratings, but nor should we assume that we know what students need better than they do. Boswell's adage that 'the path to Hell is paved with good intentions' warns us that the kindness of a deed is not assured by kindly intentions alone.

The nature of the connection between kindness and teaching rests in the fact that both kindly acts and pedagogical acts require the actor to identify with the concerns of the other. This involves conceptualising teaching and the learning of students as irreducibly social (Ashworth 2004). In serving the needs of the student, the good teacher attempts to see things from the student's perspective. This is an essential prerequisite of kindness. An act is kind in an academic setting in as much as it is pedagogically sound, but thinking from the perspective of kindness involves more than instrumentality. To be a kind teacher involves more than just a technical judgement of utility. It imbues the act of teaching with particular qualities and values. One source of difficulty with kindness is its confusion with leniency. In wanting a kind teacher, the student may be confusing this with one who will be lenient, soft, prepared to overlook errors and shallowness of thought. In wanting to be kind, a teacher might not be motivated by the learner's needs but simply avoiding responsibility for the student's confrontation with the inevitable pain of learning. The confusion with leniency rests on seeing kindness as emotion and an elision with the ideology of romantic feminised safety analysed above (Philips and Taylor 2009).

There is also risk from another direction, however, of reducing kindness to performativity through the surveillance and regulation of the necessary emotional labour many organisations now require of many employees. As teaching performance becomes increasingly accountable, so the personal quality of kindness is replaced by more manageable routines of 'due care'. Student satisfaction surveys operationalise the measurement of the care the student-consumer has received, and staff performance is scrutinised through annual performance review. Demonstrating that one 'cares' about students is transformed into a performance indicator. Such performances are regulated in ways that reduce the risk to the organisation and protect it from acts of kindness that might go beyond the mechanical performance of duty. The legal concept of 'due care' and the associated business concept of 'due diligence' are attempts to avoid such difficulties by placing care within a set of professional requirements or standards. In the same vein, ethics committees attempt to simplify complex ethical judgement by the application of rules (Clegg 2007). The manifold practices of audit, managerialism and commercialisation, which are so well documented in the wider higher education literature, operate against the personal qualities of kindness that we have nonetheless described as commonplace. It would be a mis-reading of accounts of performativity, however, to see it as squeezing out all such human acts. Indeed, how otherwise would it be possible to account for the criticisms of the systems of surveillance that detract from meaning and pleasure of teaching and research? In her subtle account of research performativity, Hey (2004) analyses the pleasure to be derived through from research performance and the simultaneity of the recognition of both the pleasure and its traps. Lynch's (2010) analysis of carelessness in academic life rests on an understanding that we know what carefullness looks like and that we recognise its practice. Sayer's (2005) comments about the forms of sociological research are pertinent, because so little research has been undertaken on kindness and care or more broadly into lay normativity – those things that matter to us a human actors. Lynch, Baker, and Lyons' (2009) 'care conversations' provide ample evidence of the importance, value, and pleasure care involves and of the willingness of people to articulate their values contra to dominant utilitarianism and neo-liberalism's championing of markets. Similarly, we would argue, that kindness in the pedagogical context goes beyond any requirement of 'due care'. It involves the unpredictable judgements of students' needs. There is always a risk of misjudgement in pedagogical encounters, which by their nature are unpredictable and unstable. While one can, and should, be held to account for the exercise of due care, kindness is a quality for which one can only hold oneself to account and is based on different normative criteria from those of audit. The difference between being held to account and holding oneself to account is crucial. It involves alienation and responsibility. Only when holding the self to account is one acting with human agency and in terms of one's own and other's life projects (Archer 2000, 2007). It is, of course, important that teachers, doctors, and other public servants are held to account by the public they serve. The problem arises when this requirement leads to a substitution of a personal quality, kindness, by a public one, a duty of care. As teachers we are rightly held to account for exercising a duty of care to students, but the recognition of the mutual humanity of teacher and student involves holding the self to account in the exercise of kindness.

Our argument for kindness has so far been largely philosophical and from first principles. We have noted the obviousness of the kind teacher and the ways kindness cuts against perfomativity and instead insists on human values in the pedagogic encounter. We have also insisted that to talk of kindness involves public values as well as private and the exercise of the intellect as well as affect, and we have rejected the argument that to exercise kindness involves a therapeutic turn in teaching. We now want to illuminate our argument by turning to some data. These data were not collected with the aim of exploring a concept of kindness. Rather, they arose as a consequence of revisiting a previous study and following through an insight which we did not fully theorise at the time but which now appears to us to relate to the discussion of kindness. We are thus bringing the normative lens we have developed to data that were collected in a more orthodox sociological context, in a study that was originally focused on understanding pedagogical practice in a particular local context.

Students' stories

The data we have chosen to interrogate from the perspective of kindness came from a previous study in which we asked third-year social science students to reflect back on how they how they approached studying, whether they thought they had changed over time, and what had influenced any changes in approach, and in particular whether the personal development planning element of the curriculum had had any impact. The research explored students' sense making in relation to their ways of studying, and 'bracketed' assumptions about the meaning and usefulness or otherwise of personal development planning, and explored what, if any, sense such ideas might have in the life-world of the respondents (Ashworth 1999). The study was based on open-ended questions about why students came on the course, in order to contextualise their experiences, how they approached studying, whether they thought they had changed over time, and what had influenced any changes in approach. Twenty interviews were conducted by independent researchers with no connection with the course toward the end of the students' third year of study. Interviews lasted between 30 minutes and an hour, with the majority being closer to the hour. The initial analysis was based on an in-depth reading of individual transcripts and analytical codings were developed only after each interview had been analysed in an open-ended way. The themes that emerge were, therefore, derived inductively through a number of iterations. The full methodology has been described elsewhere (Clegg and Bufton 2008). The original analysis focused on time and retrospective meaning-making, meanings of support and autonomy, and student's sense of self. In our original analysis we commented on the ways students' accounts clearly distinguished tutors who were perceived as caring and who engaged with them as students. Across the data, students singled out particular tutors as being helpful, tutors whom they felt they knew and could approach, and although we have chosen to concentrate on limited number of cases in this paper they are not untypical. The characteristics were described in terms of the personal attributes of the tutors (Clegg and Bufton 2008, 8). We are using these data, therefore, to illuminate our concept of kindness as a quality that students described as being something they recognised and described in terms of the feelings of care that one individual has for the life projects of the other. Our data are also illustrative of students' perceptions of experiences of lack of kindness and of institutionalised depersonalisation. Of course these data are students' accounts and reconstructions of events and the meanings they attributed to them, not of events themselves. Given the importance attached to the relational in Noddings' (2005a) account of care, and our emphasis on the ways kindness is not simply dependent on the intentions of the teacher but rather is a quality that imbues the act with meaning, students' understandings are important. We have no way of telling from these accounts what the intentions of staff were, nor of mis-recognition on the part of students; what is significant for our normative argument is that students have a language of description and appear to distinguish situations, and that they connected what they perceived as kindness and unkindness to their perception of how they were learning. The acts of perceived kindness related in these data had a clear academic dimension and implications for how students viewed their work. They concerned what it felt like when they perceived that they were attended to, respected, or treated with care rather than indifference. Students were not directly prompted to describe the relational and emotional, rather they chose to comment on what they felt about how they were treated and how this impacted on their studies. Our analysis does not provide direct evidence of the significance of kindness but is illustrative of a quality that students felt they could describe, and whose lack they perceived. They give us no insight into whether the lecturers themselves conceptualised their actions as kind or simply as instances of due care. But it is significant that students perceived such acts as expressing a personal quality rather than simply a professional role.

Students gave unprompted descriptions of their relationship to tutors in their discussion of what had helped them studying:

I mean I've got numerous – I mean there, there's only one tutor in this year which I just cannot connect to at all. I can't – I just, I just haven't got any time for him. I just feel like he's not interested in teaching, he doesn't really want to be here, he doesn't really want. It's as if – the attitudes comes across he doesn't really want to help us get a good mark, yet you'd think, um you're a lecturer, doesn't it, you know, wouldn't it be more beneficial for you if we were getting good marks and you're our tutor and lecturer and seminar tutor? Um … and it – consequently with him that's the module that's letting me down. Whereas with the others I've got such a good rapport with quite a lot of my other tutors that you know my marks are a lot higher. His is the one that I, I got 54 percent in his module, and the others I'm high sixties, seventies.

I'd say that was, yeah, I mean, if, especially like as soon as you, as soon as you get into a rapport they start to respect you and you start to respect them, so you want to try harder, and you want to try harder for them and for yourself. If there's no rapport with the, with the tutor, if they don't seem to care about you – not doing your work or doing your work, then there's no sense of 'oh I need to get this done, I want to get this done, I don't want to let him or her down, I haven't done it'. That's what it is for me, anyway. Certainly my dissertation tutor I, you know, I've got a good, a good relationship with him, where you know, he'll say, 'oh to that meeting bring such and such' and I will have it done because obviously I don't want to let him down and I want to get the work myself as well. (Jane)

The second tutor described above is illustrative of what we might call the kind tutor: one who evidences concern for the success of the student's project. This is in stark contrast to the first tutor who, from the student's perspective, appears to have no interest in their success. The rapport described is expressed in terms of respect and care about the student as a person, and the perceived concern for the personhood of the student and their project. This evokes a responding obligation towards the tutor not to let him down. The description of the tutor with whom there is no rapport is interrogated in terms of his perceived lack of interest in helping students and a puzzlement over the motivation of a lecturer in this role in terms of his own (imputed) interest in his students getting good marks. The student is exploring the possible motivation behind someone who appears not to be inhabiting the identity of a good or kind teacher, one who appears to be indifferent to his students' success. While the quote does not use the language of kindness, the dynamic is an exemplar of many of the characteristics of kindness we have discussed. Moreover, it points to the ways kindness is productive: it produced a positive response in the student; conversely the tutor where there is no rapport depresses her marks. This suggests that students perceive a reciprocity inherent in kind personal encounters, although as we have argued kindness as such does not demand a response; but if the actions are read as being authentic in the concern for the success of the student, then the student wants to respond back. It is of course possible that the second tutor was simply being instrumental, but this would involve a reading of the data that assume the student was a poor interpreter. The quote, however, suggests that the student is a thoughtful meaning-maker who tries to make sense of what she perceives to be the first tutor's lack of involvement. While being thoughtful does not ensure a valid interpretation, and we have no way of independently assessing this, it is indicative that the students make these sorts of judgement about the meaning of pedagogical acts and intentions. Here is another example:

Um my dissertation tutor, I've – he's taught me all throughout my three years. Um, so I feel like I could talk to him if I needed to. Um, he did suggest prioritising the work, um, sort of, at the end of last semester, because the dissertation's so difficult

Um, [name] she's taught us for a couple of years as well, and I just feel like we know her. Um, and she's really good, she – um, we had our last lecture on

Monday and she, she said, you know if we ever need her just email her or come to her and see her and I suppose if you ask [name] she'll guide you in the way you should do your essays and stuff like that. And also we see a lot more of her than we do the normal tutor. (Beccy)

What is striking about the above quote is Beccy's sense of feeling that she really knows her tutor and recognises her tutor's care for her own project (good marks/progress with the dissertation), which are aspects we distinguished of kindness. This is all the more remarkable because the course is a large one and the setting is a large, urban new university so apart from the dissertation there is very little one-to-one contract between staff and students. The context for the communication that the student interprets as evidence of the lecturer being someone they know and could contact is a lecture not seminar, yet even in this context the student perceives the tutor to be showing concern. Beccy appears to feel this is more than just the 'due care' of the professional tutor. Rather she interprets her tutor's offer of help as having a personal dimension. Moreover, this has a temporal dimension as part of a relationship developed over time.

There was ample evidence across the data that students had a tactful understanding of the pressures on staff and that they did not have unrealistic expectations of the time staff could spend in one-to-one situations. They were active interpreters who were able to offer considered reflections and express their interpretation of the tutor's life-world and to relate this to what they saw as the tutor's care towards their own life projects. This intertwining of feeling and intellectual/academic projects and concerns (marks, essays, dissertation) resists the easy dualism of feeling versus reason; rather, the affective appears to enhance intellectual achievement. The good teacher, one who is perceived as having particular personal qualities beyond simply exercising due care, appears to be the effective teacher by virtue of the personal not despite it. The contexts in which kindness was identified were intellectual and pedagogical, and this was evident across the data and not simply confined to the two cases above.

There were also instances of what we regard as a concrete example of an individual act of kindness that went beyond the strictly pedagogical but that, nonetheless, in the context of the interview the student thought relevant to describe:

I went to, um, one of my lecturers that at the time I was doing, um – can't remember which module it was…I think social policy and I think I went to see him about, um, an assessment problem, and he asked me generally how things were, and that was when I started talking about – I had, I'd had housing difficulties in my first year cos I went through clearing so I got put in a really secluded environment with, living with a thirty year old woman, and I was only eighteen, so I didn't really enjoy my first year and – and he gave me like some numbers to ring and he was really helpful, but I didn't get this from my support tutor. So I didn't find my support sessions very helpful I suppose (Lori)

In this instance what starts as a conversation about assessment leads to the resolution of a broader problem for the student. The irony of the description of the 'support' sessions is that they did not offer the support, whereas the actions of a tutor who the student is clearly having difficulty remembering in terms of his module is remembered two years later in a research interview because the student perceived him as having showed concern and helped.

In the quotations above, students describe qualities that we are identifying under the broad rubric of kindness: a relationship where the students feel respect is accorded and that the tutor has their interests at heart. In contrast, a lack of kindness is not necessarily experienced as active unkindness, but rather as a sense of a lack of relationship:

> I mean I think it's important to have a bit of a closer relationship to tutors, really, because, obviously you can't expect a tutor to know everybody's name or recognise everyone's face, or anything like that, but I don't really feel like there was any close communication between tutors and students. And I think sort of from what my friends have said, they'd agree with that as well, that there's not a um, a close enough relationship maybe. And obviously it's going to be hard because of the numbers, but, I don't – yeah, like, cos even the seminars are sort of, most of the seminars that I've been to, I'd say the average attendance is about ten people, so there should be quite an intimate relationship, but there isn't at all. Um, and I don't know, I don't know why. (Emily)

The coda of 'I don't know why' is interesting as it indicates she feels she has tested out a number of hypotheses and still does not understand. She uses a situational logic to explore whether it is class size, but even where the teaching is in relatively small groups it appears as if something is lacking; one way of thinking about this might be in terms of care and kindness. Emily goes on to give a clear account of what the university feels like without those qualities we described as involved in kindness:

> There's so much bureaucracy like in, in university it's hard to feel that it's more personal. Um, but I had troubles with my enrolment, for some reason I got lost in the system somewhere. And sort of, I felt a bit like nobody knew my name and I could have left Uni and no one would have realised. And I mean, luckily I didn't do that, but you do sort of, you feel – it's very anonymous. And I think, I don't know, I think if the – yeah … it'd feel better if there was more of a relationship between you and the university … I think just the whole thing needs to feel more human, really … I think yeah maybe more communication – because then the, the tutors would get to know students more as well, um, and also I think that might help with attendance as well, like, maybe if, um, if you build a relationship with a tutor I think you'd feel a greater sense of obligation to go to their lectures and seminars. Um, so, yeah, whereas if you haven't got any relationship with them you don't feel like you owe them anything. (Emily)

Like Jane in the first quote she suggests that if she perceived the organisation and tutors as caring about her, and as relating to her more as a human, then this would create reciprocal obligations. The impersonality of the organisation is perceived as irrational even in its own terms (in terms of securing student attendance). This sense is compounded by this student's experience of routine process where a lack of kindness appears almost designed in:

> I think just the whole thing needs to feel more human, really. Um, there needs to be more interaction, I'd say, definitely, um, because you sort of interact via computers and use a computer as a kind of middleman, but then when you're actually feeling desperate and stressed and a computer doesn't help with any of that and it's far better I think actually go and see someone with a problem, um, rather than actually write it down via email. (Emily)

There are also examples in the data of what students perceive as positive personal enactments of unkindness. Jane, for example, who as we have seen has distinguished tutors with whom there are varying degrees of rapport, provided the following vivid description of waiting at the administration desk:

> Um, you have to wait around for about five minutes you know, until they've finished their conversations and had their cup of tea and talked about what happened in Eastenders last night before they actually come and help you – you stand … and they do look at you and they recognise that you're there but they carry on with their conversation. Um … and that's just, it's not – or they like, she'll be sitting in her chair and the desk is over there, um she'll look at you and she'll be having a conversation with you from there chair over there, she won't get up and talk to you. And um, I, I find that very inconsiderate and – as if 'oh, do I really have to get out of my chair to come and speak to you, what do you need this time?' kind of thing. (Jane)

There is something personal about this; of recognition actively being denied. It is, however, also a matter of design. The administrators in this particular case are the gatekeepers to tutors in this building, which was designed with a reception desk and staff offices behind key-coded doors. But Jane also distinguished people in the same role (in this case librarians) who acted very differently:

> There's a couple of library assistants down there which, they seem, I don't know. It was one that really, she seems to have this constant smile on her, and she's very like, snobbys not the word, its more, um, it's as if it's jealousy that she's working as a librarian and we're studying and she doesn't like it and she's always um, she always finds ways to put you down or to make things harder for you. She's not very – instead of saying things that you could do, she says the things that you can't. And um, you know, she's not very helpful ….
>
> I mean there are lots of good librarians at, you know, down at [name]. But just one or two just make it a lot harder than what it has to be. Um you know, and if I'm standing in the queue and I can, you know I'll, I'll, I have done in the past, 'you can go in front of me cos I don't want to go and speak to her'. So you know I'll wait until the other, you know, the other person's free. (Jane)

Making things seem harder could be seen as unkind. It is interesting that the hardness is not seen as a quality of the task but with the way help is (not) offered; obstacles are erected in ways that are perceived as personal and ill-intentioned. That something cannot be done may be the case, but if one is told it cannot be in a way that suggests the person is actively being unhelpful then this would appear to be unkind, and in this instance systematic to the extent that Jane chooses to wait for another person.

Concluding reflections

Our data are illuminative because they capture both sides of the argument: the carelessness of the academy and a recognition of the kindness of individuals who appear, nonetheless, to communicate their concerns despite the institutional setting. The structures of carelessness Lynch, Baker, and Lyons (2009) describe can be seen as arising out of the fundamental reshaping of higher education institutions towards what Slaughter and Rhoades (2004) describe as 'academic capitalism' and Marginson and Considine (2000) describe as the 'enterprise university', although of course the gendered dynamics of the university predate its modern forms. Marginson and Considine prefer the term to others in circulation because they argue that:

> 'Enterprise' captures both the economic and academic dimensions, and the manner in which research and scholarship survive but are now subject to new systems of competition and demonstrable performance ... Money is a key objective, but it is also the means to a more fundamental mission: to advance the prestige and competitiveness of the university as an end in itself. (Marginson and Considine 2000, 5)

The idea of the university as an end in itself is important because it seeps into the design of the buildings and the messages about whom and what matters. The gate-keeping function of administrators and the systems within which students can get lost are symptomatic of institutions whose guiding principles are not those of teaching and the student good, but of an internal organisational logic. Our data illustrate the central paradox: the lay normativity of students means that they place value on the kindness of staff who appear to continue to act in personal ways, and a system that does not value such acts as being virtuous in and of themselves.

To return to our reflections on kindness and unkindness, we are suggesting that we know (or think we know) when people are well intentioned towards us and that this makes a huge difference. Just as our judgement about our own kindness might be fallible, it is possible of course that our students misjudged the source of perceived kindness – but what is absolutely clear is that they do make judgements about authenticity and that they respond to kindness and to its absence, or worse, where people appear unkind. This brings us back to our starting point that kindness is not about 'due care' – it is not simply an impersonal professional obligation, it is something more than that. A 'requirement' to be kind would transform itself into a form of performativity through processes of routinisation as already described. It would be possible, however, to look at how the organisation designs its systems, designs its buildings, places people, how it rewards or disparages activities and so on, and to ask whether seen through the lens of kindness these are likely to increase or decrease the possibility of kindness towards other people: students, colleagues across the boundaries of job descriptions, visitors. It would also be possible to collectively interrogate our sense of professionalism based on an idea of virtues as Bruce MacFarlane (2004) has suggested. This is very different from organisational requirements. Many of the processes and systems of mass education have been designed to make things fairer by making them more uniform, but as our data suggest, unsurprisingly, students' perceptions are that the individuals they encounter do make a difference, and that the personal qualities with which they imbue enactments and encounters matter. Our analysis suggests that it would be valuable to explore teachers' perceptions through the normative lens of kindness and to investigate whether and how teachers feel that they can bring personal values such as kindness and care to their interactions with students, and the extent to which these are being re-engineered as due care and professional competencies under existing regimes. What is subversive about kindness, and indeed love of the discipline, is that it cannot be regulated and prescribed. But perhaps universities could try to stop making it quite so hard.

Acknowledgements

The authors would like to acknowledge the support of Leeds Metropolitan University in offering the Visiting Chair that led to this research. They also thank those members of the seminar group at the university who contributed to their ideas about kindness.

References

Archer, M.S. 2000. *Being human: The problem of agency.* Cambridge: Cambridge University Press.

Archer, M.S. 2007. *Making our way through the world.* Cambridge: Cambridge University Press.

Ashworth, P. 1999. 'Bracketing' in phenomenology: Renouncing assumptions in hearing about student cheating. *International Journal of Qualitative Studies in Education* 12: 707–21.

Ashworth, P. 2004. Understanding as the transformation of what is already known. *Teaching in Higher Education* 9, no. 2: 147–58.

Aurelius Antonius, M. 167 A.C.E. *The meditations, Book XI.* Trans. George Long. Cambridge, MA: Massachusetts Institute of Technology.

Ball, S.J. 2003. The teacher's soul and the terrors of performativity. *Journal of Education Policy* 18, no. 2: 215–28.

Beard, C., S. Clegg, and K. Smith. 2007. Acknowledging the affective in higher education. *British Educational Research Journal* 35, no. 2: 235–52.

Carr, W., and S. Kemmis. 1986. *Becoming critical: Education, knowledge and action research.* London: Falmer Press.

Clegg, S. 2007. The possibilities of sustaining critical intellectual work under regimes of evidence, audit and ethical governance. *Journal of Curriculum Theorizing* summer: 27–44.

Clegg, S., and S. Bufton. 2008. Student support through personal development planning: Retrospection and time. *Research Papers in Education* 23, no. 4: 1–16.

Clegg, S., S. Bradley, and K. Smith. 2006. 'I've had to swallow my pride': Help seeking and self-esteem. *Higher Education Research and Development* 25, no. 2: 101–13.

Douglas, M. 1966. *Purity and danger: An analysis of the concepts of pollution and taboo.* London: Routledge and Kegan Paul.

Ecclestone, K. 2004a. From Freire to fear: The rise of therapeutic pedagogy in post-16 education. In *The disciplining of education. New languages of power and resistance,* ed J. Satterthwaite, E. Atkinson, and W. Martin, 117–35. Stoke on Trent: Trentham Books.

Ecclestone, K. 2004b. Education or therapy?: The demoralisation of post-16 education. *British Journal of Educational Studies* 52, no. 2: 112–37.

Ecclestone, K., and D. Hayes. 2009. *The dangerous rise of therapeutic education.* Abingdon: Routledge.

Ehrenreich, B., and D. English. 1979. *For her own good: A 150 years of the expert's advice to women.* London: Pluto.

Elliott, J. 1985. Facilitating action-research in schools: Some dilemmas. In *Field methods in the study of education,* ed R. Burgess, 235–62. London: The Falmer Press.

Furedi, F. 2004. *Therapy culture – Cultivating vulnerability in an uncertain age.* London: Routledge.

Gilligan, C. 1982. *In a different voice: Psychological theory and women's development.* Cambridge, MA: Harvard University Press.

Griffiths, M. 2003. *Action for social justice in education: Fairly different.* Buckingham: Open University Press.

Grummell, B., D. Devine, and K. Lynch. 2009. The care-less manager: Gender, care and new managerialism in higher education. *Gender and Education* 21, no. 2: 191–208.

HEA. 2010. The UK Professional Standard Framework. http://www.heacademy. ac.uk/assets/York/documents/ourwork/rewardandrecog/ProfessionalStandards Framework.pdf (accessed February 25, 2010).

Henkel, M. 2000. *Academic identities and policy change in higher education.* London: Jessica Kingsley.

Hey, V. 2003. Academia and working class femininities. *Gender and Education* 15, no. 3: 319–35.

Hey, V. 2004. Perverse pleasures – Identity work and the paradoxes of greedy institutions. *Journal of International Women's Studies* 5, no. 3: 33–43.

Lanchester, J. 2009. It's finished. *London Review of Books,* May 28, 3–16.

Leathwood, C., and V. Hey. 2009. Gender/ed discourses and emotional sub-texts: Theorising emotion in UK higher education. *Teaching in Higher Education* 14, no. 4: 429–40.

Lynch, K. 2010. Carelessness: A hidden doxa of higher education. *Arts and Humanities in Higher Education* 9, no. 1: 54–67.

Lynch, K., J. Baker, and M. Lyons. 2009. *Affective equality: Love, care and injustice.* Basingstoke: Palgrave Macmillan.

Lynch, K., M. Lyons, and S. Cantillon. 2007. Breaking silence: Educating citizens for love, care and solidarity. *International Studies in the Sociology of Education* 17, no. 1: 1–19.

Lyotard, J.F. 1984. *The postmodern condition: A report on knowledge.* Vol. 10. Manchester: Manchester University Press.

Macfarlane, B. 2004. *Teaching with integrity: The ethics of higher education practice.* London: Routledge.

Marginson, S., and M. Considine. 2000. *The enterprise university: Power, governance and reinvention in Australia.* Cambridge: Cambridge University Press.

Morley, L. 2003. *Quality and power in higher education.* Maidenhead: Open University Press and SRHE.

Mortiboys, A. 2002. *The emotionally intelligent lecturer.* Birmingham: SEDA Publications.

Noddings, N. 2005a. *The challenge to care in schools: An alternative approach to education.* 2nd ed. New York: Columbia University Teachers College Press.

Noddings, N. 2005b. Identifying and responding to needs in education. *Cambridge Journal of Education* 35, no. 2: 147–59.

Noddings, N. 2010. Caring in education. http://www.infed.org/biblio/ noddings_caring_in_education.htm (accessed February 25, 2010).

NSS. 2010. http://www.thestudentsurvey.com/ (accessed Ferbuary 25, 2010).

Paechter, C. 2006. Masculine femininities/feminine masculinities: Power, identities and gender. *Gender and Education* 18, no. 3: 253–63.

Phillips, A., and B. Taylor. 2009. *On kindness.* London: Penguin.

Rowland, S. 1996. Relationships between teaching and research. *Teaching in Higher Education* 1, no. 1: 7–20.

Rowland, S. 2008. Collegiality and intellectual love. *British Journal of Sociology of Education* 29, no. 3: 353–60.

Rowland, S. 2009. Kindness. *London Review of Education* 7, no. 3: 207–10.

Sayer, A. 2005. *The moral significance of class.* Cambridge: Cambridge University Press.

Sennett, R. 2002. *Respect in an age of inequality.* London: Penguin.

Skelton, A., ed. 2007. *International perspectives on teaching excellence in higher education: Improving knowledge and practice.* London: Routledge.

Slaughter, S., and G. Rhoades. 2004. *Academic capitalism and the new economy: Markets, state and higher education.* Baltimore, MD: The Johns Hopkins University Press.

Young, M.F.D. 2008. *Bringing knowledge back in: From social constructivism to social realism in the sociology of education.* London: Routledge.

Index

Page numbers followed by 'n' refer to notes